ADDITIONAL PRAISE FOR
START THINKING RICH

"In *Start Thinking Rich*, Adrian Brambila and Dr. Brad Klontz deliver the straight dope—everything we always needed to hear about money but the experts were too afraid to share."

—**Jordan Grumet,** MD, author of *Taking Stock*
and *The Purpose Code,* and host of
The Earn & Invest Podcast

"In a world of feel-good apologists, Dr. Brad Klontz is never afraid to tell you what you need to hear. In the case of his most recent book, what you need to hear is that—whether you like it or not—wealth is a function of the thoughts that drive your behavior and, ultimately, your net worth."

—**Paul Ollinger,** Comedian and host of *Reasonably Happy* podcast

START THINKING RICH

21 HARSH TRUTHS
TO TAKE YOU
FROM **BROKE** TO
FINANCIAL FREEDOM

DR. BRAD KLONTZ AND ADRIAN BRAMBILA

WILEY

Published by John Wiley & Sons, Inc., Hoboken, New Jersey.
Published simultaneously in Canada.

For general information on our other products and services or for technical support, please contact our Customer Care Department within the United States at (800) 762-2974, outside the United States at (317) 572-3993 or fax (317) 572-4002.

Wiley also publishes its books in a variety of electronic formats. Some content that appears in print may not be available in electronic formats. For more information about Wiley products, visit our web site at www.wiley.com.

Library of Congress Cataloging-in-Publication Data is Available

Names: Klontz, Brad, author. | Brambila, Adrian, author.
Title: Start thinking rich : 21 harsh truths to take you from broke to
   financial freedom / by Dr. Brad Klontz and Adrian Brambila.
Description: Hoboken, New Jersey : Wiley, [2025] | Includes index.
Identifiers: LCCN 2024024141 (print) | LCCN 2024024142 (ebook) | ISBN
   9781394276523 (hardback) | ISBN 9781394276530 (adobe pdf) | ISBN
   9781394276547 (epub)
Subjects: LCSH: Wealth. | Finance, Personal.
Classification: LCC HB251 .K594 2025 (print) | LCC HB251 (ebook) | DDC
   332.024/01—dc23/eng/20240628
LC record available at https://lccn.loc.gov/2024024141
LC ebook record available at https://lccn.loc.gov/2024024142

Cover design: Paul McCarthy

SKY10084079_091024

We dedicate this book to all the hustlers out there
who are committed to making a better life for themselves
and their families. We believe in you.

CONTENTS

CONTENTS

INTRODUCTION

People hate this statistic, but almost 90% of millionaires are self-made. Why do people reject this proven fact? Because it implies individual accountability if you don't become a millionaire. Instead of embracing personal responsibility, it's much easier to blame the system, other people, or the circumstances in which we were born and raised. *Start Thinking Rich* is here to blow those excuses and myths out of the water. This book serves as an invitation to learn the timeless truths about how to become rich and what pitfalls to avoid if you're sick of being poor and want a way out. If you're looking for a cuddly, uncontroversial book that soothes you and makes you comfortable in your situation rather than empowering you to change it, this is *not* the book for you. But if you're ready to take an honest look at your spending habits, your subconscious biases about money, and your self-sabotaging money behaviors and make wealth-building moves, this book will be life-changing for you.

There is a big difference between being *poor* and being *broke*. Broke means that you have no money. It is a temporary condition. Many people have money at the beginning of the month but have none at the end. We know people making six-figures a year who are broke. They get their money, they spend their money, and then it's all gone. We don't want you to be broke. This book is designed to take you from broke and stuck to financial freedom. But to do that, you first need to stop being poor. When we refer to "poor" throughout this book, we are talking specifically about a "poor mindset." While broke is temporary, an unexamined poor mindset can be permanent and keep you broke forever. If you want to get rich, you need to stop thinking poor and *Start Thinking Rich*.

This book is your manual to help you *Start Thinking Rich*. If you want to climb the socioeconomic ladder, you need to do things differently, but it all starts with having the right mindset. The first mindset shift is to take ownership of your current situation around money. In other words, it is accepting that you are where you are right now financially because of how you, or your parents, or your grandparents think about money. This concept can be a bitter pill to swallow but allow us to repeat it: if you aren't willing to take responsibility for shifting your poor mindset to a rich mindset, you will be broke forever. This is easier said than done, in part because of all the bullshit and noise about money that surrounds you. For example, social media is full of lies about how rich people think and behave around money. We wrote this book as the manual we wish we had when we were younger. We are proud of where we are, but the fact is, we would have arrived here even faster if we had known all the things we are going to share with you in this book.

We promise to tell you the truth about yourself, money, and how to get rich – to the best of our knowledge and ability. Adrian Brambila, the son of immigrant parents from Mexico, rose to TikTok stardom by redefining "real wealth," and showcasing his journey of earning $1.7 million in one year while living in a van.

Brad Klontz, PsyD, CFP® is a financial psychologist, professor, and researcher who has co-authored eight books on the psychology of money. He comes from a broken family and grew up poor but still became a millionaire in his 30s. Today, he is the world's leading expert in the psychology of money.

We first met on social media in 2019, as we resonated with each other's messages around the importance of mindset in creating wealth. Since then, we've learned so much from each other, so it was natural for us to become friends. In the past several years, we have collaborated on content and courses to help people become successful with money and on social media and joined forces for this book based on a shared passion to help others achieve financial freedom.

Together, we are combining our expertise, grit, and firsthand knowledge to write the most comprehensive book about money mindsets the world has seen. We use our proven money-making, saving, and investment strategies to take readers from "poor me, I'm broke," to "I'm rich and it's awesome!" With a combined social media following of over three million, we know how desperately people want to learn the secrets to going from broke to rich. We also know that many of the readers of *Start Thinking Rich* are going to find these harsh truths controversial. Even though they are backed up by statistical evidence, there will be some resistance. That's perfectly okay. Dr. Brad is a psychologist and has mind hacks that will bypass your natural psychological resistance to getting out of your own way so you can become the millionaire you want to be.

Start Thinking Rich is not just a money strategy book. It's a conversation about the hard lessons we've learned and the ways we've improved our financial health. It delivers actionable solutions to increase and diversify your income, save what you make, and grow your money in your sleep. It combats your inherent mental blocks to getting rich. Using Dr. Brad's research and financial psychology expertise, and Adrian's immigrant family upbringing and business building strategies, we'll challenge every excuse you can think of that will keep you stuck in a poor mindset. We truly believe that you have the potential to become a millionaire. You just need to find your path and stick with it.

Dr. Brad: Growing up poor in a working-class town in Michigan, my childhood was full of financial struggles, family drama, and trauma, including the violent death of a sibling. Despite these challenges, I made three promises to myself: (1) to build a loving and enduring relationship with the future mother of my children, (2) to establish a secure and nurturing environment for my family, and (3) to attain financial success, affording me the freedom to pursue my passions, prioritize family time, and provide my children with opportunities I never had. Today, I'm proud to say that I've accomplished and continue to pursue these goals.

However, the toughest obstacle I faced was the lack of role models who had achieved such aspirations themselves. How could those who hadn't succeeded in these areas teach me how to do so? How could they impart the necessary mindsets and strategies? Frankly, I wasn't sure if achieving these goals was even possible for me, let alone how to accomplish them. So I had to learn the hard way, through trial and error, making numerous mistakes along the way.

The purpose of this book is to provide you with the guidance I wish I had received earlier in life. I aim to be the mentor I never had, speaking candidly and directly, just as I do with my coaching clients behind closed doors, free from fear of censorship. While the truths shared may initially seem harsh, I urge you to keep an open mind and be willing to challenge your beliefs. Know that I have faith in your ability to create the life you desire.

Adrian: The first time I met a really rich person was when I got invited to the auto-tune singing rap star T-Pain's house in Atlanta, Georgia. I had just landed the opportunity of a lifetime to dance for him professionally as a robot dancer and I remember my jaw dropping when we pulled up to his house. Dozens of pimped-out vehicles, a mansion the size of a castle complete with its own salon, arcade, and club had me in shock. T-Pain was only four years older than my broke college self and that opened my eyes to believe that anyone is capable of achieving great wealth. T-Pain came from nothing and used to sell fish out of a stand in Florida. One day T-Pain showed us a song before it launched publicly. I remember when he launched it looking at the numbers and realizing within 10 minutes of launch it had over a million downloads on iTunes. Back then each iTunes download was $0.99, so in other words I watched someone make over a million dollars in minutes. It was this moment that set me on the path to discover ways where I could also launch something and make a million dollars. I haven't replicated T-Pain's success by any stretch, but I have radically changed my family tree having made over

$100,000 in a year, in a month, in a week, and even in a day through internet entrepreneurship.

My mom grew up poor in Bakersfield, California, and my dad grew up in poverty in Jalisco, Mexico, and they did everything in their power to make sure I didn't have the same struggles they did. They saved every penny so that I could go to college and graduate debt free. Make no mistake, this is a HUGE advantage I was given, and I'll always be forever indebted to them in gratitude for their selfless financial act, especially considering where they came from. Sometimes I think in my head "my family didn't suffer through decades of poverty, immigrate to the United States, and pay their life savings for my college for me to be a broke-ass Mexican American. I have no other choice but to take us all the way to the 1%." I became a millionaire by the time I turned 30. When I first became a millionaire I hired my dad, then my mom, and now even my wife, and we all work together. This book is the tactical playbook and tough mindset you need to go from poor to rich. It's the life lessons of two authors who started from the bottom and became multi-millionaires in different ways. It's the data you need to help you conquer your biases and the stories you need to inspire you to take action and *Start Thinking Rich*!

Start Thinking Rich offers a clear, easy-to-understand map to wealth creation. Here's a snapshot:

THE THREE PATHS TO BECOMING A MILLIONAIRE

Self-made millionaires became rich by taking one of the following paths:

1. *The Employee.* The employee got rich by playing the game. They figured out how to rise in the ranks at the office. They went to

college. Some went to graduate school. They became accountants, doctors, lawyers, and engineers. They maxed out their 401(k) and/or IRA each year. According to *The Millionaire Next Door*, 70% of millionaires are employees or self-employed professionals. According to a study by Fidelity, thousands of people are becoming millionaires each year through their 401(k)s and IRAs.

2. *The Silicon Entrepreneur.* This millionaire took a big gamble, and it paid off. They cashed out their 401(k) and sunk it all into their venture. They took out loans and raised capital. Then, they hit it big, despite all the odds. According to the Department of Labor, 70% of businesses fail. When they are being honest with themselves, the Silicon Entrepreneur will admit they got lucky. Sure, they had a great idea, and they were able to execute, but so did a large percentage of their colleagues who failed.

3. *The Grinder/Slow Hustler.* This is the entrepreneurial route that Adrian and Dr. Brad took. They had day jobs and socked away as much money as they could while working nights and weekends to start their businesses. They bootstrapped their operation. They did NOT put their families or futures at risk by cashing out their retirement accounts to fund their businesses. They did NOT take on debt. When their side hustles surpassed their day-job income they went full time. Now they teach people the mindsets, habits, and strategies they need to do the same.

While they took different paths, all these self-made millionaires had the same money mindset. *Start Thinking Rich* will drive home the point that we make choices every day that either make us richer or drag us further into the poorhouse. The liberating fact of the matter is, whether we're rich or poor, it's our choice.

The rich get richer because they:

- Live below their means
- Save more than they spend

- Buy assets versus liabilities
- Don't rack up credit card debt
- Don't make purchases to impress other people
- Constantly seek education, such as reading finance books
- Invest for the long term

However, the rich can become poor fast if they:

- Live above their means
- Spend more than they save
- Buy liabilities versus assets
- Rack up credit card debt
- Make purchases to impress others
- Never read books about finance
- Don't invest

Regardless of the path, we've helped thousands of people *Start Thinking Rich* by adopting our 21 harsh truths about money, which we cover in this book. *Start Thinking Rich* is a wake-up call for anyone who's ever felt stuck in the rat race, trapped in cycles of poverty and hopelessness, and victimized by the system. To us, it's all a game, and we're going to show you how to play it. This book invites you to wipe the poor-mindset cobwebs from your eyes so you can see the countless possibilities in front of you. For years, we have used our tenacity, grit, and expertise to help people achieve financial freedom. Now it's your turn.

In *Start Thinking Rich*, we transcend conventional wisdom, blending academic insights with real-life experiences through our personal stories, case studies, and actionable advice. Our goal is to be unapologetically direct and to challenge you with truths that may initially sting but will ultimately pave the way for transformational financial change. Statements like "get rid of your poor friends if you want to get rich," and "you're not allowed to use a credit card if you can't pay it off every month" are not just our attempt at being provocative and getting your attention. They are real-life lessons we break down for you to help you start thinking rich.

Our approach is one of tough love, but ultimately, hope. We'll help you take full responsibility for your circumstances, so you realize that it is not your fault if you were born poor, but you don't have to stay that way. We're not in the business of sugar-coating things for you. Our chapter headings may deliver a jolt and feel like a slap on the head, but once you get over the initial shock, our goal is to offer you compassionate guidance, which we hope feels like a pat on the back from a caring friend. We are being blunt with you because we care about you, and we want you to create the life you want. To *Start Thinking Rich*, you need to shed your poor thinking, dismantle your mental barriers, and embrace new habits. We believe that you have the ability to cut the bullshit, choose abundance, and do what it takes to go from a poor life to a rich life. Let this book be the wake-up call you need to transform your financial habits, *Start Thinking Rich*, and join the new millionaires club.

CHAPTER ONE

BEING POOR SUCKS

Money doesn't buy happiness? We call bullshit. Being poor sucks. Only two types of people say money won't make you happy: (1) broke people and (2) people who've never been broke. Broke people say it to make themselves feel better. "Sure, we don't have money, but that's okay because it wouldn't make us happy anyway." This is a comforting story to tell yourself when you're feeling hopeless, but it's also self-destructive. Telling yourself that more money wouldn't improve your circumstances is the fastest way to kill your motivation and stop you from doing what it takes to create a better life. By contrast, people who've never been broke don't know how miserable it is to go to bed hungry, miss their kids' teacher conferences because they need two or three jobs so they can feed them, to be one illness or injury away from eviction, or miss out on opportunities because they can't afford to participate.

Not only is quality of life affected by money, but growing up poor can mess with your brain. Researchers found that poverty early in life is linked to a reduction in the size of the hippocampus, the part of the brain responsible for dealing with stress and being able to remember things accurately. Children who grow up in poverty also have increased activity in the amygdala – the part of the brain that processes emotions and motivation – when exposed to things that make them feel like they might be in danger. Being poor alters the parts of the brain that help us determine what is an actual threat, how we react emotionally, and the actions we take or don't take to deal with it. In other words, being poor can make it harder for us to learn, harder to accurately understand what is happening and why, to identify real threats, make accurate judgments, and solve problems. This can lead to a self-perpetuating cycle. A child living in poverty may not do as well in school, which could affect the kinds of education and jobs they can get later in life.

In adulthood, being poor causes a whole host of new problems. People stuck in poverty face more sickness, die younger, are more likely to suffer from depression and abuse drugs, and have higher levels of stress. It can be hard to find hobbies, eat healthy, spend time with family, or take vacations when all you can think about is how you're going to pay for housing. The bottom line is that BEING POOR SUCKS. But the good news is that you *can* go from poor to rich. There IS a way out of the poverty suck-fest, and we are going to show you exactly how to do it.

CAN MONEY "BUY" HAPPINESS?

Guess what? It turns out that money CAN buy you happiness. Pick up any book on wealth and finances, and you'll likely see a reference to an outdated study that claims money can only make you happy up to a certain amount. The study, which has now been debunked, found that emotional well-being only increased in relation to income up to $75,000 per year. Interestingly, this number closely matches the average income in

2

the United States. The view of these researchers was that once you have enough money to meet your basic needs, at approximately $75,000 per year, your happiness plateaus, and more money won't move the happiness meter above that amount. A later, more comprehensive study found very different results, and confirmed what most of us already thought was true. The new study found that higher incomes WERE associated with higher levels of happiness, far and above the $75,000 mark, as you can see in Figure 1.1.

Figure 1.1 Average real-time reports of feeling good and overall life satisfaction based on level of income.

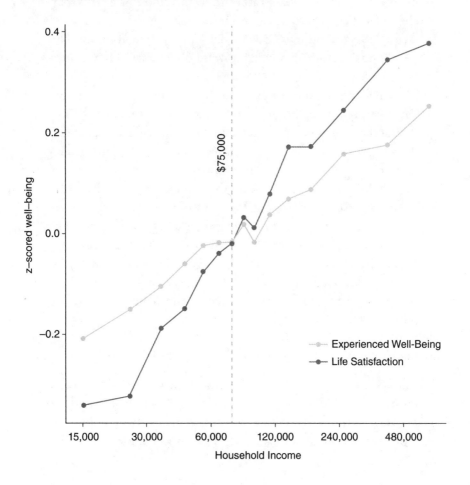

This chart clearly shows that the higher your income, the happier you are.

Adrian: In my college days, I was addicted to reading stories spawned from this popular study of millionaires and billionaires whose vast wealth seemed to bring more misery than joy. I held onto the belief that $75,000 was the golden number for happiness, a notion reinforced by countless financial self-help books that painted any income beyond that as a trade-off with one's quality of life.

With this mindset, I ventured into the world post-graduation, happiness as my compass rather than the allure of a hefty paycheck. I settled for a role in a call center, earning a "happy" $27,000 a year (38% toward my $75,000 goal – yay!), content in the belief that I was steadily marching toward my perceived happiness threshold.

But let me tell you, it was a bust. Something was off – big time. Fast forward through nine years of the grind, and *bam*, the first year of the pandemic hits, and I'm making over $1.2 million, living the dream on wheels in my tricked-out sprinter van traveling around the country. The "big sacrifice" for making $1.2 million? Just hooking up to Wi-Fi once a week. Here's the real deal: there's a whole other community out there: folks like Dr. Brad and me, who've cracked the code on using money as a tool to elevate their quality of life while simultaneously increasing their earnings. We're here to share those secrets with you. Being poor can lead to a deep dissatisfaction with life. But being rich and testing limits of possibility? The satisfaction has been underestimated. And it is life changing.

Being poor not only sucks, it can be downright depressing.

Adrian: My dad told me a story about a time when he hadn't eaten for days. As a kid in Mexico he would often go to bed hungry. So one day, he trespassed onto a farmer's land, dug up an onion, and took a big bite out of it. He told me that he was so hungry, that dirty, bitter onion was unbelievably delicious. At first, when I heard that story, I applauded his ingenuity. He found a creative way to beat his hunger. But after thinking about it for a while, I couldn't help but wonder something. How desperate would I have to be to bite into an onion like it was a juicy burger, and rave at how great it tasted? How hungry would I have to be to trespass onto someone else's property, get down on my knees, and dig up an onion with my bare hands. He did something so far out of his character in stealing that onion, it reminded me that people can resort to drastic measures if it is a matter of life or death.

Dr. Brad: When my dad left, I was just two years old, and my mom was pregnant with my sister. She was a part-time teacher, and her salary was too low to make ends meet. With two young kids, times were tough. To put food on the table, she had to rent out the basement of our three-bedroom, one-bathroom, 1,300-square-foot house to a revolving door of tenants. She had to take on more work and put my baby sister in daycare. I was a latch-key kid, and as early as in preschool, when I was just four years old, I walked home without adult supervision, which was over a mile away. One day I saw my mom sitting on the couch crying. Our television had broken again, and we didn't have the money to get it fixed. My mom relied on the television to babysit my sister and me when she got ready for work, took a bath, or cooked. In her desperation I saw her drop to her knees in front of the television and pray to God to fix it. After several minutes of prayer she stood up, turned the knob, and the television came on. It was a miracle.

BEING POOR CAN KILL YOU

In ancient Imperialist China, prisoners were tortured by "slow slicing," or inflicting small cuts all over their bodies, otherwise known as "death by a thousand cuts." The idea was that one or two little cuts would hurt but wouldn't be as alarming as losing a limb. This reduced the level of acute trauma and allowed the torturers to extend their work over days or even weeks. The prisoners would slowly bleed out, little by little, each day until they died.

Being poor can feel like death by a thousand cuts. Living paycheck to paycheck is a cut. Not making enough to save for retirement, another cut. Not being able to move out of a dangerous neighborhood, another cut. Not being able to put your kids in decent clothes, another cut. Not being able to put your kids in a good school, no money for a child's college tuition, and lack of access to healthy food, a bigger cut that leads to poor health and fewer opportunities. Some cuts are tolerable, like keeping the thermostat low and wearing sweaters in the house so the utility bill is more affordable (not a bad idea for everyone). Others lead to significant loss, such as not being able to afford insurance or not saving for retirement.

Imagine being strapped into a chair like one of those prisoners. Your captors give you a high-interest credit card so you can stop the bleeding from the wound of poverty. But the relief you feel is just temporary and creates a financial cut that is much bigger and can take years to heal. When you wake up to what's happening, you may take out a loan against your car to pay down some of that high-interest debt. Another gash in your finances opens to close part of the credit card wound. But then the inevitable unexpected life event occurs, and you can't make the payments. They take your car and now you can't get to work. Your boss fires you because you're always late from taking the bus. Now you have a high-interest loan, bad credit from not being able to pay your loan back, and no income. All of those cuts are causing you to financially bleed out all over the floor. Poverty becomes a vicious cycle, and the hole gets deeper and deeper. No wonder you feel powerless and hopeless. Sadly, this is the reality for millions of people in the United States.

Being poor can be a matter of life or death. It can shorten your life and wreak havoc on your mental health. People trapped in the hell of poverty experience increased anxiety, chronic disease, lower life expectancies, unstable housing, inadequate childcare, unsafe neighborhoods, under-resourced schools, and hunger. As of 2022, there were 38 million people living below the poverty line in the United States. Worries about money can be as harmful to your health as heart problems or diabetes. Being poor not only sucks, it can kill you.

Desperation born from poverty can lead people to do things that don't align with their values, including stealing. Most feel terrible about what they're doing, but they feel like they have no other choice. When a person sees their children crying from hunger, they'll do whatever it takes to feed them. To the untrained eye, being poor may seem hopeless, especially if it's all you've ever known. But the great news is that you can stop being poor, and we are here to help you do it. But fair warning: you must be willing to eat a few onions.

But first, the good news! We are blessed to live in a country where people like Adrian's parents can come from abject poverty and build wealth for their families in as little as one generation. We are blessed to live in one of the few countries on earth where people can go from poor to rich through their own efforts. Were we born with a silver spoon in our mouths? Nope. We had to work hard for everything we've earned. For example, Adrian's parents had to be smart with their finances, avoid trying to keep up with the Joneses, save what they could, and keep their vision of the future for their kids in the forefront of their minds. Even when they were poor, they had a rich mindset.

As you've probably noticed by now, we're not going to sugarcoat things for you. If you're looking for someone to agree with you that your situation is hopeless, this isn't the book for you. If you're looking for someone to tell you that it's not worth the effort to go from poor to rich, this isn't the book for you. If you are looking for us to give you soft, gentle nudges, this isn't the book for you. We care about you too much to beat around the bush or sell you a lie. However, if you're willing to do the work of building a rich mindset and working toward financial freedom, we are here to help you. But this journey will require you to be courageous, get honest with yourself, accept some uncomfortable truths, get real about your twisted beliefs about money and your bad financial habits, and get creative with solutions so you can stop being poor and start thinking rich. Will it be all sunshine and rainbows? No. Will we give you the education and motivation you need to help you create the financial life you want by the time you finish this book? Absolutely. While we can give you a rich mindset, you need to put in the work to become successful. You must be willing to accept some harsh truths to get to a place of lifelong financial security, and you are going to need to take action. Start taking action NOW by completing your first "Start Thinking Rich Challenge."

Chapter 1 *Start Thinking Rich* Challenge

Take a moment to list out all the ways your life could improve if you had more money. How would it feel to be financially independent, where you could have the life you want without needing to work anymore? Create a vision of what your life would look like. Where would you be? Who would be with you? How would you spend your money? What would your day-to-day life look like? What emotions would you want to be having? What stressors would no longer be keeping you up at night? Just make sure your dreams are bigger than Adrian's were when he first did this exercise back in 2015:

I want to make $60K from my career and grow my online revenue to $15K. I want to have $400 in disposable income every month. . .

I'm going to dedicate this journal
entry to my affirmations.
I want to make $60k from my
career by the end of 2015 and want
my online revenue to grow to 15k
a ~~month~~. for the year 2015
I want to have $400 in disposable income
every month to *LIVE & TRAVEL &
EXPERIENCE.*

Feb 4 2015

Adrian wasn't kidding when he said that that $75,000 study brain-washed him as a young adult! Don't make the same mistake he did. DREAM BIG AND DON'T HOLD BACK!

CHAPTER TWO

ONLY POOR PEOPLE THINK THE SYSTEM IS RIGGED

W hat follows is an open letter Dr. Brad sent to critics of capitalism via his social media platforms and email newsletter.

To My Capitalism-Hating Friends, from Dr. Brad,

I love you. I appreciate your sensitivity, your sincerity, your sense of fairness and your desire to make the world a better place. I also appreciate your thoughtful insights into the downsides of capitalism, which are many. But you and I are different. I am not an economist, politician, or sociologist. I am a clinical psychologist. I have dedicated my professional life to helping real people improve their day-to-day lives.

In my work in the trenches, highbrow political musings about capitalism, socialism, etc. are TOTALLY USELESS for people who want and need to change their lives TODAY. Even worse, suggesting to people that they CAN'T change their plight because the "system is rigged" is just HORRIBLE. You're HURTING the people you say you want to help by spouting that disempowering nonsense. Please stop doing that.

People like me – who grew up poor – can't afford to wait for people like YOU to change the entire system of government to give us a leg up. We can't afford to believe that the system is rigged, and we are powerless to create a better life for ourselves and for our families – and the evidence just does NOT support this claim. Politicians have been promising to make our lives better to get our votes for years – but nothing has changed.

As a clinical psychologist, my role is to help people achieve their goals and reach their highest potential. My focus has been in financial psychology. I have conducted psychological studies on thousands of individuals from all socioeconomic backgrounds. I've studied the mindsets, habits, and lifestyles of people who grew up POOR and have been able to climb the socioeconomic ladder. Their stories are inspiring, their psychology and behaviors can be taught, and their results can be replicated.

I will continue to share these mindsets and habits to help inspire people who want to create a better life. I will continue to dispel myths about the rich that keep people poor. I will continue to call out self-destructive beliefs about money. I will continue to do my best to give people the tools they need to change their lives – because NOBODY is going to do it for them. I will keep focusing on helping people win the game we were all born into.

I appreciate your desire to make the world a better place. When you've successfully changed the game, I will immediately shift gears and do my best to teach people how to win at the new game you've created for us.

Your ally in the trenches,

Dr. Brad

THE CAPITALISM GAME

Today, *capitalism* feels like a dirty word. But we invite you to open your mind and redefine what capitalism means. Let's start with the literal definition from Merriam-Webster: Capitalism is "an economic system characterized by private or corporate ownership of capital goods, by investments that are determined by private decision, and by prices, production, and the distribution of goods that are determined mainly by competition in a free market." The key words in that definition are "competition," and "free market."

The free market is an arena where people and businesses compete for the prize of wealth and success. As such, we see capitalism as quite simply, a game. For those who don't know how to play it, capitalism may seem like a rigged system where the rich get richer and the poor stay poor. But that's because they're playing the wrong game. It's like showing up to play football with a pickleball paddle. No matter how good you think you are at pickleball it just is not going to translate into football. The games are very different, from the strategies to win to how you keep score.

In a similar way, the "game" of generating wealth is completely different from the normal way people think about and manage their money. The wild thing about wealth is that no specific career has a direct correlation to the mindset, behaviors, and tactics required to play the game of generating wealth the best. Sadly, even many financial advisors live paycheck to paycheck! Just because you've excelled in some other area of your life, such as your profession or athletics, doesn't mean you will be naturally more gifted than someone else at generating wealth. That's why about half of the people who are making over six figures still live paycheck to paycheck. When it comes to wealth, most people never take time to learn the rules of the game and then after years of hard work and nothing to show for it, they cry "the system is rigged!" But in reality they are trying to play pickleball in a football game.

Many people are playing the wrong game. Some just throw their hands up and quit. People who have given up have fallen prey to a mindset of helplessness. They push the idea that the system is rigged, and if they get their hooks into you, you'll start to believe you're powerless too, just like them. You'll feel helpless and give up. But people who go from poor to rich understand that THEY have the power to change their circumstances. They see the game and work to understand how to play it. If you interact with people who grew up poor but found ways to advance, then you'll start to believe it's possible to succeed no matter where you started. You'll learn how the game works, how to play it, and commit to the realistic, actionable steps you can take to win.

> Dr. Brad: When I was younger, I hated capitalism and rich people. I was bitter about the unfairness of it all. Why was I born into a family with no money when others had it so easy? Why do some people have nicer cars and bigger houses when we were working even harder than most? But luckily, as I got older I met people who knew how to play the game and had built success from nothing. I quickly realized if they could do it, then so could I.

Love it or hate it, capitalism is the game into which we were born. Maybe capitalism is the best system humans have ever seen, or maybe it isn't. Our opinion doesn't matter, one way or another. We're not writing a book to change capitalism or to keep it. We just want to equip you with the tools you need to win. Recognizing it's a game is a huge part of a rich mindset. Some people say that money isn't real; there's no gold backing it. They'll ask me, "Doesn't that worry you?" I say, "Worry me? Nah, of course I know it's not real!" It's just a piece of paper. It means nothing except for our shared delusion that it means something. We're all in the game of capitalism. Money is a game. It really helps to understand that and not get too attached to any of it. We're all playing the game right now, whether you want to or not. So, the question is, how can you win the game? It's all about mindset.

Adrian: Capitalism is a game. I first started playing it for $27,000 a year at a call center at Prudential Retirement; it really sucked. No matter how hard I worked or how far I went to try to impress my boss, I could never advance. One time, I picked up the phone and through some solid rapport building I learned I was speaking to a close acquaintance of Prudential's CEO. He sat on a university board with the CEO of Prudential. I delivered my standard service, and he complimented me on my exceptional work. When I went back to the office the next day, a few of my peers gave me the heads up that my manager was talking about me. I didn't know if it was a good or bad thing. When I got called into the office of my boss's boss I knew something was up. She told me that the CEO of Prudential had heard about my interaction with his friend and had sent his compliments to the call center. I was the talk of the entire call center. The CEO had never done that before. You know what happened next for me? Absolutely nothing. Despite accomplishing something that had never been done before in the call center I had to wait for my annual review 6 months later to get a raise of $1 an hour. It was at that point I realized that I was playing the wrong game.

When you play the wrong game it can be incredibly frustrating. You can try with all of your might, but effort won't lead to success if you don't know the rules. I grew up playing Zelda and

Final Fantasy. When I first started playing, I sucked! I had to research the game manuals and Reddit forums to learn how to play, and once I did it became easy to win. Capitalism is a game and once you know the rules your frustration can turn into fun. What used to take me a whole year to make at the call center I've made in a month, in a week, and even in a day. It's because I learned (and am still learning) the ways to play the game of capitalism. Later in this book we will give you the cheat codes that grew my income from $27,000 a year to $2 million.

The reality is, the more value you contribute to the world, the more money you'll make. We are not talking about your value as a human being; that is, of course, priceless. We're talking about your economic value. Your economic value is determined by what people are willing to pay for your product or service. This harsh truth is why noble professions such as firefighters and teachers will never make seven figures. They contribute priceless value to society, but in terms of economic value, they are stuck in a game with low income ceilings. Even if the president of the United States flew you to the White House and gave you the Presidential Medal of Freedom for your outstanding work as a teacher, you'd be back home the next week making the same amount of money. If you find yourself frustrated with your profession's low income ceiling, don't get mad, just start playing a different game.

THE SCIENCE BEHIND A RICH MINDSET VS. POOR MINDSET: LOCUS OF CONTROL

How do you make the shift from a poor mindset to a rich mindset? It's all about control. Psychologist Julian Rotter found that a person's behavior is reinforced by their beliefs about why things are happening in their lives.

The amount of power someone gives to things that happen to them determines their locus of control. Those who think the system is rigged and they are powerless to change it have an *external locus of control*, meaning they put all the control on external circumstances. But people who believe they can change their circumstances and become wealthy will be able to do so. That's called an *internal locus of control*.

An internal locus of control is crucial for having a rich mindset. It leads to higher levels of achievement, higher net worth, stronger motivation, a greater drive to succeed, a dedication to personal growth, and more goal-directed behaviors. The bottom line is that people with an internal locus of control are more likely to become wealthy. They have a burning desire to learn higher-paying skills. Then they leverage those skills to make more money. They use financial knowledge to get their money working for *them*, instead of the other way around. If you want to overcome a system that seems stacked against you, you need to develop an internal locus of control.

In the other direction, an external locus of control creates a poor mindset. It perpetuates feelings of helplessness and hopelessness, and comes with the tendency to give up easily. How can you tell if you have an external locus of control? Observe your reaction to a stressful situation. Do you blame others? Do you become depressed and hopeless? Or do you gather yourself and start working on a plan of action? Do you max out your credit cards or master your spending? Do you run from discomfort and conflict or face them head on? If you tend toward an external locus of control, don't freak out. You're already changing it by reading this book. The great thing about mindsets is that they are changeable. It starts with acknowledging where you are and taking small steps to shift your perspective. When you find yourself feeling helpless, ask yourself, "Am I really 100% powerless in this moment?" Over time, you'll start to see that 99.99% of the time, you are not totally powerless to improve your situation. Once you see that you have the power to take even one little step forward, you've already shifted to an internal locus of control.

TWO SIDES OF THE GAME

When it comes to personal finance, there's the rich game and the poor game. The poor game is, "I make money, I spend it, then I'm sad I have no money." There are many reasons people do that. They may think, "I'll never have enough money so why bother trying?" In certain countries where inflation is ridiculously high, the game is to buy things immediately when you get paid. When the prices of things go up due to skyrocketing inflation, a coffee cup you buy today will be worth more tomorrow, but your currency may be worth less. Dr. Brad worked with a couple, and one of them was from Venezuela. This person experienced massive inflation as a child. They operated under the belief that you get a dollar today and it's worth ten cents tomorrow. So, the game was different there. The smart move was to take that money and spend it as soon as you got it. If that's the game you're in, that's the game you should play.

The problem arises when the game we are playing doesn't match the reality we live in, or we don't know how to play at all. So the poor game is "I make it, I spend it, it's gone," or "I don't have it so I'll just borrow it." Too many people playing the poor game go to predatory lenders, such as those who offer payday loans, which are always located in poor neighborhoods. These loans have incredibly high interest rates and take advantage of people. But you only fall prey to these corrupt practices if you're playing the poor game.

THE GAME

So how do you know if you're playing the wrong game? It comes down to this simple question: Are you getting everything you want out of life? If the answer's yes, then congratulations! You're playing the rich game and you're winning. If the answer is no, then you need to admit that you're playing the wrong game or using the wrong strategy. When you have had enough, it's time to switch your mindset from the poor game to the rich game.

The rules of the poor game:
- Blame everyone else for your circumstances.
- Spend everything and save nothing.
- Try to get-rich-quick.
- Try to impress others with stuff that makes you look rich (e.g. designer clothes).
- Don't trust investing.
- Stay closed-minded, thinking you've got it all figured out and know it all.
- Rack up credit card debt and borrow from predatory lenders.
- Give up your power and resign yourself to being poor forever.

The rules of the rich game:
- Take responsibility for your circumstances.
- Save and invest a percentage of every dollar you make.
- Try to get rich slowly.
- Don't worry about impressing others with stuff.
- Use investing to protect and grow your money.
- Keep an open mind, always looking to increase your education, whether formally or informally.
- Pay off your credit card in full each month.
- Believe that you have the power to change your life.

THE RICH PLAYBOOK

Imagine a coach in front of a whiteboard giving you the plays for success on the field. There are strategies that will get you into the end zone, and there are pitfalls that will pound you into the dirt. Here are some plays you need to run if you want to win the rich game.

The Credit Play

Having bad credit is like trying to run to the end zone with 50-pound ankle weights. A low credit score puts you at a severe disadvantage, one in which you'll pay the highest possible interest rates, costly overdraft fees, and big security deposits. You may feel like this is unfair, and it probably is. That said, these lenders know people with a low credit score are a high risk and there is a good chance they won't pay back the loan. So, they charge more up front, to offset the cost of possibly being stiffed in the long run. A shitty credit score creates shitty financial outcomes. If you have a balance on your credit card, prioritize paying it off in full each month. Leaving a balance on your credit card and paying interest HURTS your credit score. We thought this was common knowledge, but many people have been fooled into thinking otherwise.

> *The Credit Play: Pay off your credit cards in full each month (more on this in Chapter 20: "You're Not Allowed to Use Your Credit Card If You Can't Pay It Off Each Month"), decrease your expenses, and never take out a high-interest loan.*

The Get-Rich-Slow Play

Get-rich-quick schemes prey on desperate people trying to make enough money to get out of debt and feed their families. They also prey on foolish people who think they can bypass consistency and hard work. But the real way to build wealth is by getting rich slow, not quick. As frustrating as that may seem at first, a life of lottery ticket duds and tears at the computer because you've lost all your money to day trading is worse. Instead, build your wealth steadily over time.

> *The Get-Rich-Slow Play: Instead of spending that $10 on a lottery ticket, invest it and watch it grow to $20, then $40, then $100. It's not as exciting as the fantasy of winning it big overnight (which you*

won't), but it's a guaranteed way to get rich (more on this in Chapter 9: "Lottery Tickets Are for Lazy People").

The Multiple Streams of Income Play

The best way to make yourself financially invincible is to have multiple streams of income. If one stream dries up, you'll have other avenues for making money. Having many sources of revenue helps you stay financially stable in the face of unexpected circumstances. We each have over 10 streams of income and are always looking for the next one.

The Multiple Streams of Income Play: Get at least 10 streams of income to become financially invincible (more on this in Chapter 19: "People Who Binge Netflix Without a Side Hustle Will Be Poor Forever").

The Consumer Play

Americans are addicted to buying shit they don't need to impress people who don't care about them. The CRAZY part is that studies show that most self-made millionaires are frugal and downplay their wealth. It's the people with LESS money who are trying to show off. It's all quite pathetic. But the system is designed to prey on suckers by making them feel bad about themselves, so they buy more stuff. Marketing plays on our fear of missing out, and makes us feel ugly, insecure, lonely, and worthless. They design ads to hit you at your basic human needs. Entire teams of scientists sit around to come up with devious strategies to separate you from your money.

The Consumer Play: Don't buy shit you don't need. And be honest with yourself about how much you REALLY need (more on this in Chapter 12: "Only Broke and Insecure People Flex Luxury Brands").

The Team of Experts Play

Sure, you have pliers in your garage, but that doesn't mean you should do your own dental work. Still, year after year, people with no accounting experience try to do their own taxes. The fact is, people playing the rich game consult with experts, while people playing the poor game try to do it all themselves. If you're not an expert in whatever money service you need, hire an expert. Get a CPA and outsource your taxes. If you're starting a business, get an attorney to help you. A couple hundred dollars in the beginning can save you thousands down the road. Sit down with them for an hour and ask your questions; you don't have to have them on your payroll. If you're nervous about investing, hire a financial advisor to help you.

The Team of Experts Play: Hire experts and seek help when you have questions, because that's what rich people do (more on this in Chapter 15: "Only Poor People Are Afraid To Ask for Help").

A NOTE ABOUT CHANGING THE SYSTEM

It's important to acknowledge that we live in a very unfair world. Without a doubt the system *has* been rigged, very much so, in many places on earth today, and pretty much everywhere in the past. For centuries in the United States, laws have been biased against marginalized people. Anytime there are laws that oppress people, that's an injustice we ALL need to address as a society. We should also support efforts to make our society an even playing field, in every way possible. One way to make things equal is to use the money we make to create change, whether that's donating to charities or using your platforms to speak out against exploitation and oppression. We're not suggesting the system we live in is the best one or even a good one. But what we are saying is that if you believe that success is impossible, you'll be operating from a destructive mindset that will keep you poor forever.

It's admirable to spend time trying to change the system, but don't do it at the expense of working to improve your life. You can do both simultaneously. People tend to do one or the other: live for today *or* plan for the future. But you need to do both.

Money is neutral. In the hands of a greedy bastard, money can do great harm. In the hands of a generous and ethical person, money can change lives for the better. The fact is, greedy people are working the system. As a result, they may enjoy some advantages. But in our experience, karma usually catches up with them because nobody wants to do business with a selfish crook. The irony is that people who think money is bad and the rich are evil wind up working for or giving all their money to those greedy rich people. So in a way, you're hurting the disadvantaged by letting the "evil rich people" win. But if people want to make a difference and level the playing field by using their money for good, well that's an even higher level of the game.

We would all benefit if we lived in a world where people are able to thrive, feel safe, become successful, and go on to contribute to a prosperous society. That's why we should play the game not only for ourselves, but for the sake of those who need it the most. Wouldn't it be great if the fairness seekers had the most access to money in the world? But what we're doing when we endorse the idea that good people should reject money, is leaving all the money in the hands of the bad people. It makes no sense. Capitalism is a game, and you're playing it whether you want to or not. You might as well play to win!

Chapter 2 *Start Thinking Rich* Challenge: The Control Test

Let's take a quick test of your locus of control. For each situation, what would be your default mindset? Don't overthink it, just go with your gut response. Choice A or Choice B? Track your answers.

1. Situation: You got fired.
   A. I lost my job because of my asshole boss and greedy corporations and there's nothing I could have done about it.
   B. I didn't love my job. I could have shown up earlier for work with a better attitude and become indispensable. I could have also become less dependent on my job by developing multiple streams of income.
2. Situation: You lost all your money investing.
   A. I lost all my money in the stock market because the system is set up for billionaires and politicians. I never stood a chance.
   B. I put all my money into one asset and it increased my risk of losing everything. Next time, I'll talk with a financial advisor about better investments and creating a diverse portfolio.
3. Situation: Your relationship sucks.
   A. My relationship sucks because my partner won't change. It's not my fault!
   B. I'm 50% responsible as an equal partner in this relationship. I need to examine my own behavior to see how I'm contributing to the problem. If I make some positive changes, it will have a positive impact on our relationship.
4. Situation: You are broke.
   A. I'm always broke. I don't make enough to pay my bills, so I rack up credit card debt and borrow money from friends and family. They'll see how hard my life is and feel sorry for me, so I probably won't have to pay them back anyway. It's my greedy company's fault for not paying me a higher wage.

    B. My financial situation IS pretty grim right now. I'm going to reduce my expenses and get a roommate until I'm able to increase my income. I'm going to focus on learning some higher-paying skills so I can earn more money in the future.

5. Situation: Something bad happened.

    A. Life's not fair, so why even bother trying. I'm going to eat this cake, drink until I'm numb, and binge-watch Netflix.

    B. Life's not fair and it doesn't owe me anything. If I want a better life, I have to learn how to overcome life's inherent unfairness and use my energy, time, and resources to better my situation. Nobody is going to save me except for me.

LOCUS OF CONTROL TEST RESULTS

For every time you answered "A," give yourself a point. If you have more than zero points, you are stuck in a poor mindset. The goal is to get that number down to zero. The fact is that YOU, and only you, are in control of your destiny, even when the odds are stacked against you. Terrible things WILL happen to all of us. We may lose our jobs, the people we love most will get sick and die, and the economy will hit another recession. It's true that we can't control everything. But what we can control is how we prepare for hardships, how we experience and react to them, and what we do next.

CHAPTER THREE

YOU DON'T WANT TO BECOME A MILLIONAIRE, YOU JUST WANT TO SPEND A MILLION DOLLARS

We want you to take three minutes and write down everything you would do if we gave you a million dollars. Set a timer for three minutes and come back when you're done!

What did you write down? A new house or car? Quit your job? Buy a one-way ticket to travel the world? Your answers to this question reveal whether you have a poor or a rich mindset. Without the right mindset, even if you suddenly became rich, you would just blow through your money and find yourself right back where you started. Ask a person with a poor mindset what they'd do with a million dollars, and they'll likely list all the things they would buy and perhaps even the extravagant trips they'd take.

But someone with a rich mindset would chuckle at such immature behavior. A person with a rich mindset would do just one thing with the money – invest it. They would use William Bengen's 4% rule, which states you can spend 4% of the value of an appropriately diversified portfolio each year based on the first-year amount and still have enough to last your entire life. Not only that, it could last FOREVER, creating multigenerational wealth. That means a person with a million dollars in an account may take a distribution of about $40,000 per year. They may use these funds to start a business, build up a down payment for a house, or travel. But this rich mindset approach ensures they will always have that $1 million. That million dollars will be an asset that spins off cash for the rest of their lives. They would BE a millionaire, rather than just spending a million dollars. A person with a poor mindset would spend it all and eventually find themselves begging for their old job back.

Here's a list of some of the most cringeworthy things we've heard people with a poor mindset say they'd do if we gave them $1 million:

"If you gave me a million dollars, I would:"

- Quit my job
- Buy a new car
- Buy a house
- Take a vacation and fly First Class
- Get a new wardrobe

- Get a Rolex
- Invest the money in a new business (even though I have never owned a business before, and most businesses fail)
- Party and show off; YOLO!

How much money do you think would be left after that list? Without investing it, it's only a matter of time until it's all gone. Then you would be right back where you started.

Now, here is a list of things people with a rich mindset would say:

"If you gave me a million dollars, I would:"

- Continue working
- Consult with a financial advisor, CPA, and/or an attorney
- Invest ALL of the money and at an 8% average annual return (for example), I'd have:
  - $1.5 million in 5 years
  - $2.2 million in 10 years
  - $3.3 million in 15 years
  - $5 million in 20 years
- At *most* I'd take out $40,000 a year (using the 4% rule) and use it to:
  - Invest in myself by learning a high-value, high-paying skill
  - Build an emergency savings fund
  - Wipe out any credit card debt
  - Start a business (it's okay if it fails because I will have another $40,000 next year so I can try again)
  - Add it to my savings so I can eventually put a 20% down payment on a house

A million dollars is like a sword. In the hands of someone who doesn't know how to wield it, at best it's just a hunk of metal and at worst they're likely to hurt themselves. Those with a poor mindset work for money, while those with a rich mindset know how to make their money work for *them*.

THE SECRET MILLIONAIRES

The truth is, millionaires are being created every day from IRAs and 401(k)s. Retirement investing is one of the biggest ways people are becoming millionaires today. Investing in IRAs and 401(k)s allows ANYONE to climb the ladder. Anyone with an income can open an IRA. Anyone can invest in the stock market. So why don't more people take advantage of these opportunities? Because retirement accounts aren't flashy. You can't show them off like you would a new car or a Rolex. It's highly unlikely that someone will brag about their 401(k)s to their friends. That's why we call them the "Secret Millionaires." If you want to join the Secret Millionaires Club, you have to act like you *don't* have a million dollars, and then work and spend accordingly.

Spending a nest egg is the exact opposite of wealth-building behavior. Most self-made millionaires don't live lavish lifestyles or have expensive tastes, because if they did, they would never have become millionaires in the first place. Wealthy people know they need to be better than 99% of the population when it comes to money. Being aware of the poor mindset behaviors that separate people from their money will help you develop the rich mindset methods that can take you from a broke fool in a new Porsche to a smart investor in a used Toyota who is growing a portfolio, and building generational wealth. The ugly truth is this: most people are trapped by their attachments to shiny, bullshit material possessions. We'll show you how to escape that trap and find true financial freedom. We promise – it feels way better than driving a sports car.

The sad news is that nobody is going to give you a million dollars, and if someone did, you'd probably blow it anyway. But chances are, you've received a lump of unexpected cash here and there, say from a tax return, a birthday gift from your rich grandmother, or maybe a bonus from work. The question is: *What did you do with it?* Did your actions fit the poor mindset or rich mindset approach? Did you spend it right away or do you use it to increase your net worth? If you're classifying that unexpected money as surplus to be spent, you're probably stuck in a vicious cycle of living paycheck to paycheck. But if you think of each bit of extra money as a seed to be planted in your financial freedom fund of investments, you're literally growing money. Money doesn't grow on trees; but it DOES grow in investment accounts.

DON'T WAIT UNTIL YOU CAN "AFFORD" TO INVEST; START INVESTING NOW

Traditional wisdom claims you must pay off all your debt before you build an emergency fund, and you must build an emergency fund before you invest. We call bullshit on that approach because it doesn't work for most people. Take, for instance, a person who makes good money, but has trouble saving. They may be waiting until they have a healthy savings account before investing, but when they see money in their account, they spend it. For years, the cycle continues. They put money in savings, start to build it up, then take money back out of the account. If they don't invest at the same time they are saving, they'll never get to the investing part. Or consider the person who wants to pay off all of their debt before they start investing. They knock out their credit card debt, but they have student loans. After years of paying those off they take out a mortgage to buy a house. For many Americans, they don't pay off all of their debt for decades!

If you want to build wealth, you need to start investing NOW, even if you can only invest 1% of your income. As you tackle paying down debt and building up your emergency fund you can increase the percentage of your income you invest until you hit your goal. We recommend you work your way up until you are investing 30% or more of your income. Designate a percentage of your income to investments, regardless of whether you have reached your emergency savings goal or paid off credit card debt. Even if it's 1%, it will pay off in the future. Prioritize having 30% of your income to use toward your financial freedom. You could put 28% toward your high-interest debt, 1% into an emergency savings fund, and invest the remaining 1%. Let's get real; there may never come a day when you're completely out of debt. This percentage plan can help you ensure you're not left empty handed later in life.

> Dr. Brad: I know someone who got injured on the job while working for a big corporation. He couldn't work anymore, so the company was on the hook for workers' compensation. They offered him one of two options:
>
> 1. $300,000 in cash up front
> 2. Disability payments for the rest of his life.
>
> He took the lump sum of cash up front, which for a $40,000 yearly salary, adds up to seven and a half years of compensation. If he had taken the annuity payment of $40,000 for the next 30 years, he would have been able to live comfortably for the rest of his life. Instead, the lump sum of money lured him into a false sense of security. He sold his mobile home and bought a new house, took his whole family to Disney World, bought a brand-new truck, and lived as if he was rich. In no time, all the money was gone and due to his injury, he wasn't able to work and bring in more money. After a year and a half of living lavishly, he had to move back into the trailer park, suffer through his injury at a crappy, low-wage job, and sell his new truck. What the corporation knew that most people don't is that most people will see that large number and throw logic and reason out the window.

WHY WE SUCK AT MONEY

When it comes to money, our brains are stuck in the caveman era. To plan for the future, we need to overcome all of our ancestral hard wiring in our brains that tells us to spend what we get right away, live just for the moment rather than plan the future, save nothing, and share everything. This is how ancient tribes survived when they were in the wild with no refrigerators to save food and under the constant threat of predators. But in modern times, we can save and plan ahead; we just don't do it because of this ancient conditioning.

ANCIENT BRAINS IN A MODERN WORLD

The whole concept of saving goes against our evolutionary biology and psychology. Most of our time on Earth has been as hunter-gatherer groups of no more than 150 people. You couldn't save anything because carcasses would rot if you didn't eat them right away. In fact, if members of the tribe tried to save and not share resources, they would be banished, which meant certain death. In many tribes, the true measure of wealth wasn't how much you saved, but how much you gave away to the other members of your community. Saving or hoarding resources was seen as selfish, and members who tried to do so lost status, which made them vulnerable because their survival depended on the protection of the tribe. We are fighting against evolution when we save our money and resources. It goes against what we've learned during most of our time on Earth. That's why most people are terrible at it.

SHORT-CIRCUIT YOUR HARD-WIRING

While we are not creatures of saving, we are creatures of habit. The way to short-circuit your hardwiring when it comes to money is to create a no-brainer investment strategy that essentially does all the work for you. If you set up your investment deposits to automatically come out of your account each month, you bypass that part of your brain that sees the resource and wants to use it. The money will already be gone from your account without you lifting a finger. It will take more work for you to stop the payments, which bypasses another inherent instinct to use as little energy as possible, rather than allow the automatic investment to happen without effort. Our brains developed "laziness" as a survival skill because long ago, we could have been chased by a saber-tooth tiger at any moment, so conserving our energy was crucial. Now, we don't have to worry about being chased, but our brains are still geared toward saving energy and spending resources. Auto-investing bypasses both of those mechanisms.

DON'T BE AFRAID TO INVEST

Most people who grow up poor are afraid to invest. They don't trust financial advisors, banks, or the stock market. They have seen financial institutions take advantage of poor people and have heard stories of people losing all their money. But the sad truth is, this avoidance just keeps them poor. Investing isn't as scary as people think it is if they do it like rich people do it. A poor mindset puts investing on a pedestal as this distant, intimidating thing. Or it makes people "invest" in get-rich-quick schemes that take all their money. But it doesn't have to be that way, and you don't have to be rich to invest like the rich. You can go onto an investment app, like Acorns, Vanguard, Fidelity, Charles Schwab, or Betterment and invest $30 per month (the cost of one premium streaming service). Adrian likes using Acorn's feature of investing spare change when he uses his credit card. So every time he swipes he is investing!

It's that simple. Taking small action like this may be all your mindset needs to shift into wealth mode. You'll see your portfolio grow and realize, "Hey, I'm an investor now." Investing is crucial and is life-changing.

"BUT WHAT SHOULD I INVEST IN?" RESEARCH TARGET-DATE FUNDS

Unfortunately, we can't tell you specifically what to invest in, for many reasons. We don't know your tolerance for risk, your tax situation, or your timeline. For advice specific to your situation, you need to consult with a financial advisor. But for DIY investors, many experts recommend "target-date funds" to keep investors on track for their investing goal. Target-date funds are exchange-traded or mutual funds that change over time, reallocating and rebalancing your money the closer you get to your target date. For instance, if you're young, a target-date fund would invest your assets in more risky investments, like stocks. But as you get older, your funds would be shifted to more stable investments, such as bonds. It requires very little expertise or knowledge about financial planning, and DIY investors who invest in target-date funds at places like Vanguard, Fidelity, or Charles Schwab will outperform the majority of investors who are trying to "beat the market" by trading stocks. It is an incredibly inexpensive option that gives you access to the exact same investments that only rich people could access in the past.

FINDING THE RIGHT FINANCIAL ADVISOR FOR YOU

Most rich people hire financial advisors to manage their investments. In fact, 70% of millionaires work with financial advisors. Frankly, they are just too busy making money and/or enjoying their financial freedom to want to worry about what the stock market is doing day to day. And the *last* thing they are going to do is sit at their computers trading all day long trying to "beat the market." But a good financial advisor does more than just invest for their clients. They help with the details of a client's financial life, including cash flow planning, tax planning, retirement planning, estate planning, educational planning, and insurance planning. But finding a good financial planner isn't easy. In fact, the majority of people calling themselves financial advisors are not required by law to do what is right for the client. We know this sounds CRAZY, but it's true.

After the stock market crash of 1929 that led to the Great Depression, the federal government stepped in to try to protect investors from fraudulent practices by investment advisors. So they passed the Investment Advisors Act of 1940, insisting that financial advisors hold to a *fiduciary duty*. Quite simply, a fiduciary duty means two things: (1) the advisor is required to put the clients' best financial interests above their own, and (2) advisors need to disclose their fees and any potential conflicts of interest. Sounds pretty simple, right? Wrong!

The fact is, the majority of financial advisors out there today are NOT fiduciaries. For example, insurance companies and broker-dealers lobbied Congress and got excluded from the fiduciary duty. Now, you've got to ask yourself, why would they NOT want to be held to the simple duty of putting their clients' interests first and not withholding information about fees and conflicts of interest? Were they worried that doing the right thing by clients would cut into their profits too much? Regardless of what motivated them to work so hard to not be held to a fiduciary standard, it's good to know where their loyalties lie when you are choosing a financial planner. The ONLY financial advisors who are legally obligated to be fiduciaries are Registered Investment Advisors (RIAs), which are monitored by the Securities and Exchange Commission (SEC). Dr. Brad is a managing principal of YMW Advisors, an RIA that manages close to $700 million. They charge clients a percentage of assets under management, with most clients paying less than 1%. If you are looking for a financial advisor, we recommend you work with an RIA. If you have $500,000 or more to invest and want to work with Dr. Brad's fee-only RIA, you can learn more about his company at www.StartThinkingRich.com/Invest.

BECOMING A MILLIONAIRE IS POSSIBLE!

It's not your fault that you want to spend a million dollars. But to become a millionaire and stay one, you must overcome your ancient hardwiring. But the good news is, it's absolutely doable. You don't have to have superpowers to become a millionaire; you just need to be smarter than your survival-based brain. When most people see a million dollars, they think of how to spend it. But if you learn how to save and invest it, that million dollars could sustain you and your family for life.

Chapter 3 *Start Thinking Rich* Challenge

Now that you know the differences between what a rich mindset and a poor mindset would do with $1 million, what would you do now if we gave you $1 million? Compare your answers to the list you made at the beginning of this chapter. How has it changed now that you know how to make your money work for you and not the other way around? What would you invest in to make your life better? Pay attention to any urge to buy rather than invest and save. Challenge yourself to think about how you would use the money to build net worth and enhance your life.

CHAPTER FOUR

YOUR BELIEFS ABOUT MONEY ARE KEEPING YOU POOR

You've been lied to about money. Many of us were raised to believe that money can't buy happiness (it can, to a significant degree), and even worse, that rich people are bad and poor people are somehow more virtuous. But money isn't inherently good or bad. It's a tool, like an ax. An ax can be used to chop firewood to keep your family warm, but it can also be used to murder someone. Before we can start building a wealthy lifestyle, we have to dismantle the lies we've been told about money.

It's time to shred your false mindsets about money. Everything you've been taught about money being "bad," "a happiness killer," or "the root of all evil," is wrong. Not only that, but much of what you've been taught about how to become rich and how rich people spend their money is also wrong. These false beliefs about money are keeping you poor. In this chapter we are going to identify and challenge what we call "poor mindsets." If any of these mindsets sound familiar, your beliefs are hindering your relationship with money. You're not alone. Many people out there have the same tendencies. Being broke can be temporary, but a poor mindset can keep you poor forever. The first step is recognizing your poor mindset and changing it.

POOR MINDSET NO. 1: RICH PEOPLE ARE EVIL

This one is ingrained in many of us, especially if we grew up reading the Bible. In psychology, the term used for people who push money away because they think it's bad or they don't deserve it is called "money avoidance." Dr. Brad has written extensively about this in his books and research articles because it's a huge roadblock to wealth for many people. Money avoidance causes a host of financial problems unless it's resolved. Here are some of the beliefs that lead to money avoidance:

> "Money is bad."
> "You can't get rich without taking advantage of others."
> "Money destroys relationships."
> "There is virtue in having less money."
> "Rich people are greedy."
> "If I make too much money, my friends and family will look down on me."

If you have any of these beliefs, you're not going to have any money. You will repel money and the people who can show you how to get it. If you start to have some success, you will sabotage yourself. That's why it's important to challenge this belief, and we are here to help.

GOD DOESN'T WANT YOU TO BE POOR

Many religions talk about money, and much of that talk isn't good. For example, if you grew up in the Christian religion, like we did, you've probably heard at least one of these phrases from the Bible:

"The love of money is the root of all evils."
"It is easier for a camel to pass through the eye of a needle than for a rich person to enter the kingdom of God."
"If you want to be complete, go and sell your possessions and give to the poor, and you will have treasure in heaven."

These verses can turn into beliefs about money that dictate our financial lives. Taking these verses out of context or looking at them in a vacuum could lead you to believe that money is bad and rich people are evil. It's also easier to believe that money is bad than it is to do the work of becoming wealthy. However, the Bible says a lot of other things about money, suggesting that the truth about money is much more nuanced. Consider these Bible verses:

"The blessing of the Lord makes a person rich, and he adds no sorrow with it."
"And this same God who takes care of me will supply all your needs from his glorious riches, which have been given to us in Christ Jesus."
"A wise man saves for the future, but a foolish man spends whatever he gets."
"Idle hands make one poor, but diligent hands bring riches."

We're not religious scholars, but perhaps the message here is that when you have abundance, you should be careful to maintain your humility, not lose touch with the struggle of others who may be less fortunate, and make efforts to help the disadvantaged when and where you can. Those with a rich mindset will be open to a nuanced view about money and wealth, exploring the good while being conscious of the risks. We believe that whatever higher power you believe in wants you to live a life of abundance.

Money can be used to fund beautiful and amazing things. It provides for families, furthers humanitarian causes, brings security, and offers freedom, so we can focus on what's important to us. When we're financially free, we have more time and resources to do good in the world. Wealth can help you add more even value to the world. So consider becoming wealthy as a moral imperative and do the good work to get there.

> Adrian: Like most college kids I was dead broke. The only way I could really make a positive impact in the world was through donating my time to volunteer. So I spent my time volunteering across a variety of organizations and causes, from helping victims of the Cedar Rapids flood of 2007, to teaching dance to at-risk youth. Today, my impact is exponentially greater than back when I was a broke college student. Because of my financial freedom, I can contribute in ways beyond my time and have chosen to fund things like gifting people cell phones to funding sustainable food gardens for schools in South America. Unless you are the next Gandhi or Mother Teresa, it is a fact that you can make a bigger impact in the world the more money you have.

POOR MINDSET NO. 2: MORE STUFF WILL MAKE ME HAPPIER

The more people put money on a pedestal, the more likely they are to have worse financial outcomes. The belief that more money and more stuff is going to magically solve all your problems is a dangerous one. Dr. Brad's research calls these "money worship" money scripts, and they lead to lower income, lower net worth, and higher credit card debt. Money worship beliefs can destroy your financial life. Here are some of those harmful beliefs:

"Money would solve all my problems."
"It is hard to be poor and happy."
"You can never have enough money."

The fact is, all the shiny new toys in the world will NOT bring you lasting happiness. Think back to when you were a kid and you got an amazing birthday present. You probably spent the day, or even the week, playing with it. But soon enough, your excitement faded as things settled back to normal. With any new purchase you may feel a burst of excitement, but it quickly fades and often we are left with stress from a fat credit card bill.

Adrian: I believe that every object you own owns a piece of you. The more stuff you own the more trapped you become. My old condo used to look like everyone's – every drawer, cupboard, and closet filled to the brim with completely unnecessary stuff. It took moving to Europe to learn how amazing life can be when you don't own anything. My wife and I have taken this money script to the max when we spent a whole year living in a van. Today our house isn't on four wheels anymore, but if you were to open random closets and drawers you would see a lot of empty space!

POOR MINDSET NO. 3: RICH PEOPLE ARE BIG SPENDERS

The belief that rich people are big spenders could be one of the most destructive beliefs about money ever. This belief is supported by prominent displays of wealth all over reality television and social media. We see celebrities in their Lambos. We see billionaire entrepreneurs in their private jets. We see movie stars in their mansions. But is this an accurate depiction of how *most* wealthy people spend money? The simple answer is NO – not even close. A quick analysis of the situation can help. The reality is that most millionaires in the United States are "self-made." Think about what it takes to become a self-made millionaire. Being a millionaire means that you have acquired a net worth of at least one million dollars. The *only* way to acquire a net worth of a million dollars is to *not spend* a million dollars. Get it?

The psychology of self-made millionaires goes directly against what we see on social media. Most of them describe themselves as frugal. A study of over 1,000 clients of financial planners revealed a shocking secret. When separated into two groups and analyzed, Dr. Brad found that the group with $11 million in net worth spent only twice as much as the group that had a net worth of $500,000. Even though their net worth was 22 times higher, they spent only twice as much on things like homes, cars, vacations, and watches.

The sad reality is that if you are obsessed with material items, you will never become financially free. As soon as you start to get ahead you will look to buy your next toy – a fancy watch, a luxury car, designer goods. If you want to become wealthy, you're going to need to start thinking rich.

POOR MINDSET NO. 4: YOU CAN'T TRUST PEOPLE AROUND MONEY

The belief that people are always out to take advantage of you is a scarcity mindset, and another money worship belief. As with all poor mindsets, you probably came to this belief honestly. Perhaps you grew up in poverty and saw lots of stealing and scamming. Or perhaps you had your lunch money stolen by a bully at school. The problem with this mindset is that becoming financially free requires a degree of trust around money. For example, many people who grew up poor were never exposed to legitimate investing. They were never exposed to financial professionals, such as financial advisors or accountants. They have heard stories of people who "invested" and lost all of their money. Interestingly, when you do a deep dive into these stories of "investing," it turns out it wasn't investing at all – it was speculation – trying to get rich quick. Studies on rich people find that they are much more likely than those in the middle class to trust financial professionals and hire them. So while you can't trust just anybody with your money, there are accredited professionals in whom you can and should put your trust, so they can guide you in growing your money.

RICH MINDSET = MONEY VIGILANCE

We've discussed some of the beliefs that keep people poor, but what kinds of beliefs make people rich? In Dr. Brad's research, these beliefs are called "money vigilance," and the richest people have them. So how do you shift your mindset to one that brings abundance, rather than focusing on scarcity? Here are a few examples of these money vigilance mindsets:

"It is important to save for emergencies."
"It is extravagant to spend money on oneself."
"I treasure every dime I earn and refuse to waste any of it."
"No expensive dinner, fancy outfit, or expensive car is worth a lifetime of financial security."
"Flip burgers now, own the restaurant later."
"I take care of my money, so my money can take care of me."

When you respect your relationship with money, your money will take care of you.

Adrian: My immigrant family came to this country with nothing. My father didn't speak English and worked hard doing manual labor cash jobs. It was back-breaking work, but he never gave up. Many people in the United States believe that the American Dream is dead. But to immigrants, that dream is alive; you just have to work hard enough to make it a reality. My parents saw America through the lens of an abundance mindset. Instead of focusing on everything they lacked, they saw a land of possibility and opportunity in front of them. They were used to living poor, so they were used to going without fancy clothing or frivolous expenses. They took everything they made and saved. Every penny held the promise of a better life. They never wasted their energy crying about what they didn't have. Instead, they focused on working for what they wanted.

Growing up, Adrian learned from his parents and grandparents that there was no money problem that hard work couldn't solve. Every day, his grandmother would walk for miles to other villages from her rural town in Tamazulita, Mexico (because she couldn't afford a bus ticket), in the hopes of being able to buy goods to sell them in her community. If she couldn't buy goods that day, she would knock on doors in her town and ask if she could make people dinner to make extra money, sometimes using ingredients she would forage from that day in the wilderness. She instilled the value of hard work into her family. Adrian's dad did exhausting work detailing cars at the Toyota dealership and climbed the ladder to Parts Manager. When Adrian started building wealth, he felt guilty because his work didn't feel "hard" enough. He wasn't taking long bus rides or doing hard manual labor. He was pushing buttons on his computer. If Adrian had not become aware of this belief, he would have sabotaged his financial success.

Since Adrian's dad worked so hard for every penny he earned, he worried it was too risky to invest in the stock market. Instead, he went the safer route of CDs and Treasury notes. During a family conversation, Adrian asked his parents how much they lost in the 2008 crash. They said they didn't lose any money because they hadn't invested in the stock market. While it's nice that they didn't lose money, they also prevented themselves from building 10 times the wealth they accumulated through the safer routes such as investing in the S&P 500.

> Adrian: My parents were the first people on both sides of their families to move from lower class to upper middle class. My mom told me a memory she had as a young adult hearing her dad say he had finally been able to save $1,000 in the bank after all the kids had moved out the house. He shared that achieving this had finally made him feel "rich."
>
> My parents came from nothing and so they felt the safest investments were Treasuries and CDs. I was able to build off their conservative spending and saving habits to learn about the power of investing in the stock market among other investments. I built on their work ethic and found other ways to make money besides having a normal 9-to-5 job.

Unless we challenge the status quo, we are doomed to repeat the same financial habits as our families. Some of you have good financial behaviors you can emulate from your parents like Adrian's parents' good saving habits. Others might need to challenge the financial behaviors and habits they saw growing up.

> Dr. Brad: I remember working with this one guy who is now close to billionaire status. He was also an immigrant who didn't speak English when he and his mother first came to the United States. I was fascinated with him. He was dealing with every systemic barrier possible, from language, to culture, to education. I became obsessed with his mindset. When he was a teenager, he worked at a fast food restaurant, flipping burgers and working the fry machine. While his coworkers were blowing their paychecks, this guy was saving every dollar so he could one day own that restaurant. Not only did he save enough to buy it, but he now owns

hundreds of them. What set him apart from his coworkers was his willingness to sacrifice. As an immigrant, he understood the sacrifice and grit required to improve his circumstances.

Whenever we post on social media about the willingness to sacrifice being tied to our potential to become rich, we always get the same comments:

"Why should I have to sacrifice?"
"I want to enjoy the money I've worked so hard to make."
"YOLO!"

But our level of success is in direct proportion to our willingness to sacrifice. When you are willing to make the sacrifices to have the future you desire, remarkable things are possible.

Dr. Brad: That fast food worker didn't make enough to buy the restaurant overnight. He had to take gradual steps to get there. He realized he needed to learn a trade so he could make more money. So he used what he'd saved from his restaurant job and went to school to learn to be a mechanic so he could make a solid hourly wage. For five years, he worked as a mechanic and slept on his mother's couch. He ate noodles for dinner, rode the bus and bought his clothes at Goodwill. He was saving 95% of his income. In five years, he had enough to buy his first restaurant. But he continued to sacrifice, working, saving, and keeping his expenses low. Now, he owns hundreds of restaurants. He retired his mother who now lives a life of luxury. He can buy anything he wants. I find his story so inspiring. It makes me sit back and think, "What was I complaining about earlier?"

Many immigrants who came to America are broke but have a rich mindset. They are willing to sacrifice for a better future. Their beliefs about money keep them on track to success. Instead of harboring negative beliefs about money being evil, they see it as a tool. They are so dedicated to creating a better life, they are willing to sleep on couches, eat onions, and wear clothes from the thrift store. The average American is not willing to make the same level of sacrifice. As such, they never reap the same rewards.

MINDSET HACKS

Nobody just decides to create a whole new belief system and wakes up the next morning as a new person. It takes practice. Smart people who are trying to achieve a goal will put systems in place to make it easier for them to succeed and harder for them to fail. Here are some tools that may help:

1. *Credit card debt*: Take all of your credit cards out of your wallet and lock them away. Remove your card information from major retail websites, like Amazon, so you're not tempted to rack up debt with online shopping. Place the key to your credit cards under a note that says, "Is this purchase worth giving up my dream of (insert goal here)?" Place pictures of your goal next to the note, so you have to look at what you'll be missing if you use your credit card for frivolous purchases. Maybe it's a house for your family, or a restaurant you want to own. Maybe it's a young, retired person playing golf. It can be whatever you think will motivate you and prevent you from shredding your future for that fleeting moment of retail bliss.

2. *Saving*: There are a few tricks that can help:
   - Direct deposit a percentage of your paycheck each month to your savings account, so you don't even see it and won't be tempted to spend it.
   - Label your savings accounts. It's easy to pull money from a general savings fund, but it's much harder to pull from an account labeled, "My Daughter's Future," or "My Dream House."
   - Get roommates. Rent is skyrocketing across the country. Dealing with a few roommates while you save for a house of your own will get you to your goal much faster.

- Live in a van. Adrian did it! Find unconventional ways to save money. You can even turn it into a game. How can you spend $40 a week feeding yourself? Can you learn to sew patches in your clothes so you don't have to buy new items? Can you live without streaming subscriptions and read books for a year? Get creative and challenge yourself to have fun with it.

3. *Invest*: Of course, it's a good idea to invest your money, but that's not the only investment you can make. You can also invest your time and energy into learning a new trade or skill that will bring you more income.

4. *Find ways to make money in your sleep*: We will get into this more in Chapter 19: "People Who Binge Netflix Without a Side Hustle Will Be Poor Forever," but if your only source of income comes from your paid labor, you're missing out on huge financial opportunities. People who have figured out how to get rich make money in their sleep.

5. *Sacrifice*: Consider buying a new phone or going out and spending money on alcohol as financial dream killers. Make the sacrifices now and you'll be able to order anything you want when you're rich. The irony is, you'll be so used to being careful with your money, you may not even care as much about fancy gadgets and extravagant dinners.

When you train your mind to be strong and get used to going without certain luxuries, it becomes a superpower. While everyone else is spending $300 on dinner, drinks, and entertainment on the weekend, you'll be saving. Sure, it may feel like you're missing out, at first. But in 5 or 10 years when you are a financially free millionaire and they are still slogging away at their 9-to-5 jobs, living paycheck to paycheck, you'll see that it was worth the sacrifice.

Adrian: When we lived in a van, we gave up a lot of luxuries. We didn't have air conditioning, there were no appliances, like dishwashers or washing machines. Our entire life's possessions were in the van with no room to buy more items or clothing. We didn't watch TV that year. Instead of binging shows, I read books and hiked the country. I built my social media followers with just a couple hours of Wi-Fi access a week from 100,000 to 1 million followers, which launched the personal brand I have now! That year living in a van we saved 95% of every dollar we made by living such an extreme minimalist lifestyle. It took a few weeks to get used to living in a van, but I surprised myself with how much liberation it created. I had more mental capacity to think and the freedom from consumerism was excellent for my mental health. This sacrifice of living "tiny" ended up being a decision that catapulted me into financial success! You'll find that once you start making sacrifices, the same is possible for you.

Dr. Brad: When I got out of college, I had a massive amount of student loan debt. The interest rate was insane, and I knew I needed to pay it off as fast as possible. So I got two beat-up cars, one for $500 and another for about $2,500. They were constantly breaking down, so I would drive one while fixing the other one. I lived in a house with no furniture, just a mattress on the floor. I had a hand-me-down ping-pong table and lawn chairs in my living room. My cupboards were bare. I had one fork, one plate, and one cup. It's a miracle that my wife decided to marry me when she saw how I was living. I did that for three years. I didn't buy any new clothes. I didn't go on vacations, and I used all of my salary as a clinical psychologist in schools on Kauai to pay off my debt. And I didn't stop there. I also started a couple of side hustles, doing substance abuse evaluations and giving tennis lessons on the weekends. I did whatever I could to make money so I could pay off my loans while simultaneously funding my retirement accounts. I paid off $100,000 in student loan debt in three years and I was proud of that accomplishment.

The fastest way to crush your financial wellbeing is with unchecked money beliefs. Even if you make a million dollars, a negative association with money will sabotage your financial well-being every time. Before you make a single dollar, it's important to investigate your money beliefs and find out all the ways you sabotage yourself when it comes to earning, saving, and investing. When Dr. Brad tells his students and followers that most millionaires are self-made, he encounters a ton of resistance to that idea. Even when he presents studies and data to back it up, people don't want to believe they are broke because of their choices and not because of fate. The question is, how is that belief helping them? Sure, it makes them feel better about their situation, thinking it's out of their control. But when those with poor mindsets find out most millionaires are self-made, they come face to face with the reality that they could be rich but are failing to do so. But it isn't a moral failure. It's a mindset failure, and mindsets can change.

Chapter 4 *Start Thinking Rich* Challenge

Write down all of your beliefs about money. Then think back to the memory that started each belief. Many destructive money beliefs begin in childhood. Maybe your parents taught you to never talk about money, so you developed money avoidance beliefs. Maybe your parents believed money was evil and passed that down to you. Once you've discovered the source of your harmful money beliefs, write new beliefs from a rich mindset, such as, "Money is a tool and I use it for good." Or "I take care of my money, so my money takes care of me." Display your new money beliefs on a mirror or wall where you can see them every day and think about them before you make any new purchases. Use this new money mindset to help you set up automatic payments to investments and savings. Label your accounts to keep you on track. Congratulations on your rich mindset! For a free test of your money beliefs developed by Dr. Brad and used in his research with over 100,000 people, visit www.StartThinkingRich.com/moneyscriptstest.

CHAPTER FIVE

YOUR TEACHERS CAN'T TEACH YOU HOW TO GET RICH

N ot only is everything you've been taught about money WRONG but you're also trusting the WRONG people. If people haven't done something themselves, how are they going to teach YOU to do it? It's just common sense. Why would you trust teachers to teach you to be financially independent when they aren't financially independent themselves? Why would you trust your college professors to teach you to run a business, if they haven't been successful entrepreneurs? Why would you trust your employer to take care of you and help you become financially independent, just so you can leave them? Why would you take investing advice from your uncle, who lost all his money day trading? Many people have blindly trusted these people to teach them, and yet:

- The average American has $96,000 in debt.
- Fifty-six percent of Americans don't have enough savings to cover a $1,000 emergency.
- Forty-nine percent of Americans will never be able to retire comfortably.

Instead of trusting the wrong people for the wrong things, you need to accept the fact that people just can't teach you what they don't already know. So, unless you have a close relationship with someone who has achieved exactly what you want to achieve and is willing to mentor you, it's on you to stop wasting time and start learning about money, business, and investing. Unfortunately, our school system fails to teach students the basics of personal finance. So, instead of relying on your mainstream education to teach you how to become financially independent, find people who are living your dream life, and learn from them how to create it for yourself. Instead of trusting your employer to support your desire to be financially free, and therefore not need them, spend your nights and weekends learning how to build your side hustle so you can eventually leave your job. Instead of relying on Social Security or your company's pension to take care of you when you are old, learn to invest for yourself.

Sure, the false sense of stability from that regular paycheck is quite alluring, but there is plenty of risk involved in relying on only one source of income. What if you wake up tomorrow and your company decides they don't need you anymore? About 40 million Americans lost their jobs in 2023 alone. What if there are big layoffs at your company this year or what if your company goes bust? Don't be fooled into thinking that a "stable" 9-to-5 job offers financial security. There is no such thing as a sure thing when it comes to selling your time and labor. A corporation will ALWAYS put their financial interests above yours. That's just a fact of life. The bait of a "stable" 9-to-5 is there to pull people into a trap. But we're going to teach you how to diversify your streams of income so you can become financially invincible (more on that in Chapter 19: "People Who Binge Netflix Without a Side Hustle Will Be Poor Forever").

> Adrian: I went to college and the degree I earned ensured that I would be in the middle class. However, college did not teach me how to make it to where I am today. I had to learn how to become an entrepreneur and millionaire on my own and through relationships I sought with mentors.

DON'T TRUST BROKE PEOPLE TO GIVE YOU ADVICE ON HOW TO GET RICH

The worst thing you can do is take advice from someone who hasn't lived their own advice, or worse, attempted and failed. This might sound harsh. But should you trust a friend to give you investing advice if he lost all his money trading stocks? The problem is, he might tell you that investing is "too risky," when in reality he was gambling; he wasn't investing at all. Or worse yet, are you going to take financial advice from your broke friend, who lives in his mother's basement trading crypto, about the latest shit coin that is certain to increase 1,000× in the next few weeks? Or should you put your life's savings in the hands of a twenty-year-old financial advisor who is fresh out of college, has huge student loan debt, no money invested for himself, leases a brand-new Mercedes, and wears a Rolex? With all of the terrible advice out there, whom CAN you trust? The last thing you need is someone in your ear with a can't-do attitude based on their own inexperience, shortcomings, traumas, or failures. To get solid advice, you need to talk to someone who has gone from where you are to where you want to be or is at least a step or two ahead of you, talking the talk, walking the walk, and succeeding. At StartThinkingRich .com/resources we have a curated list of trusted sources of information on personal finance, entrepreneurship, and investing that we have found useful on our journey.

YOU CAN'T TRUST THE SYSTEM TO MAKE YOU WEALTHY

The traditional 9-to-5, working-for-someone-else-until-you-retire or-die-job just doesn't cut it anymore. Gone are the days of graduating from high school, getting a company job, working for 50 years, retiring with a gold watch, and riding your company's pension into the sunset. The system has changed dramatically, and for most Americans, for the worse. Company pensions, where your company carries the risk of funding your retirement, are sadly a thing of the past. This didn't happen by accident. Companies have been systematically offloading the burden of funding your retirement for decades now to free up their balance sheets. Once they are no longer responsible for supporting you in your old age, their profits surge. In other words, your company literally stopped caring about you – at least caring about what happens to you in your old age. The entire retirement savings system shifted, but most Americans never got the memo. You can no longer count on your company to take care of you. The best you can hope for now is a 401(k) match, and if your company offers you one, you are lucky, because most are not even required to do that.

As if that isn't bad enough, for many people, one job doesn't even earn them enough money to make ends meet, let alone have enough for emergencies and retirement. This is by design. Today's companies expect workers to sell their labor and time for the lowest wages possible so they can fatten the pockets of shareholders while leaving the workers to struggle. The system is set up to make companies and their stockholders more and more wealthy, with little incentive to take care of their employees.

The truth is, your employers are very unlikely to want you to become financially free. Why would they? If you left, they would lose out on your labor and would have to invest money to train your replacement. You've got to think outside the box to truly free yourself from the 9-to-5 grind. It's time to take charge of your own hustle. We aren't saying you need to quit your job right now. It took Adrian five years for his online side hustle (teaching people how to dance the robot) to make enough money to take him to full-time entrepreneur. Dr. Brad built up his side hustles for over a decade before he left the "security" of his day job working in the public school system in Hawaii. But time is going to pass quickly, so you might as well work for yourself when you're not working for your boss. Set yourself up with more sources of income. Build up your side hustles on nights and weekends like Adrian and Dr. Brad did. Make yourself rich, not just your company's shareholders. Invest so you can become a shareholder yourself, where YOU can get paid for doing nothing. Find people who have broken free of the paycheck-to-paycheck system and learn how they did it, so you can do it too.

FINDING YOUR TEACHERS

If your teachers are living paycheck to paycheck, or don't really know how actual rich people invest, you can't rely on them to teach you about financial independence. Period. So where DO you learn to be financially free?

Picking up this book is an excellent start, but don't let it be your only resource. There are many books out there (go to StartThinkingRich.com/books for a list of some of our favorites) that can educate you on becoming wealthy. There is an abundance of knowledge on YouTube, podcasts, and social media. In fact, there has never been a time in history where people have so much free access to great information. But with all the information and "experts" giving advice, how do you know whom to listen to and what advice to follow? The key is this: find people who are succeeding in doing what you want to do and study them like your ideal life depends on it.

Dr. Brad: Never ask people for advice around a particular goal if they haven't achieved it themselves. It is unhelpful at best and dangerous at worst, because they're VERY likely to tell you all the ways it's too difficult or downright impossible. Before I wrote my first book, I heard a lot of chatter about how hard it was to do; things like:

- "Oh, it's hard to get it published."
- "It's impossible to get a literary agent."
- "Everybody thinks they can write a book and that everyone else should care."
- "It takes forever."
- "Most people who start it never finish."

This was all quite discouraging. I began to think to myself, "Who am I to think that I can write a book, given how challenging it is?" Thank God I came to my senses and saw that I was talking to the wrong people, people who'd never written a book.

I realized that I needed to talk to someone who had done what I wanted to do. But where could I start? I didn't know any authors. One day I was at a bookstore and I found a book by a guy who graduated from Wright State University's School of Professional Psychology, the same graduate program I had attended. He was the only published author I knew at that point, and I didn't even know the guy. But I found him online and emailed him. I mentioned our university connection and asked if I could pick his brain for 30 minutes on how he wrote a book and got it published. He was kind enough to say yes because of our university ties. I didn't squander this opportunity. I took several hours to put together a list of questions I wanted to ask him.

Over the course of our 30-minute interview, my mindset changed from "writing a book is hard and almost impossible," to "I know it's absolutely possible because I'm talking to a guy who did it!" I'd already written the book in my head by the time the conversation ended. It wasn't even in this author's consciousness that it was too difficult or impossible. His mindset was "you can absolutely achieve it if you want to write a book." That's all it took for me to shift my mindset, and here I am writing my ninth book!

If you talk to people who've failed in their pursuit of a goal, like writing a book, they are likely to tell you it's ill-advised or downright unachievable, like a mountain that's impossible to climb. But authors who have done it can show you that it is possible because it's a mountain they've already scaled. They can show you the map, where the tough spots are, and how to get around them. It matters whom you talk to, whom you ask questions, and what advice you get. The context of their experiences and their mindset matters and can set you on a path to success.

WHAT QUESTIONS TO ASK THE EXPERTS

If you want to get into politics, it's going to be tough to book an "ask the expert" sit-down with the president of the United States, but that's okay because it's not necessary. You could start with your local city council representative. If you want to become an entrepreneur, a meeting with Elon Musk is probably out of reach for you, at least for now. But you could start with a local business owner, or someone in a neighboring town who's in a related industry. The key is this: all you need to do is find someone a step or two ahead of where you are today. Often these people are closer than you think, perhaps a family connection, a friend of a friend, or an Instagram DM away. Remember, you don't need the entire road map to your destination before you get started; you just need marching orders for your next step or two. After you've found this person and learned all you can from the resources they have to offer (e.g. their social media profiles, their website, books they've written), you may decide it's time to reach out to them and see if they'll let you ask a few questions. After you share where you are on your path and your goal, here's a list of questions you could ask them to get you started:

- How did you get where you are?
- What are the biggest mistakes you have seen people make who are in my position and are trying to succeed at this?
- What advice would you give someone who wants to do what you do?
- To what do you credit your success?
- What do you think are my next steps?
- Are there any books, resources, or education that you think are essential for succeeding in this?
- Are there any professional groups or associations I should join?

Remember, the time they are giving you could be your biggest gift. Listen closely to what they are saying. Do NOT argue. Do NOT interrupt. This is not your time to brag or try to get them to do you a favor. In fact, do NOT ask them for anything else whatsoever. When they pause in their responses, you could ask: "Is there anything else?" before you move onto the next question. If you are out to coffee or lunch, make sure YOU insist on paying. If you show that you're willing to give your full attention to their advice, to put in the time, and do the work, many people are open to sharing what they know. Just don't waste their time if you haven't made the effort to educate and prepare yourself before reaching out to them.

People approach us all the time and ask us for business advice. "What business should I start?" "How do I start a business?" We always respond with these questions:

- What is your area of expertise?
- What is your experience?
- What is your training?

If you can't answer those questions, you're not ready for a business mentor yet. Don't be lazy; do your homework. Ask good questions – not questions that can be easily answered by a simple Google search. If you find that you lack the skills, experience, or training for what you want to achieve, then fix this. College can teach you about business and a college degree may be able to open some doors for you, but real-world business experience will always trump what you learn in a textbook.

DO WHAT IT TAKES

Once you've learned from the experts, don't stop there. Knowledge is useless unless you do the work and apply what you've learned. If your mentor tells you that you need to spend 500 hours perfecting your skill set, do it. Don't be afraid to take business or trade courses online or at your community college. But don't stop there. Find people succeeding in the real world outside of the university walls. Get crystal clear about your goals and decide if you're willing to do what it takes to succeed.

> Dr. Brad: I remember working with a high school student in my role as a clinical psychologist. She was a drummer, and she was upset because she was number two in the drum line. She wanted to be number one, but she thought the guy in the number-one spot was just better than her. I saw her self-defeating mindset and I told her that she was correct. I told her that compared to him she was terrible. In fact, if you are starting out something new, you are terrible

61

at it too. Whether it's tennis, soccer, or playing an instrument, everybody sucks at it when they are starting out. But there is only one way to get good. You have to want it. You have to be willing to put in the work. You have to be willing to practice. Hey, it's okay if you just don't want it bad enough. But it's important to tell yourself the truth about that and not blame anyone else.

So I invited the student to do a little mental exercise. I asked her how often this other student practiced the drums. She guessed that it was about six hours a week, and she knew that he worked with a private teacher too. Then I asked how much she practiced. She said about one hour per week. "All right," I said. "If you want to beat him, you need to practice seven hours every week for the next 52 weeks." She looked at me like I was crazy. She said there was no way she wanted to do that. So I said, "Perfect! Now you know you just don't want to do what it takes to be first chair, and that's okay." When she reframed it for herself, she chuckled, relaxed, and stopped torturing herself over her position.

If you don't want to be financially free, even when we show you there's a proven path, that's fine. But own your decision. Don't waste your breath with excuses. If you have a goal, do the research on how other people have achieved that goal. Learn what they've done and do more of it. But if you're not willing to do the research and the work to achieve your goals, just admit you don't want it bad enough. If you learn what it takes to achieve a goal and decide you don't want to do that, we can respect that. But then don't expect handouts from other people when you're not willing to do the work and invest your time, energy, and money into the things you want.

If you know what you have to offer, understand your skill set, understand your weaknesses, and know exactly what you want, it will be much easier for you to succeed. If you want to start a business in a specific area, find someone who is already succeeding in that area and do what they do. For example, if you want to be a contractor, your best bet is to find a successful contractor and study them. You'll get much further than you would by trying to figure it out on your own. Set your goal, hone your skills, and seek the appropriate people and find out how they got where they are and do what they did.

> Dr. Brad: My parents were teachers when I was growing up. My mom encouraged me to go into public service. My dad noticed that during the Great Depression, the only people who kept their jobs were government employees, so he thought it was a safe bet. I was told to either become a teacher or get a job in a federal prison. They told me horror stories about their colleagues who had quit their teaching jobs to start a business, only to have their businesses fail. They had to come crawling back to their teaching jobs at a lower salary, and with less money and less security than before. My parents wanted the best for me. In their minds, a stable, government job was the safest route for me. They didn't want me to get hurt, lose my money, or become a failure. So, when I wanted to become an entrepreneur, if I had taken their advice, I would have quit before I even began. Instead, I studied people who were successful entrepreneurs, researching what worked for them and trying to model it in my endeavors. I learned about how they thought, got into their mindset, and replicated what they did. That has made all the difference for me.

COMMIT TO TEACHING YOURSELF

We are all for education. Dr. Brad is a professor whose parents were teachers. Adrian teaches online courses. There is considerable value in getting an education and building valuable skill sets. But don't stop there. Find the people who have the wealth, success, lifestyle, and knowledge that you want to have and study them. Before you contact them, do as much as you can on your own to build your expertise, experience, and training so you know the questions to ask and you're not wasting their time. Find out whom they learned from and study those people as well. Go all the way to the top, read the books of your mentors' mentors. Be your own best educator. Then, put yourself in positions to meet people who are a few steps ahead of you and form meaningful connections. Go to their seminars, networking events, and book signings. Actively support their social media posts with frequent comments and shares. Build relationships and show that you're not just sitting there with your hand out. Prove that you have and will continue to put in the work. If you authentically grow your team of experts and inspiration, you'll become unstoppable.

Chapter 5 *Start Thinking Rich* Challenge

How to Learn from the Best

Who have been the biggest teachers in your life? How have they helped you? How have they held you back? Think about your biggest life goals right now. Write down three or more things you most want to learn. Take some time to identify a noteworthy (aka industry famous) teacher on these subjects and learn from them, either through their books, podcasts, or online courses. Find three people on social media who are doing what you want to do, work to establish relationships with them, and then ask them the most important question you can in a comment or DM. Ask people in your current network if they know anyone who is succeeding at achieving your goals, even if they are just a step or two ahead of you. Then ask for an introduction and offer to buy them lunch or ask for a 30-minute phone call where you can pick their brain with your well-thought-out questions. Apply that knowledge to become successful so one day others can ask you how you did it.

CHAPTER SIX

IT'S NOT YOUR FAULT IF YOU WERE BORN POOR, BUT IT IS YOUR FAULT IF YOU DIE POOR

I t's time to destroy the destructive myth that if you grew up poor, you'll be poor forever.

Look no further than Adrian's family story.

Adrian: At 15 years old, my dad came to the United States from Mexico with no money, a language barrier, and only the clothes on his back. He washed cars at a Toyota dealership, working his way up to Parts Manager.

In every family picture for many years, my dad was wearing his workshirt, a polo shirt that Toyota gave him. He refused to buy any new clothes until he saved $10,000. My parents worked hard, sacrificed, avoided doing anything stupid, and my dad was able to retire at the age of 56. My parents didn't start out with any money, but they had something even more important than money. They had a rich mindset, the mindset we are teaching you. They were willing to sacrifice to become wealthy. There's no big secret to this. It's not that profound. They lived in a poor neighborhood, they didn't buy clothes, they didn't go out to eat or drink alcohol, and they didn't lease a luxury car to impress their friends. They still had fun, but they did so in ways that didn't cost much money. For example, they joined a Mexican soccer league and had a blast playing the game. They worked hard, played soccer, and raised their kids. First, they saved $10,000. Then they elevated that goal to $50,000, then $100,000, and so on until they eventually became millionaires. It took them a long time, but they did it.

Recently, I was with my family in Oceanside. I rented a beach house for my whole family to come and celebrate my birthday. I asked my parents to take me to my childhood home, so I could see where I grew up. It was an incredibly impoverished neighborhood. The streets were filthy. I don't ever want to go back there. But my parents lived in that neighborhood longer than they may have needed to so they could get ahead financially, and so my sister and I could have the opportunities we enjoy today. Their ultimate goal was to make sure that my sister and I had a better life than they did. They taught me what they could and taught me well, and I took their lessons about saving and accelerated them. Now, I've become a multi-millionaire who can afford to hire my retired parents. My parents came from terrible tragedies and a level of adversity that is hard to imagine. But they did what it took so that we could have something better. Sometimes it takes a generation or two to adopt a rich mindset and put it into action so that it elevates the family and begins to create generational wealth.

YOU CAN'T COMPETE WITH AN IMMIGRANT

Adrian's family rags-to-riches story is just one of countless others and is why we say that you can't compete with immigrants. Many came from poverty the average American can't even fathom and are willing to work harder and sacrifice more than the average American would even consider. But their mindset and habits show what is possible. Only a highly motivated person is willing to do what it takes to spend decades changing the trajectory of the family wealth. Most Americans would NEVER be willing to do this. Most would much rather live a life of comfortable mediocrity than do what it takes to climb the socioeconomic ladder. After all, life isn't that bad, is it? You've got heat in your house, you've got a car, you can numb out with your iPhone or Netflix. Why put in all that time and effort? In fact, we don't blame you if you don't want to do it. Only a "crazy" person would live like that, right? Only a person who's obsessively dedicated to transforming their family's life on such a deep level, they're willing to spend a generation doing it. We just want to say, we give you permission to not want to become wealthy bad enough. If it's not your thing, that's okay. We can respect that.

EARNER SKILLS VS. WEALTH SKILLS

Getting rich comes down to two skill sets: earner skills and wealth skills. Earner skills are used to bring in money. Your income is your best wealth-building vehicle. Wealth skills are what you do with that money once you've earned it. There are many people who won the lottery only to lose it all. Many people who are born rich go broke. Why do so many people born into wealth blow it? Because they lack wealth skills.

The old "shirtsleeves to shirtsleeves in three generations" adage comes from the early twentieth century and is often attributed to Andrew Carnegie. The idea is that wealth built in one generation is cursed to be lost by the third generation. It's a warning that unless we teach our children and grandchildren about the values behind earning and managing wealth, they will squander it and wind up right back where we started: in shirtsleeves working for hard-earned dollars. The harsh truth is, it's not your fault if you were born poor, like Dr. Brad and Adrian's parents, but it is your fault if you die poor.

WHY YOU SHOULD TRY TO "BLAME" YOURSELF IF YOU'RE POOR

In Chapter 2, we discussed Dr. Julian Rotter's work around locus of control. This concept applies to wealth building and wealth management as well.

Whom do you have to blame if you're not finding as many ways as possible to save 30% of your income?

You.

If you haven't developed a high-earning skill set, whose fault is it?

Yours.

If your poor parents didn't teach you healthy financial behaviors, but you didn't make the effort to educate yourself in adulthood, who's to blame?

That's right, it all comes back to YOU.

This might sound a bit harsh but it's GREAT news. Imagine living in a world where you actually were powerless, where there was no hope of bettering your life. Imagine that because of your status at birth, you couldn't attend school. How depressing! In many places in the world and throughout much of history that was indeed the case. But thankfully it is NOT the case right here and right now and for you.

If you are reading this book, you're already taking responsibility for your financial health. Good for you! You just need a few mindset tweaks and some motivation, discipline, and education and you can go from broke to rich. You need a rich mindset to get your head right. You need to employ strict money discipline and stick with it. You need the wisdom to stop sabotaging yourself and to keep those success habits going. Finally, you need some education to learn higher paying skill sets and wealth-building strategies, such as investing.

FLEX YOUR MONEY DISCIPLINE

Developing discipline requires consistency. You can strengthen your discipline by making some simple rules for yourself and sticking to them. Here are some money discipline rules everyone should follow if they want to start thinking rich:

1. Pay off your credit card in full each month. If you can't do this, get rid of them.
2. If you're not maxing out your retirement savings every year (your Roth IRA, 401(k), etc.), you need to get focused, develop a strict budget, and stick to it.
3. Do an honest inventory of your finances every month. Where did you overspend? How can you save more?
4. Journal every day about your financial goals. Reflect on your progress. Revisit and revise your goals as needed. Think about them every day. Keep them in your conscious mind. Studies show that people who keep their goals front of mind and hold themselves accountable are more motivated, do better in school, do better at work, make more money, and have a higher net worth.

OVERCOME YOUR LEARNED HELPLESSNESS

The concept of learned helplessness shows just how important it is to own our power in any given situation. In the 1960s, a psychologist by the name of Martin Seligman conducted a series of pretty horrific experiments on dogs. Some of them were put in a cage where they got electric shocks with no way to escape. In another cage, a group of dogs received shocks, but learned that they could escape by pressing a button with their noses. In the next phase of the experiment, the dogs were placed in a room where one side of the floor would intermittently shock them, but if they jumped over a partition onto the other side of the room, the floor was not electrified and they didn't receive a shock. The dogs that had previously learned to escape tended to jump over the partition to avoid being shocked. But this is the terrifying part of the experiment. The dogs that had no escape in the previous experiment stayed on the electrified side, laid down and whimpered and took the pain. It appeared to the researchers that they had just given up, that they decided that escape was impossible and that they were helpless.

These troubling experiments by Seligman, especially if you are a dog lover, highlighted a phenomenon that happens when we perceive a series of negative events to mean that we have no control over what happens to us. Learned helplessness occurs when we have decided that we no longer have control over our lives. Those poor dogs learned that they would be shocked no matter what they did, so they stopped trying to escape, even when escape was possible. The same thing has happened to millions of us, especially if we grew up in environments in which we felt helpless and hopeless. The problem, just like with the dogs, is that when we get older we DO have control over more and more aspects of our lives, but we may have slipped into a mindset that we are powerless and the situation is hopeless. Meanwhile, it is obvious to those who know, that your escape from your current situation is just a hop or two away.

One way to push past learned helplessness is by reminding ourselves that we have control over what happens to us, even if it's only a small level. Seligman discovered that we can overcome learned helplessness by creating empowering experiences for ourselves, ones that help us learn new skills, find new opportunities, and build up our sense of control over our circumstances. The more we see our ability to overcome adversity, the greater our internal locus of control becomes.

In terms of money, many of us have been born in cages of poverty and hopelessness. We may have learned that it's useless to try and escape, even if there is a clear and simple way out. Our inner puppy may be despondent and ready to lie down and quit. But we have the opportunity to save ourselves from those horrible electric shocks of poverty and injustice. It's not your fault if you were born into an electric cage, but it is your fault if you decide to stay there. So get out of the cage ASAP.

STOP WASTING YOUR TIME AND FOCUS ON FINANCIAL FREEDOM

Social media is the biggest time and energy drainer out there. People waste hours scrolling, looking at what other people do with their money, obsessing over celebrities, and arguing about trivial bullshit. They spend all this time debating and obsessing online, but imagine how their lives would change if they focused on financial freedom. Time is a currency. Show us how you spend your time, and we'll tell you what you value AND where you will be in 10 years.

You have to decide if the things you spend your time and money on are adding value to your life or extracting your resources, like your time, energy, and money. With every minute and every dollar you spend, you're making a choice about what's important to you.

There's a guy in New York who has a high-demand, high-paying skill set. He's a tech programmer and he hustles harder than most. He works four jobs, all remotely. His ability to meet the requirements of four ful-time jobs and not raise any red flags just shows how lazy most Americans are, and how low the work productivity expectations are in America. With all those jobs combined, he's making around $500,000 per year. But every weekend, he goes out and blows every single dollar. On the guy's Instagram page, you can see him at the strip club making it rain dollar bills. Friday night, he's at the strip club. Saturday night, he's having cocktails at strip clubs and going to fancy parties in New York. Sunday night, there's a post of him saying, "I have no idea where all the bread goes." All he has to do is look at the last 48 hours of his posts to see where all his money went. While he is one of the hardest workers we know, he is a classic example of the high-income, low-net-worth trap.

It wouldn't be surprising if that programmer has some deeply ingrained negative money beliefs that make him spend his earnings as fast as he gets them. If we don't address these negative money beliefs, they will cause us to sabotage our finances, one way or another. The truth is, if you believe money is bad, you'll never hold onto it for very long.

In addition to the common belief that money is bad and the people who have it are evil, many people are dealing with massive amounts of envy. People hate hearing that a large percentage of millionaires are self-made. The reason they hate it is because that means becoming wealthy is possible, but they either don't know how or are just not willing to do what it takes. Often, when we are struck with envy, it's because we believe the person who has what we want doesn't deserve to have it and that we are more deserving than they are. This goes hand in hand with believing that rich people are evil and don't deserve what they have.

The truth is, no amount of excuses, complaining, or envy will change our financial situations. We all have control over how we react to setbacks and hardships. We can choose to be like those dogs in the learned helplessness experiments and lie down and let ourselves continue to get shocked. Or we can get up, even when it's hard, and free ourselves from our financial cages.

For the readers who are ready to give up the powerlessness, complaining, and excuses, here's how you make sure that even if you were born poor, you don't die poor:

YOUR IDIOT-PROOF GUIDE TO GOING FROM POOR TO RICH

What would we tell someone who asked us how they could go from poor to rich? We would first teach them the basics of going from poor to middle class, and then from middle class to rich. The formula is actually quite simple:

1. Graduate high school.
2. Get a job.
3. Get as much education as possible (statistically speaking).
4. Don't spend more than you make. Live within your means.
5. Invest a percentage of every dollar you make. Most experts recommend 10%, but it depends on how rich you want to get and how fast you want to get rich. Dr. Brad invested 30% of every dollar he made. He has never had less than three jobs his entire adult life. Adrian was saving 95% of his income when he lived in a van. If you invest five dollars per day at average market returns – the S&P 500 has on average over 10% returns per year the past 100 years – you'll have over a million dollars in just 42 years.
6. Don't do anything stupid like try to get rich quick – this is the hardest one.
7. Put an investing system in place with the very first job you get. Transitioning from college into the workforce or out of high school, you're going to think you're rich because you've never made money before. Dr. Brad's first post–graduate school job paid $32,000 per year and he thought, "Holy shit, I'm rich!" Get yourself used to living on less than you make and invest the rest.
8. Invest in a financial freedom fund, not a retirement fund (call it something more motivating). You'll be more inclined to contribute

to a financial freedom fund from a young age, when retirement seems so far away.

9. Don't buy a bunch of stuff. Avoid materialism and embrace minimalism.

10. The harder and smarter you work, the more money you make. Find people who are succeeding at what you want and research what they did to get it.

11. Get a partner who compliments your money mindset.

Chapter 6 *Start Thinking Rich* Challenge

1. Write down all of your personal barriers to financial freedom.

2. Write down all of your negative money beliefs, behaviors, and excuses you've used to prevent yourself from attaining financial freedom.

3. Find role models who've had similar barriers as yours but found ways to thrive despite them. To help combat potential excuses and convince yourself that success is possible for you, it might be helpful to find role models who look like you, have experienced similar types of adversity, are from your hometown, or come from a similar background.

4. Research the mindsets and habits of these role models to learn how they overcame those barriers.

5. Research the practical steps they took to become successful. For example, what specialized skills or knowledge do they have? How did they get those skills and that knowledge?

6. Create a plan for your own financial freedom that demolishes excuses, negative money beliefs, and bad money behaviors, and puts you on track to achieving your own success.

YOU DON'T DESERVE MORE; YOU'RE GETTING PAID WHAT YOU'RE WORTH

This one may sting a little. But if you are not increasing your economic value in the marketplace, you will see that reflected in your bank account. This isn't about your value as a person. This is about your economic worth. When you go to work, your bosses aren't paying you because they think you're neat and want you to have money. They're paying you to supply them with the skills, talent, and labor you can offer that are of value to their company.

Think about it from the standpoint of entering the workforce. If you don't have a degree or trade certification that gives you a set of skills to offer employers, you'll have to start at the bottom at an entry-level position. An employer must take the time, energy, and effort to train you so you can do the job they need you to do. This costs money. You'll likely be paid an hourly wage with raises based on your performance and how much you're able to expand your skill set. But there's a cap on how much you can grow your paycheck on an hourly wage. If you want to make a big salary, you need big skill sets, talents, and expertise.

If you went to college or a trade school to learn a skill, you would automatically be entering the workforce at a higher pay grade than someone who has no degree or certifications. Not every job is available at an entry-level position. An average high school graduate, for instance, can't just walk in off the street and start doing electrician work. Certifications are required, so you don't fry the whole building while you learn on the job. Employers will pay good money to make sure an expert does the important, high-stakes work for their company. Think about it. Would you want an eighteen-year-old kid off the street who borrowed his mom's scrubs to perform surgery on you? Or would you rather find an educated and experienced MD who is Board Certified and knows what he's doing? Experts get paid what they're worth. People who have taken the time to master a trade or skill get paid more. If you feel you're not getting paid enough, the question is, What are you doing to increase your value?

Adrian: When I graduated college, I got a job that paid $27,000 a year. I worked for Prudential Retirement in the call center. All day, every day, I helped angry people with their 401(k)s. It would have been naïve of me to think I deserved to get paid more for that job. I was doing a low-skilled task at an entry-level position. But did I just surrender myself to a life of minimum wage? No! I hustled.

I read a new book every week about business to expand my knowledge and learn how to make money online. I started posting YouTube videos in 2010 when I heard it was a way to build an online business. For perspective in 2010, being a YouTuber wasn't a thing yet and I was doing this out of all places in humble Dubuque, Iowa, where often people's response to me saying I was a YouTuber was: "So. . .you're uploading what? Like cat videos?" Not only did I need to put in the time to learn, but I also needed to have discipline and work consistently on building my economic worth because no one was going to do it for me and no one in my environment even knew how to support me.

In 2010, I landed an internet audition through YouTube to be a back-up dancer for T-Pain. But as fast as the opportunity came, the concert tour ended. I was finishing my senior year in college in Dubuque, after having lived a life that not many people in Dubuque, let alone the world could relate to. So, as awesome as that experience was, people in Iowa didn't give a damn. I remember in an internship interview I had at an insurance firm, I told the interviewer that I'd danced professionally for T-Pain. He noted it and said: "So I see here you danced for T-Pain. That's great and all but what does that have to do with selling truckers' insurance?"

So I took to YouTube to start teaching my new professional skill of dancing the robot. But I had to learn that discipline and consistency of posting online and all the things that come with starting an online business. At first, I thought I would create these videos and suddenly make a bunch of money. But just like at my 9-to-5 job, my income was equal to the amount of time, energy, and skill set I was giving it. I needed to develop digital marketing skills before I would see an increase in my income from that side hustle. It took me two years of daily efforts, learning, and striving before I made my first dollar online.

Some might say I wasted two years working for free. But I spent those two years increasing my economic worth. I educated myself and learned a higher value skill set. During those first two years the only person who really watched my videos was my mom.

Shout-out to all those awesome moms out there supporting their kids' dreams!

I originally wanted to work in marketing. So when I graduated college, I applied to 50 different marketing firms. I only got three interviews and they all said "No." It wasn't until I spent those two years working on my side hustle, learning SEO, and building a blog that gained a thousand visitors per month that I actually had something to offer a marketing firm. So when I applied to all the marketing agencies in Cedar Rapids, Iowa, a few years later, I had internet marketing experience, I had a great portfolio and profile of my own, and a website with traffic and income. The marketing agencies stayed the same, but I changed by increasing the value of what I had to offer them. At the time, I believed that my employer, no matter how hard I worked, would not be able to give me the income I wanted. So I focused on increasing my worth as an entre-preneur, and after working on my side hustle for six years, I was able to quit my job. Now my income is 100% based on my ability.

Dr. Brad: For me, the clearest path to becoming more valuable in the marketplace was education. I noticed that people who had degrees got paid more. I also noticed that they didn't seem to sweat quite as much. So I wanted to go all the way up and get a doctorate. But not just any doctorate; if I was going to take out loans and put in all that work, I wanted the highest paying doctorate. So I went to the library, grabbed the Department of Labor's *Occupational Outlook Handbook* (now available for free online), and looked up which degree pays the most. I knew I wanted to work in mental health, so the question was, "How do I get paid the most in this field?" That's when I found Clinical Psychology in the handbook.

At the time, that was the best course of action for me. But that's just one of many possible approaches. Now, as a clinical psycholo-gist, I have higher value skills than before I went to school and worked as a gravedigger. But even with that doctorate in clinical psychology, there was a ceiling for how much I could make. I enjoyed my work, but I got paid by the hour and I was working 70 hours a week so I had maxed out the value of that business model. I was getting paid what I was worth, but I wanted to increase my value so I could make even more. That's when I went back to school and pursued a master's certificate in financial planning. By becoming a financial planner, I added an entirely new skill set and then combined the two to create an expansive business model that scales higher.

If you can blend two skill sets, it's a quantum leap. So if you've hit a ceiling in terms of income but you want to increase your value, consider adding a new skill set and finding ways to combine your skills together in a unique way which puts you in high demand. High demand equals high economic value. Instead of accepting the fact that you're at an economic limit, find the ways you can grow and diversify your skill set.

Your boss isn't in control of your income. You are. Your boss and your low-paying job are just reflections of your mindset. It is within your control whether or not you get paid more. Those of us with the high-earning mindset keep looking for more ways to bring in diverse streams of income.

THERE ARE NO GLASS CEILINGS ONLINE

A harsh reality of the 9-to-5 world is that "value" can be subjective. The systemic problems that occur in the workforce often get brought to light when someone who is qualified and increases their value through certifications or higher education doesn't get the raise or position as promised. Sometimes it's their fault and sometimes it's downright discrimination. You can rationalize why these deserving people don't get the promised opportunities. But the reality of organizations is that they don't always deliver on promises. Glass ceilings, the idea that you can't advance no matter what you do, gives you two options.

1. Find another job
2. Go online

Option two and the idea of e-lancing is starting to become more widely considered, with huge opportunities to work remotely from marketplace websites like Upwork.com and Fiverr.com. If you have anything to offer as a skill set or professional experience, you can e-lance your services in today's market. Thanks to the forced remote working movement that occurred from the pandemic, hiring e-lancers is much more common. The beautiful thing about the internet is that there are no glass ceilings. The internet doesn't care what you look like, your experience or background, or even if you have a criminal record. Your income is 100% based on the value you give to the market. With a little bit of application and marketing your skill set, you have the ability to create uncapped internet income streams.

MEET STEFANIE K.

From humble beginnings as an orphan in Korea, Stefanie was adopted by Midwest farmers in the United States. Raised in a hardworking household, she embodied the values of a strong work ethic and diligence from a young age. Eager for independence and wealth, despite facing disabilities like ADHD, she persevered, working tirelessly since the age of 14, determined to carve her own path in life. However, the journey was far from smooth. Early adulthood presented numerous challenges, and she found herself in difficult situations, including stripping to make ends meet after leaving home.

Despite the hardships, she remained determined in her pursuit of a better life. She found her passion in marketing roles after being given opportunities as a brand ambassador for various big corporations. Eventually, she transitioned into organizing events and promotions for prominent agencies, solidifying her reputation in the industry; however, her personal life took a tumultuous turn as she entered into a financially dependent and abusive relationship, where she lost not only her independence but also her voice.

Her dreams evolved from conventional notions of success to a desire for freedom and resilience. Instead of settling for a stable job and retirement plan, she longed to explore the world and create unforgettable experiences. After a turbulent divorce, she became a single parent to five children, one with special needs. Her focus shifted to providing her children with a rich and supportive life, no matter what. Throughout the trials and tribulations, her dreams remained unwavering. She yearned for true independence and financial stability, aspiring to build a business that not only provided for her family but also empowered others, particularly women and minorities facing similar challenges. Despite the setbacks, she held onto the belief that through determination and resilience, she could turn her dreams into reality.

It was this determination that led Stefanie to Adrian's online courses, which changed everything for her. She studied at night and on weekends so she could learn how to make money online. Within months of completing the courses, she found unfathomable success for herself, generating over $20,000 in monthly profits. This newfound knowledge and confidence allowed her to leave her corporate job so she could prioritize her family and pursue her passion for travel and living life on her own terms.

Despite all the adversity she faced, Stefanie didn't just sit back, complain about her circumstances, and accept her fate. She started thinking rich, took charge of her life, learned new skills, and increased her economic value. To learn more about Adrian's courses for making money online, go to StartThinkingRich.com/Earn.

GO FUND YOURSELF

Here's a harsh truth that pisses off people with poor mindsets. Nobody is going to invest in you if you don't invest in yourself. In other words, nobody invests money into people or projects that "need" money. When you ask people to fund your projects before you've proven yourself and put your own time, energy, and money where your mouth is, you destroy your credibility. You come off as lazy, entitled, and just plain annoying.

We get people all the time in our DMs asking if they can "run a business idea" by us. They come at us with these half-baked business proposals or just an idea. They want us to give them money to live on while they develop their new business or product. We always respond the same way: "Go fund yourself."

What these people don't realize is that the ones who get funded for a new business idea are the ones who have an established track record of success in developing and selling businesses for millions of dollars. Investors are excited to give them money because they will make them rich, NOT because the startups "need" the money. It is incredibly difficult to get funding for your first business venture. Most entrepreneurs fund themselves, sleeping on their friends' couches and working out of their garage. A great test is to go to a bank to see if they will loan you money for a business. If they say "no," then don't expect an "angel" investor to swoop in and donate money to what the bank sees as a risky bet.

Sure, some entrepreneurs had parents who gave them a starting stake. No shame in that. In fact, we hope to be in a position to do the same for our kids someday IF they demonstrate a superior work ethic and present us with an airtight business plan. But most entrepreneurs worked late nights and weekends getting their start-up off the ground, while maintaining a job. They saved and sacrificed to make that business a reality. Business investors know that most businesses fail after about seven years. So why would they want to give you their hard-earned money while you go and experiment for a year if you've never done this before? We hate how the media glorify entrepreneurs who are good at fundraising, as if that is the same as running a business successfully. Fundraising just isn't as powerful a skill as running or scaling a business. We've built multiple million-dollar companies and have never asked for money. We bootstrapped them ourselves, focusing on one sale at a time and growing the business through the money earned.

Imagine you were able to get an investor to give you money from just a business idea. Wouldn't that be awesome? One of Adrian's old friends successfully pulled off raising $60,000 from a prominent family in his college city for a video app idea. He ate up the attention and status that it provided, knowing that he was a funded startup. Having no previous financial or business experience, he burned through the funds and had to ask for more. Shockingly, the wealthy investor said yes, but with a catch – it would be a convertible loan note. This is a fancy way of saying he would be indebted to the investor. Long story short, the guy ended up mismanaging the funds and overspent on the development teams and programmers. His "successful" fundraising abilities landed him with a six-figure debt. This is the stark reality of people who fundraise money for their ideas without first learning how to actually grow or run a business.

> Adrian: I have friends who have asked me for money, or sometimes opportunity. If they ask me for money, I'll offer them $500 to let me take a video of our conversation for my YouTube channel. In that conversation, I get to look underneath their financial hood and ask tough questions. It's like a financial workshop that my followers can learn from while I'm helping someone change their financial behaviors. Of all the people who have asked me for money, only one person said yes to letting me pay them to do a financial workshop video. I ended up hiring the one person who said yes for a project. She needed help like the rest, BUT she was willing to work for it. Other people just want money and don't want to do the work.

When you ask people to give you what you're not willing to work for, it's a very bad look. It damages your reputation, which makes people not want to work with you in the future. Nobody's perfect, and there are many things that can be forgiven. But if you build a reputation as a mooch, that will never be forgotten. When you take advantage of people, you're burning bridges. Asking for handouts and taking advantage of others comes from a poor mindset. People with a rich mindset don't take advantage of people because they know that kind of behavior soils their reputation and repels opportunities. Wealthy people can smell a mooch a mile away and they want nothing to do with them.

WAYS YOU CAN INCREASE YOUR WORTH

To increase your worth you need to invest in yourself. Here are some ways to increase your value:

- Read a book every week. We're not talking about Harry Potter. Read books that will teach you a skill or expand your business knowledge.
- Listen to podcasts by people who have the economic value you wish you had.
- Take online classes.
- Go back to school and learn a skill that will complement the skills you already have.
- Find a mentor who is willing to teach you what they know.
- Get creative and combine your skill sets to create a high-value offering.
- Make yourself indispensable where you are and your boss may pay you more.
- Find new avenues, put in extra hours, work a side hustle, become an entrepreneur.
- Avoid blaming others and realize the power you have to change your financial situation.
- Take our Start Thinking Rich free masterclass by visiting StartThinkingRich.com/learn.

Chapter 7 *Start Thinking Rich* Challenge

It's time to examine ways you can increase your worth, whether that's learning a new skill or adopting a better mindset:

1. First, write down every complaint you can think of about your situation. Be thorough!

2. Next to each complaint, write down a way you can change that circumstance. For instance, if you're not getting paid enough at your job, what new skill can you learn to increase your value at work?

3. Write down a plan that includes time-sensitive goals, such as "I will master this new skill in six months."

4. Post your goals up where you can see them. Every time you feel inclined to complain, remember the actions you can take to change the things you don't like about your circumstances.

CHAPTER EIGHT

ONLY LIARS SAY THEY LOVE THEIR JOBS

What's the fastest way to kill your love for something? Turn it into a job. The majority of the workforce in America sells their labor, often by the hour, to earn wages that help them pay for living expenses, and if they're lucky, they'll have a little extra for play and travel. We sell our time and our skills to employers to serve them and their businesses, but not our own lives. Too many hardworking people in the United States are stuck working jobs they hate for a boss they dislike and coworkers they can barely tolerate. Even the ones who say they love their jobs would quit tomorrow if they suddenly found themselves in a position of lifetime financial freedom and security. Even if that's where you are, it doesn't mean you can't start working toward something you love today.

A job is different from a calling. When you're working in service of a calling, you're dedicated to something greater than yourself that you believe will make a difference. But a job? That's just something you do in service of someone else for a paycheck, whether you believe in it or not. Now, there are a few fortunate souls who have found ways to combine doing what inspires them with making a living. They may truly love what they do. But we've found that if they had a choice, they'd choose financial freedom so they don't have to sell their time and labor for a paycheck. Most people could roll back into work on their days off, but instead they choose to sleep in, travel, play golf, spend time with family, write poetry, garden, or take up woodworking.

The ultimate definition of financial freedom is being able to do what you want to do, when you want to do it, wherever you want to do it. That includes what you do for work. You can love the work you are doing, but turning it into a job that you depend on for your survival is the fastest way to kill the joy in that work. Now, not everyone wants to be an entrepreneur and some find safety in their 9-to-5 jobs. Of course, 9-to-5 jobs can be wonderful things, especially when the work is fulfilling, you love your boss, and they take care of you until you retire. But sadly there is no security in working for someone else. Many people give their whole lives to a company only to find themselves laid off just a few years before retirement, their pension dissolved, and nothing to show for the decades they gave to that company.

You can love your job to an extent; but to give your whole life to it can set you up for disappointment. If you're able to travel the world, you gain a global perspective of how work doesn't need to be a part of your identity. Ask someone who doesn't live in the United States, "How was work today?" Regardless if they are a CEO or doctor they may say, "Behind me." Living to work appears to be more of an American ideology than a globally shared perspective. Adrian's wife's Irish manager at her previous job at Deloitte said jokingly, regarding their American counterparts: "We don't work 80-plus-hour workweeks here in Ireland very much. Not that Americans are working harder than us but that we are just more efficient with our time!"

On the other end of the spectrum are the jobs that people loathe, the ones with bosses that are total dicks. Working a job like this will rob you of your joy and energy, making it hard for you to live a fulfilling life. Such jobs can kill your motivation and turn you into a bitter, resentful slacker. We all know people who are experts at doing the bare minimum to receive a paycheck. You're better than that, and you deserve better. It goes without saying that while most of us have to work to survive, life is too short to work for a soul-sucking boss, even if it pays well. In those situations, it's important to make an exit plan that will help you get out of a bad situation as fast and with as little harm to your reputation and financial life as possible.

NO JOB IS PERFECT ENOUGH TO TIE YOU DOWN

But even with the most ideal job that would bring you the most joy, if you do it for long enough, the joy will eventually fade, leaving you wanting something more. Let's say you get a job petting puppies. What could be better, right? Who doesn't love petting the soft fur of a puppy and playing with those cute little guys? Chances are, most people would love this job – for a little while. But eventually, you might notice that the puppies smell bad, and their teeth are sharp when they nip at your hands. And let's face it, the job at your imaginary puppy workplace can get a bit boring after a while. There aren't any new challenges to face or problems to solve, it's just pet a puppy, pet a puppy, pet a puppy, all day every day. And what about your puppy-petting coworkers? What if one of them is a jerk and upsets the workplace dynamic? What about that Monday morning when it's cold and rainy outside, and you'd rather stay in bed? Or that sunny Friday afternoon when your buddies asked you to ditch work to go golfing? It was fine when you played with puppies on your own whenever you wanted to, but now that you *have* to do it every day for eight hours a day, it's not as fun or rewarding.

The point is, no job is perfectly loveable. There are traffic commutes, workplace dynamics, complaining customers, difficult bosses, etc. The only way to guarantee doing work that you love is to become financially free and do it when, where, and how *you* want. Maybe that's petting puppies, maybe it's feeding the hungry, maybe it's woodworking. But true love of one's work comes from taking the "job" out of job satisfaction.

> Dr. Brad: I loved tennis so much that when I was offered a scholarship to play in college, I was ecstatic. Getting paid to play tennis, are you kidding me?! But it didn't take long for it to start feeling like a slog. There was enormous pressure to win, or I faced the possibility of being replaced, losing my scholarship, and having to drop out of school. In between matches, my teammates and I would challenge each other for higher positions, creating a fierce sense of jealousy and competition. After a while, tennis started to lose its luster. After college, I thought being a tennis teaching pro would be a great side hustle. I could make money doing what I loved, right? But I quickly found out that what I actually loved was playing tennis for FUN, with the people I liked, when I wanted to play. When I had to win to keep my college scholarship, or had to show up at a resort early every Saturday morning to teach a bunch of annoying tourists, my love of tennis started to wane. I was killing the joy of something I loved because I had turned it into a job.

Turning a hobby or beloved activity into a constraining job that your livelihood depends on is the fastest way to kill the love for that thing. There will be days when you don't want to go to work, even to do the thing you once loved. Usually, we try to have a good attitude and persevere, but that's when our job satisfaction plummets and ultimately lowers our overall life satisfaction. One of the lessons here is regardless of how much you love what you do, there are days that you'd rather not do it if you had the choice.

So protect your hobbies. Do work you enjoy, but consider keeping some of your most enjoyable hobbies and activities sacred.

Adrian: My dad's biggest complaint about his job was the commute. Every day, it would take him an hour and a half to get to work, and an hour and a half to get home. He did that for 13 years. It was stressful work, but most of the time he didn't complain about it. It was the commute that was tough. That would have been true for him even if he was working a job he absolutely loved. At a typical 9-to-5 job, we don't usually get to choose our hours, commute times, who our managers or coworkers are, or our work site. That's why some people become entrepreneurs.

When I moved to Austin, I spoke at an Internet Marketing Party event, where I met a bunch of entrepreneurs. We all had one thing in common: we have the freedom to do what we want because we don't have to sell our time to an office or factory and work with a bunch of strangers every day. I enjoy having the freedom of choice that comes with being an entrepreneur. My fellow entrepreneurs and I share the love of freedom that comes with the work.

I want to make it clear that not all entrepreneurs are enjoying the privileges of time freedom. I think quite the opposite is true for most entrepreneurs who find themselves working over 80-hour weeks. There is even a popular meme culture for prideful entrepreneurs boasting: "I'd rather work 80 hours for myself than 40 for someone else because they are my hours." While most entrepreneurs may raise their fists and cheer at that sentiment, I've always found that notion to be ridiculous. All too often, these same prideful workaholics will justify their position by shitting on salary workers. To me working 80-hour weeks as an entrepreneur is just building a bigger box than a 9-to-5. They're still stuck. I personally optimize my business for time. I'm always on the hunt for utilizing automations, AI, and outsourcing to streamline my business so it can work without me even if that means at a lesser profit. I don't have the goal of being a billionaire. I am quite happy with being a multi-millionaire who gets to work and play when I want.

WHAT YOU DO IS NOT WHO YOU ARE

If someone asks you who you are, you might tell them your name and list off a few identifying details about yourself. For instance, you might say your name is Todd, you're a dad of three kids, and you work in construction. Your job isn't necessarily who you are; it's what you do. But something interesting happens when people invest more education and time into a career. They make their jobs central to their identity. According to the Pew Research Center, among those with some college or less education, only 34% of them say their job is important in terms of their identity. That number goes up to 39% in those with bachelor's degrees, and jumps to 53% in those with postgraduate degrees. But your job is not who you are, even if you've been in school for a decade learning how to do it. This realization can be liberating and terrifying at the same time.

It's important to make a clear separation between who you are and what you do for work because it allows you the freedom to evolve. Let's say that you've studied and interned for years to become a doctor. But after five years in the field, you're burnt out and want to pivot to something else. It will be much harder to do so if your entire identity is wrapped up in being a doctor. Now we're not saying you have to throw away entire skill sets or careers. But you can use what you've learned to create a situation where you have the freedom to do the work you want to do. For instance, Dr. Brad started as a clinical psychologist but after he hit that billable-hour ceiling, he knew he needed to pivot. So, he added financial planning to his expertise and combined the two fields to create something entirely new: the field of financial psychology. He applied his knowledge in psychology to financial planning, thus breaking his earning ceiling and creating more opportunities and financial freedom for himself. He found a way to turn his education and skills away from a job with limitations and into work he finds fulfilling and exciting without needing to answer to anyone else.

Adrian made a name for himself on the internet teaching people how to dance. But when that stopped bringing him the income and satisfaction he wanted, he pivoted to internet marketing. Once he mastered that, he made another pivot and taught others how to grow their online businesses. If that stops bringing him fulfillment, Adrian has the freedom to pivot again, anytime he wants, to something else.

The unfortunate truth is, most young people find their jobs unfulfilling, especially compared to older generations. A Pew study found that only 44% of people age 18 to 29 find their jobs *enjoyable*, compared to 65% of those over 65 years old, and only 39% of young people (age 18 to 29) find their jobs *fulfilling*. Not surprisingly, overall job satisfaction is also lower in positions with less benefits and lower incomes. But sadly so many lower-wage workers sabotage their own financial lives through overspending and racking up credit card debt, keeping them stuck in jobs they don't like for even longer. This is why obtaining financial freedom as early as possible should be your number-one priority, even over any fleeting job satisfaction.

BUT MY JOB IS WHERE I MAKE FRIENDS

Some people will stay in jobs that they don't love because they have become attached to their coworkers. Maybe you met the best man at your wedding at your office job, and maybe your best friend of 20 years began at your first low-paying job right out of college. But getting attached to a job because of the friends you work with is a trap. Your friends will eventually move on, and so will you. Life happens, people start families and move out of the city, they get promotions or find positions at new companies. And unfortunately, in competitive jobs, they may be a groomsman in your wedding one day, and then stab you in the back and steal all of your clients the next. Some workplaces are incredibly competitive and cutthroat. If you rely only on your job to make and maintain friendships, you're likely to find your social calendar and your bank account empty one day.

Instead of becoming so enmeshed in your job that your finances, relationships, and fulfillment are all wrapped up together, it's better to disentangle your life from your job so you have freedom to move and grow. Become a person who can make friends anywhere, at the grocery store or on the pickleball court. When we have the freedom to choose our environments, activities, and where we spend our time, we are more likely to make deeper friendships because we are naturally surrounded by people who have similar interests and lifestyles. With coworkers, you don't usually have anything in common with them except for your job, and you don't choose how long you spend with these people. In our opinion, the workplace is one of the worst places to make friends.

JOBS ROB YOU OF CHOICE

A job takes away choice. You sell your time and your labor, so those things no longer belong to you. Not only that, but you no longer get to choose when you take vacation and what you lose if you get sick and have to miss work. You've agreed to give your employer 40 or more hours per week, with maybe two weeks off per year, and a handful of sick days, no matter how many days off you might actually want or need. That's why financial freedom is so important. It helps you buy back your time.

> Dr. Brad: One of the biggest challenges for me when I was stuck on the billable-hour model was that I didn't have the freedom to take time off without taking significant financial hits. A vacation cost me not just flights, rental cars, and hotels, it cost me even more in lost income. I knew that if I became sick for a week, I'd have to

make up the time on nights and weekends or I was going to come up short. That type of life is not freedom. It is a lifestyle of financial insecurity and fear. It wasn't until I became an entrepreneur that I was able to create a money-making model that allowed me the freedom to take a week or a month off if I wanted, without causing financial stress.

If you have a job that you currently like, that's great. But we'd wager that if you had a choice, tomorrow you'd rather go golfing, fishing, hiking, or whatever else you love most instead. That's why we argue that only liars say they love their job. Unless you love surrendering your freedom, you don't love your job. But the secret is, you don't need a "job" to provide for yourself and contribute to society in a meaningful way. You can become financially free, do what you love when and where you want to do it, and be generous with your time and money because you feel like it, not because your boss is requiring it. We're not saying that all jobs are bad. We have both had jobs we've enjoyed and found meaningful. In fact, in addition to his entrepreneurial ventures, Dr. Brad still has a "job" as a professor. Adrian, while traveling Asia for three months, spent his mornings in coffee shops working on final edits for this book. We take on projects we love, but at the end of the day, we *only* take on projects we love. We mentioned that the older generations found their jobs more fulfilling and identified more with their work. That makes retirement a difficult transition for many. When they retire, those who find their jobs to be central to their identity often feel like they're losing parts of themselves. When they rely on their jobs for their social connections, this can make the situation even worse. For these people, the transition to retirement can lead to depression and health problems, exactly at the time when they should be enjoying their freedom and living their best lives.

We expect pushback on this chapter. But to those who disagree with us, we present you with a question: Would you still do your job if you weren't getting paid for it? Are you happy with selling years of your life in service to this job? Who will you be when you retire? Even if you love your work, financial freedom will make *you* the master of your life, instead of your boss. It will put your security in your hands instead of the hands of a faceless corporation who could lay you off on a whim. Many people think the safe option is to keep working that 9-to-5 job. They submit to a life of just working and paying taxes for the illusion of job security. But businesses fail, bosses lay people off, and no job is guaranteed. Ironically, the higher you climb in a company the more you get paid and the greater the incentive for the company to lay you off to save money. So even the best 9-to-5 job isn't as safe as it seems. The more challenging yet more fulfilling option is the one that puts you in control. This may require a lot of trial and error, but we promise you it's worth it. Whether it's prioritizing investing, becoming an entrepreneur, or a combination of both, when you have the freedom to do what you want, your life will become more fulfilling. We currently have more opportunities than we've ever had before to reframe how we're looking at work, and we know you can do the same. So why would you settle for giving your working years for someone else's dream instead of your own?

Chapter 8 *Start Thinking Rich* Challenge

For this challenge we invite you to paint a picture of your ideal work life. Take some time to create an exciting vision by reflecting on the following questions. Flesh out as many details as you can, getting as specific as possible: Why are you here on earth? What is your true purpose in life? Who are you without your job? What would you do if you didn't have to go to work every day? If you could spend your time doing ANYTHING, what would it be? Take some time to contemplate these questions and write down your answers.

CHAPTER NINE

LOTTERY TICKETS ARE FOR LAZY PEOPLE

From a young age, Henry watched his father blame his problems on everyone else. His father's victim mentality tied him down, making change impossible. When he lost his job, it was his boss's fault. "He always had it out for me," Henry's father would mumble as he sat on the couch watching TV.

Henry was on a little league baseball team. As he stepped up to the plate, he remembered his father's words. "I hope the umps are fair this time. Try to get a walk." Henry's dad was teaching Henry to be passive, in life and in baseball, instead of encouraging him to step up to the plate and take some swings. In other words, he was teaching Henry to put his fate in the hands of others, just like he was doing in his own life.

Every week, Henry's dad went to the liquor store to buy lottery tickets. Even though he wasn't working, he somehow always had 30 bucks to dump into a handful of losing tickets. Over the course of 42 years, at 30 dollars a week, Henry's dad spent $65,520 on lottery tickets. If he had invested that money instead, even at just average market returns (the S&P 500 has returned an average of over 10% a year for over 100 years) that $65,520 could have grown to over $1 million. Instead of investing his way to becoming a millionaire, his dad sat on the couch whining about his situation and stayed broke.

Henry had to take out student loans and work his way through college. When he became an adult, his dad would ask *him* for money. Over time he grew to resent his father. When the time came, Henry's dad ended up in a cheap retirement home, since he had no savings.

Sadly, there are thousands of people who think just like Henry's dad. Instead of taking control of their lives, they are passive observers, wallowing in their victim mentality, which makes them easy prey for get-rich-quick schemes, like lottery tickets, pyramid schemes, crypto rug pulls, and day trading. It's time to expose these alluring traps for what they really are: a dirty trick to separate poor people from their money. If you feel hopeless or lack the discipline to do what it takes to actually get rich, you're an easy mark for one of the oldest cons.

The lottery sells us a 1 in 300 million shot at winning for the low-low price of $2.00 per ticket. Think about it, if someone on the street said, "Give me $2 and I *might* be back with a million dollars," but they never came back with anything but another extended hand, you'd think twice about giving that person your money every week. Yet people get their paychecks and head to the counter to throw their money away on lottery tickets with the same level of promise the guy on the street could offer.

So why do people do it? Why is it so appealing to "get rich quick?" Is it because we'd rather not work for what we want in life? Is it due to a lack of financial literacy and no knowledge on how to go from poor to rich?

Maybe, for people like Henry's dad, it's easier to blame their circumstances on everyone else. Are we too lazy to work for it or too undisciplined to make sacrifices today for a better tomorrow? The truth is, even if you did win the lottery (and you won't), it's not going to solve anything.

The typical lottery winners find themselves broke and alone within a few years of winnings it big anyway. Why? Because they have a poor mindset, and a poor mindset is the enemy of fortune. Think about it. People who throw their money away on lottery tickets are the ones who are struggling the most financially. The lottery is often referred to as a tax on the poor, and it is. If lottery tickets were actually a good investment, rich people would be buying them all the time too.

Dr. Brad: I fell prey to the get-rich-quick scheme of day trading. I grew up in a low-income family, and I often fantasized about being rich. While I was on the right path, getting my degree and building my expertise to get me a high-earning job, I was saddled with over $100,000 of student loan debt. I was raised to believe that debt could crush you, especially if you're poor. It was a catch-22. I was terrified of my student debt, but I also knew that I would not be able to go to school without student loans, which made me grateful that I was able to get them in the first place. Still, I was desperate to pay them off as fast as possible, which made me an easy target.

One day, a mentor of mine showed me how he made $100,000 in one year by trading stocks on margin. I remember asking him what one of the companies he just invested in did. He looked at me, shrugged, and said, "I don't know." He was just making money and I was in awe. I couldn't believe it was that easy. I thought to myself, "So this is how people get rich? I can do this!" I was thrilled at the idea that I could pay off my $100,000 debt in a matter of months. So I sold my truck for $10,000, bought a 20-year-old Toyota Tercel with a leaky roof for $500, and I started trading. NOTE: I lived on Kauai at the time and when it rained water would flood the bottom of the car and slosh around, splashing on the seats. I would drive barefoot to work so I wouldn't soak my work shoes and when I hit the gas the water would rush under the driver's seat and when I hit the brakes, I had to lift my feet off the floor as a wall of water rushed forward. I eventually just drilled some large holes in the bottom of the car so the water could drain out.

That's how my short-lived adventure in day-trading began. After a few months, things were going great. I saw my money double. I started to picture what it would feel like to be debt free.

Every day, I'd buy a stock I knew nothing about and think, "Getting rich is so easy if you just know what to do!" My mentor was 20 years my senior, had a nice house, and made more money than I did, so I thought he had it all figured out. I followed his lead and it worked out great. In no time I had turned my $10,000 into $20,000.

But what I didn't know was that I had started trading at the peak of one of the biggest stock market bubbles in history. Unfortunately, a few months after I got my start as a trader, the infamous Tech Bubble burst. Over the course of a few months, I watched most of my money melt away as I, along with the rest of the world, kept waiting for the market to go back up to where it "should" be. My mentor suffered an even worse fate, as the online broker he used started issuing him margin calls, forcing him to deposit additional cash into his account at the worst possible time. At the end of the day, I couldn't believe I fell for it. As a psychologist, I should have known better. But even with my knowledge about human behavior, I fell into the get-rich-quick trap. It was so humbling, I decided to learn about the psychology of investing so I'd never make that mistake again.

I had to figure out why a reasonably intelligent person would do something so stupid with his money, and why so many of us are vulnerable to doing the same. Over time, I realized that many smart people who are just trying to make a better life for themselves and their families slip into this type of poor mindset and self-destruction. When you grow up poor like I did, you don't know any rich people, let alone how people get rich. This lack of financial literacy sets people up for failure, just like it did for me.

Lower income people get sucked into get-rich-quick scams all the time. The fantasy of getting rich quickly is SO seductive. We see these people on social media, flaunting their "wealth" and selling day trading and crypto trading courses to desperate people who just want to improve their circumstances. Meanwhile they're leaning against a stranger's car and wearing fake jewelry. It's all designed to prey on our worst instincts and most painful vulnerabilities. Most people who are poor are desperate to not be poor anymore.

So what's the psychology behind wanting to make the most money in the shortest amount of time for the least amount of effort? The answer can be found in our ancient ancestry. Back in the caveman days, humans had to conserve as much energy as possible, so when the time came to fight for scarce resources or outrun a saber-toothed tiger, they would have maximum energy stored up to survive. But while our brains still contain that hard-wiring to conserve energy, it's no longer necessary for us to outrun predators or fight for access to a watering hole. So instead, we are prone to trying to conserve energy by purchasing lottery tickets or succumbing to day-trading schemes instead of being patient and doing the hard work of becoming wealthy.

In addition to our neurological conditioning to default to the laziest solutions, many lottery players are operating from a place of learned helplessness, like the man at the beginning of this chapter, Henry's father. As we mentioned in Chapter 2, those with an external locus of control have a poor mindset. That mindset is developed in childhood and often includes a victim mentality. As we learned in Chapter 6, learned helplessness is the mindset developed when a person (or traumatized dog) faces continuous uncontrollable situations that negatively impact them. Since they can't figure out how to escape the situation, they give up and stop trying. This frame of mind is like a sedative for one's motivations. It keeps people stuck in painful situations where they could take action to find a way out, but they don't. Prolonged stress and feelings of hopelessness, whether from an electrified floor, an abusive or neglectful childhood, or extreme poverty, can alter the brain, making it difficult to take empowered action.

Over time, learned helplessness can manifest in adulthood in many ways. Dr. Brad conducted a study with his colleagues that was published in the *Journal of Financial Therapy*, which discusses the implications of learned helplessness. It states that learned helplessness can manifest as a failure to accomplish goals, which leads to lowered expectations about future prospects, lower levels of motivation, and the feeling that no matter what actions they take, their fates are outside of their control. People with high levels of learned helplessness struggle to complete difficult tasks from start to finish. They also tend to struggle with depression, anxiety, and phobias. And listen, it's not their fault that they developed this mindset, especially when they were powerless kids stuck in an inescapable situation. But as adults, it's their responsibility to unlearn that helplessness, because success is often just a few steps away.

HOW DO YOU OVERCOME LEARNED HELPLESSNESS? FAIL!

If you've experienced some form of learned helplessness, don't worry. There is a way to get out of that psychological trap. Psychologist Carol Dweck found that the best way to overcome learned helplessness is to experience failure and take full responsibility for it. She did a study where she split the participants into two groups. One group underwent rigorous training during which they failed at many tasks and were instructed to take full responsibility for those failures, admit it was due to lack of effort, and learn how to do better. The other group received training in which they succeeded at every task. The members of the second group showed no signs of improvement in their extreme reactions to failure, while the group that failed and took responsibility showed considerable improvement.

Another way to overcome learned helplessness is by adopting the mindset psychologists call "learned hopefulness." By experiencing empowering circumstances in which we have the opportunity to learn skills and find our internal locus of control, we can reverse the tendency toward learned helplessness and become more motivated, more hopeful, and less depressed.

Mindsets can be infectious. So, if you want to overcome learned helplessness you are going to need to distance yourself from people who have a victim mentality and surround yourself with people who take total responsibility for the outcomes they are getting in life. If all else fails, get yourself into therapy as soon as possible so you can snap out of it.

So when faced with the opportunity to develop healthy financial habits over time versus spending a few hundred dollars a month on lottery tickets, which one do you think will move you into learned hopefulness and a rich mindset?

Get-rich-quick schemes target people who have fallen into learned helplessness. Being poor can cause a series of traumatic events to occur in a person's life. These events could make a person feel like a dog in that cruel experiment, locked in a cage getting shocked with no way out. But there is always a way out, and it's not in a get-rich-quick scam. Those scams lead to even more financial shocks and will put you in even worse financial stress.

Adrian: When I started teaching the Brambila Method, I had to watch out for scammers. The "make money online" course industry is one of the worst for get-rich-quick schemes. At first, I was just offering tools and free advice on social media based on what was working for me. I had no intention of ever creating a class. But I came across this other class that developed a terrible reputation on social media for scamming people. It sold an online course for $7.00 on how to become a millionaire, and the content was absurd. The class was a big circle-jerk. They convinced people to buy their class, become an "affiliate," and then earn money by selling these classes to others.

Eventually, these predators were using my educational videos and saying, "If you want to do what Adrian does, go buy this $7.00 class." I was not affiliated with this program at all. But I was getting direct messages from people who fell for the scam accusing me of being the scammer. That's when I knew that I had to create my own course so nobody would be tricked into buying these other sham courses. And that's what I did. Anyone who buys my courses will tell you, I teach the opposite of get-rich-quick. I teach my students how to build their skills and platforms by creating value for their prospective clients. From the very first day I promoted my course, I set the expectations. I told my students, "If you want to become a millionaire from this class, this isn't the one for you. You'll have to find that somewhere else. But I can teach you to make your first dollar online."

Get-rich-quick scams sucker people into giving up their hard-earned money. The scammers flex luxury brands (we'll get into how stupid that is later), and show off their "wealth" to get people to buy. To the untrained eye, it looks so appealing. Then, when they tell us how easy it is, our caveman brain gets excited. They prey on those with learned helplessness because they know that most people will try their bullshit methods, fail, and give up the first time, never questioning the method or realizing it's a scam. They blame themselves for the failure. They lose more money, which leads to more feelings of hopelessness and more desperate attempts to get out of the hole they've dug for themselves by giving what little they had to predators. It may appear sparkly and luxurious online, but it reeks of greed and false promises.

Building real wealth is not seductive or glamorous. It's sleeping on a couch and working extra hours at the fast food chain while saving every penny, not buying new clothes or going out to dinner, and learning and improving little by little. The best way to improve our financial circumstances is to improve our mindset, work consistently for a steady flow of income, and then make our money work for us. So while it's tempting to slip into the get-rich-quick mentality, real winners know that success lies in the "get-rich -slow" approach.

Chapter 9 *Start Thinking Rich* Challenge

This challenge takes courage but is worth any uncomfortable feelings that may arise. It requires you to take an honest look at your mistakes and the poor mindsets that set you up for failure. Take heart in knowing that most people who have gone from broke to rich have fallen for similar scams on their way to financial freedom. You are not alone.

- Make a list of the get-rich-quick schemes you've fallen for in the past.
- Now, examine the thoughts, emotions, hopes, and dreams that made you decide to jump in, even though the odds of winning were nearly nonexistent.
- Write down how much time, effort, and money you wasted and keep it somewhere so you can refer to it the next time your crypto-bro buddy tries to rope you into the next get-rich-quick meme shit coin.
- On another piece of paper, write all the ways you can get rich slowly, smart, and sustainably. Take the most unglamorous approach, like going back to school to grow your skill set, taking an online course to learn a new side hustle, saving 30% or more of your income, investing in a Target-Date-Fund or with a Certified Financial Planner (CFP®) (not your day-trading buddy who has no idea what he's doing), and finding ways to reduce your spending.

CHAPTER TEN

GET RID OF YOUR POOR FRIENDS IF YOU WANT TO GET RICH

Wait! Before you get triggered, slam the book shut, and miss the entire point of this chapter, let us explain. Our definition of a "poor friend" isn't what you think it is. Remember, we make a big distinction between being poor and being broke. Poor friends are people in your life who are stuck in a poor mindset, suffer from learned helplessness, encourage you to overspend along with them, and wallow in self-pity. Having a poor mindset has nothing to do with income or net worth. In contrast, broke simply means you currently have no money. Broke can be temporary. But a poor mindset can be permanent and will lead to a life of lost opportunities, financial hardship, regret, and bitterness.

You've probably heard the saying that we are the sum of the five people we spend the most time with. We are social animals and are therefore wired to adapt and conform to the people around us. If we have broke friends with rich mindsets, ones who work hard, are good with money, and are striving to make a better life for themselves, that's amazing! And their mindset and motivation will rub off on you. However, if you've got friends who have high incomes but suffer from poor mindsets – living above their means and flaunting lavish lifestyles – they will poison your mind, drain you of your resources, and lead you to a life of financial ruin. To put it bluntly, you will either lose those friends or lose your money, the choice is yours.

You may have lifelong friends who've known you since preschool, high school pals, college buddies, even certain family members that you'd hate to lose. We're not saying you have to abandon any relationship with someone who doesn't have a rich mindset. That would be cultish. But you may want to limit the amount of time and energy you invest in those relationships, or the degree to which you let them in on the details of your financial life if you want to level up.

Imagine you've just received a major promotion at work with a significant pay raise. Who's the first person with whom you'd want to share this amazing news? What would their reaction be? Do they have a rich mindset that would make them see your win as their win, congratulate you, and celebrate with you? Or would they diminish your accomplishments and make you feel guilty because they're still stuck in the same position they've been in since high school? The first friend is someone with a rich mindset. The second has a poor mindset and will pull you down with them. Even if you don't notice it right away, if you let them get too close, people with a poor mindset will have a negative effect on your life and your choices. But why is it so hard to leave relationships that aren't good for us? The answer is human psychology.

Since the beginning of human history, we have spent most of our time on earth in hunter/gatherer tribes. Those tribes were closeknit, consisting of no more than one or two hundred people. They depended on each other for survival. They made discoveries, shared resources, told stories around the fire, worshipped the same deities, and protected each other from outside threats. The desire to maintain connections with the people around us is hardwired into the deepest part of our psyche. If our ancestors didn't maintain those connections, they would have been banished, starved, eaten by predators, or killed by rival tribes. Today, that need to belong to a tribe is deeply embedded in every aspect of our lives. Leaving one's tribe can cause an enormous amount of stress and anxiety because our brains believe that if we leave our tribe, no matter how limiting or downright harmful the relationships are, we will face certain death.

We want so badly to belong, it can sabotage our success. Even if we start to do well and make decent money, if our friends and family are still living with a poor mindset, we will see ourselves becoming less familiar with them. Those who have adopted a rich mindset will have trouble relating to those with a poor mindset, which can make both parties feel disconnected. The need to belong is such a powerful driving force, it can keep us from climbing the socioeconomic ladder because we fear that we won't belong among our family and friends.

THREE WAYS PEOPLE WITH A POOR MINDSET CAN SABOTAGE YOUR SUCCESS

Friends and family members with a poor mindset will ultimately try to keep you down. It's not that they don't care; it's just that they don't want to lose you. Your success means that you are leaving them, figuratively and literally. You may leave the job you share, or the neighborhood where you both live. There are three ways we have seen this play out:

1. **Trying to Make You Feel Guilty**

   A common way that people close to you will attempt to control your behavior is guilt. It's often done subconsciously, and when confronted, few would ever admit using this tactic. The idea is that if they can make you feel a sense of shame, remorse, or obligation, they can keep you close. Watch out for comments like:
   - "Must be nice to be able to afford that house."
   - "How can you put money in a retirement account when your sister can't even pay her rent this month?"
   - "Oh, I bet you think you're too good for us now, don't you?"

2. **Cutting You Down to Size**

   Since you're on the road to success and your friend is stuck in their dead-end job, they are going to feel bad about themself. To cope with this bad feeling, they might try to make *you* feel bad about yourself instead. This is usually not done on purpose, but is done subconsciously, to protect themself from feeling bad. In psychology, this is called "projection." Because they feel bad about themself for their lack of success, they may say things to you to make you feel bad about yourself instead:
   - "Here comes Miss High and Mighty showing off with her fancy new job."
   - "They only gave you that promotion because they want to sleep with you."
   - "Wow, you're so lucky. I wish I had a boss giving me raises and everything I want. I'm still earning my living with *real* hard work. Must be nice to get all those perks at your cushy office job."
   - "So what, now you're one of those rich pricks?"

3. **Trying to Get You to Spend More Money**

   Someone with a poor mindset is not thinking about saving for the future. They are thinking about spending money today. They lack financial literacy and have no idea how people actually go from poor to rich. All they know is what they see on social media. In their eyes, if you have money, you need to flaunt it. That's one of the core mindsets that keeps them poor. So when a poor mindset friend catches wind that you're making more money, they will try to get you to spend it, and often on them!

- "Dude, you got a raise. Why are you still driving that piece of shit?"
- "You need a new wardrobe to go along with that promotion. Let's go shopping!"
- "Let's go to Vegas, baby!"
- "You got a raise! That's great! Can I borrow some money?"

If you've heard any of the phrases above, it's a sign that you need to rethink your relationships. Otherwise, you are at high risk of losing everything you've worked so hard to achieve. Not only will poor-mindset friends make you feel bad about your success, but they can infect you with their poor mindset. It's contagious!

There is scientific evidence that our brain waves sync up when we interact with others. It's called "collective neuroscience." When we talk to each other or share an experience together, our brain waves synchronize and create matching patterns. This can be a good thing, if you're among people who have a positive attitude and see the world through a hopeful lens. It can help you get rich when you surround yourself with supportive mentors who embody a rich mindset. But if you're around people who are insecure, are scared of losing you, are negative, complain a lot, blame others, or are devoid of hope, your neurons will start firing on that wavelength along with them.

This affects our behavior, as well as our thoughts. If you spend enough time with someone, you will naturally be drawn to their habits. For instance, if your best friend loves running 10K races, they may convince you to train with them for the next one. Likewise, if your friend loves overspending at fancy dinners, drinking $10 lattes, or getting bottle service at expensive clubs, chances are you'll be overspending too. But if your closest friends are good at saving and prioritize investing, you will help each other reach your goals and support and encourage each other when times are tough.

MOOCHER FRIENDS

Sometimes friends can not only hurt your success and confidence in yourself, but can also take advantage of you. Moocher friends are always in financial trouble. They never try to solve their money problems; they just borrow money from you and whatever poor souls are in their circle. If you loan them money, they never pay you back, and if you go out together, be ready to foot the bill. People like this have learned that they don't need to work for their money. Instead, they make friends with people who have money and enjoy the fruits of their labor, receiving all the perks without getting their hands dirty with actual work. Or maybe they work hard, but always seem to be struggling financially. They're terrible with money and have no discipline. So they give you another sob story about how their rent is late (as if it's a total surprise that their rent is due again like it is every month), and beg you to help them out.

The best way to help moocher friends is to refrain from giving them money. Instead, it's better for you and more empowering for them to offer them opportunities. Maybe you know of a flexible gig they could do as a side hustle, a class they could take, or a free financial literacy program that could help them. If they turn down your non-financial support, they were likely just looking for a handout and weren't serious about paying you back or changing their circumstances so they don't have to ask you for money again. Giving someone money for nothing just encourages them to continue doing nothing. So in reality, you aren't helping them, you are hurting them. Beware!

Adrian: I had a good friend who was struggling with money and credit card debt. We were close, and I'm good with money, so I wanted to help him out. So I created an opportunity for him. All he had to do was collect money from one of my affiliate campaigns. I wanted to diversify my affiliate income, because there's always the risk that a business will cut your commissions or end their program. So I decided to create a backup affiliate stream of income and I put it under my friend's name. All he had to do was collect the commission, keep twenty percent and send me the rest.

At first, it was going great. He sent me the money on time and earned some for himself. But then the payments started to come in a little late. Pretty soon, months were going by without a payment. At one point, I realized he owed me a few thousand dollars. That led to a hard conversation. I thought I was giving him an easy leg-up with this opportunity. He made extra money, I was getting paid, everyone wins. But because he lacked financial literacy and was severely strapped for cash, it put him in a position in which he felt he had to manipulate the income arrangement and take money from his own friend.

Now, I have to take accountability, because I introduced money into our relationship and shifted it from just a friendship to a business relationship. This would have been fine if our financial habits and values were aligned. It's clear reading my very last texts with him how my ambition and growth in my wealth mindset challenged his ego in an adversarial way instead of a way that inspired him to level up with me. Now, six years later as I re-read the last texts from him for this book, I'm very proud of how I handled the situation. I'm still sad that I lost a close friend in the process. But I had to realize that he was the one willing to sacrifice our friendship in service to his poor mindset.

Now, my go-to response when someone I care about asks me for money is "I'll give you my classes for free so you can learn how I make money and do the same for yourself." If they don't take me up on it, I know they were never interested in working to pull themselves out of the struggle; they just wanted someone to bail them out, and they were never going to change until they hit bottom and figured it out for themselves.

Dr. Brad: When I'm coaching my financial clients, I always encourage them to think carefully about loaning money to friends and family. As soon as you introduce money to the equation, you change the dynamic from friend/friend, sibling/sibling, or cousin/cousin to borrower/lender. But if you don't want to lose the relationship, you can't hold them accountable the way a bank would in a true borrower/lender relationship. Banks can ask for proof of purchase, a business plan, and/or collateral. A contract is signed. They can charge late fees when payments aren't made on time. They can even repossess the item their money was used to purchase to recoup expenses. Try doing that with your cousin. You'd have your whole family pissed at you.

That's why I tell anyone considering lending friends or family money that they have to completely let go of their expectations about the way they spend it. If you give them $200 so their utilities don't get shut off and they spend it on a new pair of shoes, it's none of your business. If they give you a sob story about how they can't pay their rent and you catch them later that week at the bar buying drinks for everyone, you need to be 100% okay with it. You shouldn't be surprised they are bad with money, since they have proven it by needing to borrow money from you in the first place. If you can't loan them money without worrying about how they spend it, don't do it, because it will ruin your relationship. My rule of thumb is, don't loan friends money unless you're fine with giving it away and never getting paid back. Regardless, be forewarned that when you loan someone money you have changed the relationship and you have put it at risk. At the very least, if you loan money to someone who is a financial mess they will probably start avoiding you, just like they do their other debt collectors.

Sometimes, people really are down on their luck and need someone to help them out. We get direct messages all the time from people who are struggling and asking us to give them money. Some of the stories are sad and tug at your heart strings. But if we gave money to everyone who asked for it, we would be teaching them the wrong thing and end up broke ourselves. We all need help every once in a while, and it's okay to give to someone in need. But the people who are chronically struggling with finances and asking you to loan (or give) them cash are not managing their money well. Worse, they are not taking responsibility for it and not making the hard decisions they will eventually need to make. In fact, you are just prolonging their agony by temporarily propping them up.

When they hit a rough patch financially, they might need to take some drastic measures to get back on track, such as moving back in with their parents, getting a roommate (or two), downsizing to a cheaper vehicle, or getting a side hustle. They may work hard and just be terrible with money. But if they don't get uncomfortable enough to change their mindset and behaviors because they're always being bailed out by friends and family, they will never learn how to build their own wealth.

Misery loves company. When a healthy person escapes unhealthy cycles, it highlights the misery of the poor-mindset group. Like crabs in a barrel, the unhealthy group will pull anyone who tries to escape back into the barrel. Good friends don't pull each other down. They escape the barrel and then show others how it's done.

HOW TO LET GO OF POOR-MINDSET FRIENDS

So how do we distance ourselves from people with poor mindsets without becoming completely isolated? Well, you probably won't need to cut ties completely. You can just limit the amount of information you share with them and the influence you allow them to have in your life. That might look like not sharing your financial goals, your business struggles and triumphs, and your financial status. You could limit your interactions to focus around a shared interest, such as a sport or hobby, and not share the intimate details of your financial life with them to avoid things becoming uncomfortable.

As you climb the socioeconomic ladder, you may find that you naturally drift away from them, spending less time with them while still loving and supporting them from a distance. Understand that this is a common experience for people as they start to make more money and climb the socioeconomic ladder. It's not because people become snooty; it's just that their mindset evolves and their interests and habits may have changed. Maybe you will make sure there are certain things you never discuss with these friends or family members, such as getting a raise or going back to school. Be selective about those with whom you share your goals and accomplishments. News of your promotion may not be for everyone, and that's okay. Unfortunately, there may be times when you have to cut someone off, both financially and personally. This is never easy, but it doesn't have to be malicious. You can let them go with love and hope for the best for them. Once you let go of relationships that are dragging you down, you'll have room in your life for your power group, the people who inspire you, hold you accountable, celebrate with you, and help you improve.

FINDING RICH-MINDSET FRIENDS

When striving for your financial and professional goals, it is crucial to surround yourself with people whose values and interests align with yours. As we covered before, your job isn't the only place to make friends. Join a sports team, find people online who exhibit a rich mindset and learn from them, interact with them whenever possible. Join clubs or meetups with people who are actively working on improving themselves, like mastermind groups. Take up golf, the favorite sport of the rich. Volunteer with a charity, where people of means like to give back to their communities. If you free up the time you used to spend with poor-mindset friends going out to bars or complaining about your boss, you'll leave room in your life for new, more beneficial connections. Even if you don't know anyone who's rich, you can meet people on their way to becoming rich and support each other on the way up.

We have a friendly competition going between us. We'll play pickleball, ping pong, go skeet shooting, or compare our social media followings. As we are finishing the final edits to this book, we are right now competing on who can get the most pre-order sales (currently Adrian is winning but Dr. Brad is close on his heels). That friendly competition helps us grow our skills and become better players, both on the court and in the financial world. We don't always talk about money. But we push each other to elevate our game. We make each other better. And we didn't meet on the pickleball court. We met online. Our content showed that our values are aligned, so we started watching each other's videos and interacting. Pretty soon, we were messaging each other and sharing ideas. Now we're trying to beat each other on the pickleball court and writing a book about finance together.

> Dr. Brad: I remember one time we were hanging out and I was sharing a win with Adrian and afterwards I said, "I'm not trying to brag." Adrian interrupted me and said, "Dude, brag! Brag to me. I love to hear it when you win." It's great to have friendships like this, where we celebrate each other's successes and hype each other up.

When it comes to relationships, life is too short to be dragging around the weight of other people's poor mindsets. If you want to develop and keep a rich mindset, your inner circle will be a huge factor in whether or not you can maintain that mindset. Your success and financial well-being depend on your closest friends and family. Whether we like it or not, we are heavily influenced by the people who are close to us. So choose wisely whom you trust with your financial goals and successes and where you invest your most valuable asset – your time.

Chapter 10 *Start Thinking Rich* Challenge

It's time to get honest about your inner circle. List the five people you spend the most time with. What do you talk about with these people? If money and success comes up, is the tone uplifting or sad? Are conversations motivating or depressing? Take a moment to rate each one of them on a scale of 1 to 10 with regard to their mindset, where 1 = a poor mindset and 10 = a rich mindset. Reflect on each one. For those with a score of 7 or below, do you think you can enlist them into adopting a rich mindset? One way to do this might be asking them to read this book. Ask them if they would be willing to go on this journey with you. If they refuse, it might be time for you to make some decisions about how much time you want to spend with them going forward and/or to limit the topics you talk about with them.

Now make a second list of people you're interested in getting to know better. People you can learn from who will help you elevate yourself. If you can't think of anyone you know, what books or podcasts can you engage with to get access to people with a rich mindset? What clubs, sports, or charities can you engage with to put yourself around people with a mindset you'd like to adopt? Start putting your focus in those spaces with those people.

CHAPTER ELEVEN

POOR PEOPLE BUY STUFF; RICH PEOPLE OWN TIME

Ask any truly successful person what they value most in this world and the answer will always be the same: TIME. Time is your most precious, most valuable resource. Once you spend it, you never get it back. You could have a luxury yacht, the hottest new sports car, designer clothes and accessories, and a mansion on the hill, but if you don't have time, you won't be able to enjoy any of it. The true marker of wealth is not objects or status, it's time.

If a person makes $20 per hour, a pricey coffee-house muffin isn't just $10; it's 30 minutes of their life. That weekend bar tab isn't $100; it's 5 hours of their life. That new car isn't $500 a month, it's 25 hours of their life each month. When you break down your expenses in terms of how many hours of your life they cost, it becomes clear just how valuable your time is and how much your stuff actually costs.

Wealthy individuals understand that money is simply a tool to help them purchase more of their top commodity – time. Whether you use your hard-earned cash to go on a vacation or book a five-star restaurant for dinner, true wealth is all about gaining access to experiences that offer the greatest amount of freedom and joy. As such, one of the key strategies for becoming wealthy lies in learning how to funnel your money into purchases that ultimately buy you back more precious minutes and hours each day.

The only way to escape the rat race is to learn how to make money in your sleep so you can stop trading your time for dollars. You can always make more money, but you'll never be able to make more time. This is the secret the rich have always known: if you don't own your *time*, you are *poor*.

WE HAVE LESS TIME THAN WE REALIZE

Four thousand weeks. That's the average lifespan of a person living in modern times. When you are going about your day-to-day life, it might be easy to waste time scrolling on social media or watching trashy television. But when you think of it in terms of a precious, steadily depleting resource, it becomes harder to squander. Four thousand weeks. That's it! That's all you get – if you're *lucky*.

People selling their labor and time, clocking in and out by the hour doing jobs they hate for wages that don't pay their bills, are punching away weeks, months, years, and decades of their lives. Meanwhile, rich people are playing golf, fishing, traveling, spending time with loved ones, and sunbathing near the Italian Riviera. They've learned how to maximize their time on this earth. And you can too.

Wealthy people are masters in the art of time satisfaction. Studies show that while wealthy people spend a similar amount of time working, they spend more time in active leisure, like exercise and volunteering, rather than passive leisure, like watching tv and relaxing at home. This leads to a higher life satisfaction for the affluent. So how do they free up so much time for the things they love about life?

PASSIVE INCOME

What if you didn't have to sell your time for money? Many freelancers and online marketers, like Adrian, have found a way to make money in their sleep. But there's a common myth about passive income that we need to debunk right now. Passive income doesn't mean making money without having to work for it. There is a good amount of work involved in setting up and maintaining these passive income streams and systems. You don't just flip a switch and start making money.

> Adrian: Crappy online marketing is ruining the term "passive income," which traditionally was defined for opportunities where your money makes money like dividends from a stock investment. In the online world of business the language around passive income started to broaden up since the internet is "always on" and in theory a website is working 24/7 even when you are not at your laptop. Here is a real-life example. You tell me if you would call this passive income. In 2022, I spent over 100 hours creating 500 product review videos, which I uploaded to Amazon. Even though it took me one month to make the videos, they generated $22,233 for me. Is that passive income? In 2023, without more than 10 hours of additional work, I made $43,614. Is that considered passive income? As I am writing this in May 2024, I've already made over $5,000 without any additional work from these exact same videos. Is that considered passive income? The internet has many opportunities like this that

can generate income for long after the work is done. I've started to describe these opportunities less as "passive income" and more like "work that has the potential to continue to make money without the burden of additional time."

Dr. Brad: I spent 20 years hustling, working as hard as I could. But I stayed motivated because I always had the goal of freedom in mind. I never thought, "I'm going to work for 40 or 50 years so I can live in a big house with a fancy pool and drive expensive cars and never see my kids." My goal was always freedom. Now that I've achieved it, it feels so good to know that if I want to take a month off of work, I don't have to worry about how I'm going to feed my family. If I get sick, I don't have to worry about how much paid sick leave I have to cover us or how much money I am going to lose each day I'm in bed with a fever. I kept my eye on the ball, hustled my ass off, developed multiple sources of passive income, and now I'm at a place where I own my time. I will probably always work, because I love it. But now I decide when, where, how, and with whom I work, and I invest my time in businesses and activities that feed me and help me fulfill my mission in life, while having the flexibility to spend time with the people I love most.

If you want time and freedom, you have to be willing to work and do the hard stuff in the beginning. Adrian spent countless hours studying the masters of online entrepreneurship; he read dozens of books on how to build an online business and platform and how to achieve financial freedom. Dr. Brad worked hard and got his doctorate in psychology and then became an expert in financial planning and blended the two fields together. We both worked nights and weekends while our friends were partying. We drove used cars so that we could invest more money, while our friends saddled themselves with high monthly payments for their leased luxury cars. Instead of filling our closets with designer clothes, we filled our 401(k)s with stocks of the companies selling those useless clothes to our clueless peers. While our friends consumed content on social media, we created it, and built our online platforms to millions of followers that we passionately served with our motivating content on how to achieve financial freedom. Most people don't recognize that being a legitimate "influencer" is much more than taking selfies in public. In the first year alone of being on TikTok, Adrian created over 1,000 videos. While our friends wasted time watching Netflix, we read books, implemented wealth building systems, and diversified our revenue streams so we could one day make passive income while we were spending our time doing the things we loved. That's why they're called side hustles and not "side take-it-easies." You'll never make passive income by doing passive work. We'll cover side hustles in depth in Chapter 19: "People Who Binge Netflix Without a Side Hustle Will Be Poor Forever."

WHAT'S YOUR FINANCIAL FREEDOM GOAL?

Financial freedom doesn't need to be some far-off dream for the distant future. It also doesn't need to happen all at once. It is crucial to set a goal for when and how you want to achieve financial freedom. For example, at what age do you want to be able to buy back one day of your week? How about two? When would you like to be able to work just 20 hours a week while making progress toward your financial goals, instead of needing to work 50 hours a week just to stay afloat? In how many years do you want to be entirely financially free, where your passive income allows you to fully fund your desired lifestyle?

Whether it's 10 or 20 years from now, set your financial freedom goal and then work backward to figure out just how much money you need to make right now and in the subsequent years for you to reach your goal. After you have set the goal, it is time to get specific. What's the max you can make in your current profession? Will that get you to your goal? If not, it might be time to expand your skill sets to increase your earning potential. Figure out if you need to get a side hustle or two, and how much you'll need to make at that side hustle to hit your goal. Where can you cut expenses today to allow you to grow your nest egg or invest in a business or side hustle to help you reach your goal faster? Dr. Brad spent two decades working a day job and no less than three side hustles, investing 30% of every dollar he made. Adrian lived in a van for a year and was able to invest 95% of his income. When you have an exciting goal, it is easy to cut back on spending that doesn't have as much meaning for you.

Financial freedom is more than just being worry free and financially stable. Financial freedom means time with your family, long vacations, unlimited PTO, new hobbies, self-improvement, and fun adventures. It means having the time to coach your kids' little league, volunteer at their school, or take them to the zoo in the middle of a workday. It means being available to help your child plan her wedding or spend time with your grandchildren. It means traveling to new places with friends without worrying about how much vacation time you're burning. When you're working 80 hours a week with no time off, it doesn't matter what your net worth is; you're poor.

INVESTMENT INCOME: BUILDING UP YOUR NEST EGG

There's nothing like the feeling when you wake up and see that the money you've invested is making money. The wealthiest people who've achieved financial freedom have investments that make more money than their jobs. Now that's true passive income. As we've said before, most millionaires are self-made. They started investing as much as they could, even if it wasn't a huge amount at first. It could literally be $5 per day. But eventually, that $5 will compound and start working for you. It will build, and the more you invest, the more it will grow. It's one of the most exciting things, when your money starts making money.

It all comes down to the small decisions you make consistently every day. Don't put it off. Wealth can be built on $5 per day. That consistent investment will get you to a point where, one day, you'll be able to buy back your time.

True wealth isn't measured by objects; rather it's measured by moments – those precious slivers we wisely use our money to create and enjoy. True wealth means investing in experiences rather than things – this will give us more opportunities to learn, grow, and connect with those around us – which is really what life's all about anyway!

Your nest egg is the cumulation of all of your financial freedom investment accounts. This includes, but may not be limited to, your 401(k), Roth IRA, Traditional IRA, brokerage accounts, and trust accounts. Nest egg income is the cash that flows out of these accounts. When done wisely, these accounts spin off income to you in perpetuity. Many retirees live comfortably on distributions from their nest eggs without ever touching their principal, which is the original money they put in. What makes this income different from other sources of income is that it truly can be passive. For example, "passive income" from rental units is anything but passive. It is a business, where you are responsible for finding tenants, fixing or replacing broken appliances, bookkeeping, potential evictions, paying taxes, etc. In contrast, nest egg income typically comes from investments, which ultra-wealthy individuals typically have managed by a financial advisor. Many financial advisors recommend what's called "The 4% Rule." The idea is that every year, you can take out 4% of your nest egg to sustain you financially through your retirement, without dipping into the amount of money you invested. For example, let's say that you have a $1 million nest egg. First of all, congratulations! Doing what it takes to accumulate $1 million is incredible. We have immense respect for your dedication, sacrifice, and willingness to delay gratification. With a $1 million nest egg, under the 4% rule, you would have an income of $40,000 per year for the rest of your life. This is assuming you have average investing returns. As long as you don't do anything stupid, like trying to "beat the market" by not being adequately diversified or trying to "trade," you (and your children, grandchildren, and great-grandchildren) should be able to count on that 4% distribution forever. This is how generational wealth is created.

OUTSOURCING: TAKING OWNING YOUR TIME TO THE NEXT LEVEL

Let's say you've become a master at earning money in your sleep. You're not clocking in to work 40 to 70 hours per week, and you actually have time to take care of things that you've been putting off. So you switch from one form of labor to another. Now you're running errands, doing chores, deep cleaning your house, scheduling appointments, and organizing those messy closets. Are you the master of your time?

Adrian: Most people know me from social media as the guy who lived in a van, had Wi-Fi one day a week, and was able to make over seven figures from internet marketing. How was that possible? It's because I became obsessed with outsourcing, automation, and processes that made my business run successfully on its own, without me. I knew how to outsource all business-related systems and tasks. But when we moved to a house, I was still doing my own laundry and chores. If something was broken, I'd be the one to go to the hardware store and try to fix it, usually unsuccessfully. And then it occurred to me, I became financially free so I could spend time doing what I love, not doing chores.

My wife had the idea to hire a personal assistant who managed our household. It was a light bulb moment. I realized that if I really wanted to optimize my time, because that is what wealthy people do, then I would need to outsource tasks in my personal life, as well as my professional life. Wealthy people aren't fixing faucets and folding clothes. They outsource almost everything so they have time to do what's important to them. Time equals freedom. And getting that personal assistant has been transformative. It's been just under a year and already, even on the first day, Ash and I looked at each other like, "Oh, my gosh, this is amazing." Every hour she puts in is giving us a gift of time. Now, we know that we will likely only have this personal assistant temporarily, because we support those we employ in building their own side hustles and eventual financial freedom, but we plan to continue to outsource as much as we can to give us as much freedom as possible. Another thing we outsourced was cooking. Coming from a Mexican family, cooking is a big part of culture and I had a hard time letting go of it, despite the fact that cooking and washing dishes consumed 20 hours per week between my wife and me. After hiring our chef and eating her first meal, which was so incredibly delicious and thoughtful, I realized I really don't enjoy cooking; what I enjoy is eating!

Owning your time is the ultimate milestone of wealth and success. Reclaiming your time is more exhilarating than a thousand sports cars, more flashy than a hundred Rolexes, and better than the most delicious five-star meal in the world. When you get to a place where you don't have to sell your time for money, the world of possibility opens up. Life satisfaction skyrockets. You'll have time with your family, for hobbies, and for living your life on your terms. We want that for every person who reads this book. True financial freedom is when you can finally stop punching the clock and start taking back your life.

Chapter 11 *Start Thinking Rich* Challenge

If you want to be truly rich, you need to own your time. Owning more and more of your time is a process, but it starts with the right mindset. Don't fall prey to the trappings of fake wealth – blowing your money on cars, clothes, watches, etc. Instead, focus on building up your nest egg. And make sure you have financial freedom as your TOP financial goal. To make this happen, ask yourself these questions:

- How many hours of your week do you currently own?
- How many hours of your week does your boss own?
- How many hours of your week are spoken for with life-maintenance tasks?
- What are some tasks you can outsource? NOTE: Our top recommendation is house cleaning. Not only will this save you hours of time; if you are in a relationship, it can be the best form of relationship therapy!
- What is your financial freedom goal?
- How much do you need to make now to achieve that financial freedom goal?
- What can you do to reach that goal? Do you need to increase your income to get there? If so, what skills can you learn or combine? What side hustles could you do to get you to that finish line?
- What is your nest egg income goal? How much can you invest every time you get paid to achieve that goal?

Once you have all of your answers, create a Master of Time plan for yourself and work consistently every day to meet your goals. Small actions now will have a big impact later.

CHAPTER TWELVE

ONLY BROKE AND INSECURE PEOPLE FLEX LUXURY BRANDS

We've got a message for all the "Hey, look at me! I just bought a Rolex! Check out my Louis Vuitton bag that costs more than my rent! Bro! My Lambo goes *vroom-vroom*" wannabes out there: WE ARE NOT IMPRESSED WITH THE STUFF YOU BUY. Fancy stuff is just a reflection of an insecure ego and dumping your money into it is the fastest way to go broke. It's also a dead giveaway to actual self-made rich people, who according to studies, *do not* spend like that. If they do have nice things, the truly wealthy ones aren't posting on Instagram about it to flex it in your face. In fact, quite the opposite. Most self-made millionaires proudly brag about how *frugal* they are. Actual rich people are more likely to brag about how little they paid for their used Toyota than how much they paid for their new BMW. When you flex luxury brands to try to impress your broke friends, people with money know you're faking it. The harsh truth is, most people who flex luxury brands are punching themselves in the financial dick.

There are entire industries that prey on suckers who are willing to trade their hard-earned dollars and precious time for sparkly, loud, fast, meaningless crap they can show off on social media. That's why Bernard Arnault has acquired essentially all the luxury designer brands, from Louis Vuitton to Tag Heuer, and is now one of the richest humans on earth. He knows insecure people would rather go broke and look rich than try to save money. This has made him a contender for the richest person along-side Elon Musk and Jeff Bezos. It's almost too easy to extract money from poor and middle-class people who hand over their hard-earned TIME (remember, dollars = time if you're selling your time for money) so they can show off for their friends and followers who don't even care about them. What an embarrassing waste, and an easy trap for people who grew-up poor to fall into, just like Dr. Brad did in his 20s.

Dr. Brad: When I got out of graduate school, between my public school day job and three side hustles, I started making a six-figure income. The first thing I did was buy my mom a 14-karat-gold custom Hawaiian heirloom bracelet. My dad left when I was two years old and my mom was pregnant with my sister. We went through some tough times, especially in the years before she married my stepfather. I wanted to show her my love and appreciation for all she did for me and my sister. So I spent thousands on that bracelet for her.

Around the same time, a friend introduced me to the world of luxury watches, and I decided I should get one, as I was entering the world of the wealthy with my high income. To be entirely honest, I also wanted to show people that I had made it. So I bought an

Omega Speedmaster, which set me back another couple thousand dollars. Sure, I was making pretty good income, but the problem was, I had a net worth of *negative* $100,000 due to my student loan debt. At the time, I had no idea that spending money like that is a poor and middle-class move, and NOT what most wealthy people do. I made the classic poor-mindset mistake. I wanted to thank my mother for her hard work and sacrifice and show the world that I had "made it" with my shiny new bling. After a lifetime of feeling left behind and going without, I wanted to treat myself. Later, I learned that this put me further away from my goal of being financially free.

TWO OF THE MOST IMPORTANT aspects of a rich mindset are delayed gratification and not falling prey to the trappings of materialism. Delayed gratification simply means that you have such an exciting vision of your future financial freedom that you can easily say "no" to the temptation of blowing your money on meaningless bullshit that is less important today. Without a clear and exciting vision you will not be able to override your impulse to spend now and you will be poor forever. Materialism is where you believe that owning more stuff is the most important thing in life. This is the opposite of a rich mindset. A rich mindset prioritizes experiences over stuff. These two mindsets are more important than:

- Dollar cost averaging
- Beating the market or winning the lottery
- Getting a job that pays six figures
- Buying Bitcoin early

Without the right mindset, even if you came into a bunch of money fast, you would just blow it. Your insatiable desire for more shiny objects NEEDS to be restrained. There is no dollar amount in the world that can satisfy it – which is why you need to control it.

Only people with a poor mindset fall prey to flex culture, and that will keep you poor forever. So why do people go against their own best interest and buy things they can't afford to attract a shallow mate and show off to their friends and followers? Again, it all comes down to psychology.

THE PSYCHOLOGY OF THE FLEX

Outward displays of wealth have a long history. For example, the Vikings wore their wealth on their bodies. There were no banks or "safe" places to hide one's riches so they often carried their treasures with them. Successful warriors wore expensive armor, had costly swords, and sported arm bands made of silver and gold. Those in the upper class covered themselves in fine silk with gold threads and adorned themselves with furs and jewelry. The women wore colorful beads and even brooches made of precious metals. They flaunted their ability to travel by displaying souvenirs from faraway lands, like Byzantium. They were like the Kardashians of the Middle Ages.

The ancient tribal hard wiring in our brains makes us prone to flexing those luxury brands. In order to secure a mate and carry on the bloodline, the men of the tribe had to show that they could provide for their mates and offspring. So it makes sense that they would flaunt the fur pelt to demonstrate that they are good hunters who can get food for the tribe. In modern times, men seeking female partners might flex luxury cars and designer clothes to convey the same message, "Mate with me! Behold, my prize possessions and see that I can provide for you and our future offspring." In many current cultures, outward displays of wealth not only denote status, but they can be a protective factor in avoiding being attacked by strangers. Only someone who is important, has resources, and could cause me trouble if I mess with them would have that expensive jewelry, drive that kind of car, etc., so the thinking goes.

There is an evolutionary aspect that triggers our brains to show off our success, wealth, and vitality so we can survive and increase the chances that our bloodlines will carry on. But in modern times, our survival isn't dependent on fur pelts, sports cars, or expensive watches. It's a constant tug-of-war with our ancient psychological conditioning and our reasonable, rational minds of today.

QUIET LUXURY IS THE FLEX FOR THE RICH

The opposite of flex culture is money vigilance. This is a mindset Dr. Brad discovered in his research on the ultra-wealthy. It turns out that self-made rich people are careful with their money. They know exactly where every dollar is, how it's spent, what's coming in and what's going out. They are careful with their spending, they invest wisely, and are mindful of anything that might separate them from their money. When they start making money, they focus on how much they can keep, versus what they can buy. Dr. Brad's studies on the ultra-rich show that they tend to be more money vigilant; in particular, they feel anxious about losing money, believe it should be saved rather than spent, have difficulty spending on themselves, and feel it's impolite to talk about money, let alone show it off. They also tend to be less money avoidant and have a higher internal locus of control. People in the ultra-rich category don't feel the need to flaunt their wealth. Rich people are much less likely to wear designer labels than the poor and middle class. Even among the richest people on earth, many embrace the concept of "quiet luxury," or "stealth wealth." This is marked by a preference for expensive items that are in muted tones, no logos, and nothing too flashy or obvious. Only those familiar with the luxury items would be able to spot them by recognizing the stitching or other subtle characteristics.

So most self-made wealthy people tend to be savers and investors versus spenders, and that's how they amass their wealth. In addition, with so many people struggling to get by due to inflation and stalled wages, some wealthy people may also downplay their financial status as a form of protection. While in some situations outward displays of wealth can raise your status, in many other situations flaunting your wealth can put a target on your back. In some circumstances, people may be more likely to try and rob or take advantage of you. They may feel like it's tacky to flaunt luxury items in front of people who can barely afford rent. They understand that some may hold money avoidant beliefs, assuming that money is bad and rich people are evil. So to protect themselves, some wealthy people keep their wealth subdued and hidden. As it turns out, if you really want to appear wealthy, taking a more subtle approach will work better than flashing an over-the-top, gaudy designer handbag at a party. For those who know the truth, such behavior is a sure sign you're broke and living outside your means.

INVESTMENTS AREN'T SHINY BUT THEY MAKE YOUR FUTURE BRIGHT

You could be wearing $30 sneakers, jeans, and a t-shirt from Target, and drive a Prius. But if you've been saving and investing your money, chances are, you're wealthier than the guy driving the BMW and walking around in Armani suits. The majority of status items immediately lose value as soon as they are purchased. Suits fade, BMWs eventually break down. But smart investments appreciate and grow your money, making your future brighter than the sparkliest of Rolexes. We'd take a $5 million 401(k) over a luxury watch any day.

People who forgo investments or, worse, go into debt so they can get fancy things are running a fool's errand, trying to enjoy the benefits of being fake wealthy without actually putting in the real work to become wealthy.

Adrian: We recently had some people over to our house for an internet marketing mixer. I'll never forget it. This woman and I were talking about shoes and she told me she was wearing $500 tennis shoes. They looked like regular shoes to me. I couldn't believe it. She was still in college and was wearing $500 shoes. The most expensive shoes I've ever worn are Vans. Luxury brands just don't appeal to me. I'm not impressed by them. You'll never catch me wearing Louis Vuitton or Gucci. I prefer to walk around knowing that I've got millions of dollars working for me. Now that's a good look.

Dr. Brad: I recently posted a video that went viral. We were in Vegas and I shared that even my eight-year-old son knows that everyone there flexing luxury brands was actually broke and insecure. My comment section lit up with people saying things like, "Well, what about the Kardashians?" Insecure people will always look for these outlying examples to make them feel better. But if you think about it, the Kardashians are likely getting paid to flex these luxury brands so they can sell them to broke people who want to appear wealthy. Why would a star give free advertising for a tacky brand targeting the poor and middle class? Of course they wouldn't! The inside scoop on superstars and influencers is that they don't advertise brands for free. When you see them in labels, rest assured that label is paying them to market their wares.

Adrian and I are both social media influencers; we go out of our way to make sure there are no brand logos in our videos because that's free advertising for those brands. My habitually worn Detroit Tigers hat is an exception, of course, but that's just me angling to throw out the first pitch in a game sometime. If any of our readers have connections and can put in a good word for me, please let me know!

LIVING BEYOND YOUR MEANS

When most people get a job promotion or raise, they increase their cost of living alongside it. This is known as lifestyle inflation. Instead of keeping their eye on the ball, delaying gratification, and buying more of their time, they blow their money on clothing, cars, and housing upgrades. When they start making more money, they just turn around and buy more expensive toys and gaudier objects. SIT DOWN. BE HUMBLE – these might be some of the best rap lyrics from Kendrick Lamar for becoming wealthy.

This is an easy wealth hack and a total no-brainer. If you get a raise, live as if you were still making the same amount of money as you did before your raise and invest the extra income. Pretend like it's not even there. This doesn't even involve tightening your belt or spending less. You just live within the means you've already established before your raise. And if you really want to level up, try cutting your expenses by 20% and put that in investments as well. The higher the percentage of your income you can invest, the closer you'll be to the nest egg and financial freedom goals you set in the last chapter. Those with a true wealth mindset live below their means and stack their cash.

THE THINGS YOU OWN BECOME A LIABILITY

Let's say you spring for a $250,000 vehicle, fully loaded, the epitome of luxury. You've just created a huge liability in your life, not just on your financial balance sheet (cars depreciate the moment you drive them off the lot), but also in your mind. So much of your energy will be spent worrying where to park so you don't get any scratches, where to keep your car so it won't get stolen, and worrying about anyone who drives too close to you on the freeway. You have to worry about potholes and bad weather. And then there's the maintenance.

> Dr. Brad: When my buddy takes his new Land Rover in to be serviced for regular maintenance it costs him $2,000 a pop. I drive a used Toyota 4Runner and it costs me $90.

Expensive cars have expensive parts, expensive insurance, and are expensive to fix and maintain. So you're not only paying a high price tag, but you'll also be shelling out tons of money on upkeep and repairs. The elation you experience on the first day you purchase the vehicle will fade quickly and you'll be left with a huge financial liability and less energy because you'll worry about it all the time. The popular concept of minimalism is all about being free from the weight of worrying about stuff in your life.

> Adrian: I am a big believer that the more stuff you own the more it owns you, and I'm not alone in that. Minimalists across the world share the same belief. While most people might think I was crazy for living in a van, minimalists think everyone else living in cluttered homes with stuffed closets and owning multiple cars are the crazy ones. I met pickleball legends Christina and Walter Doorman out of San Marcos, Texas, who told me that their final commitment to minimalism was getting rid of their wedding rings! Christina shared that she remembered staying up at night with worrisome thoughts of her wedding ring getting lost or damaged. Eventually she and her husband Walter got rid of them and Christina said she has never felt more free. A wedding ring is not a symbol of marriage; it's a symbol of consumerism at the most intimate level. Love cannot be bought. Your wedding ring doesn't represent love. It represents a business that made money off you.

DEBT DOESN'T DISAPPEAR WHEN THE EXCITEMENT FADES

Think about any of your childhood birthdays. If you're like many Americans, you probably woke up to a day filled with cake, ice-cream, and a stack of presents. You tore through the presents as quickly as possible, buzzing with excitement over all your new toys and gadgets. Now, do you actually remember any of the presents you got as a kid? What about your birthday last year?

We're not saying it's bad to give and receive gifts. Nor are we saying that it isn't fun to treat yourself to an exciting new purchase. But if buying gifts for yourself or others makes you a slave to credit card debt for the rest of the year, it might be worth asking if it's *really* worth it to you. We are conditioned to consume, to overspend, and to live outside our means. We are also accustomed to quickly acclimating to new items and situations, making them normal in no time. In other words, the joy you feel in a new purchase is usually temporary, and for most Americans lasts just a fraction as long as the pain you will endure in trying to pay it off later. The push to consume is constantly influencing us, on our TVs, or phone screens and devices, and on billboards and street corners. Get this latest gadget and you'll be happy! Drown your depression with this new handbag! Attract the hotties with your lifted truck!

But if you really look at the cost of impulse buying, materialism, and overspending, you'll see that none of it is worth your financial freedom. In fact, studies show that happiness from new purchases wears off after anywhere from six weeks to three months. But unpaid debt can last for seven years on your credit report. Not only that, but if you're spending money you could be investing, it will keep you broke and take years from your life (see Chapter 11: "Poor People Buy Stuff; Rich People Own Time").

LUXURY BRANDS ATTRACT CONDITIONAL RELATIONSHIPS

Let's say you spend most of your 20s driving a beat-up car. It gets you to work every day, but it isn't turning any heads. After a while, you get tired of driving the beat-up car, so you spring for a luxury car with your company bonus. Suddenly, women are noticing you on the street. Maybe you post a picture of you with your fancy new wheels and get a bunch of new followers. Friends you haven't seen in years are sending you messages asking how you got successful enough to afford such a nice car. It may feel nice for a while, but there's a catch.

People who show up when your life is looking shiny and fancy are usually only there to bask in the glow of your success. But as soon as life takes a turn, which will happen because we all have our ups and downs, those same people will probably vanish. The relationships you attract by flexing designer and luxury items will be transactional and conditional. There are countless stories of celebrities losing everything to shady parasites who wait for them to become vulnerable so they can bleed them dry. But the friendships and romantic relationships you made when you had that beat-up car may still be there for you. When you flex luxury brands, you're not only hurting yourself financially, but you are also paving the way to a lonely life full of fake friends and vultures. Stop wasting your money on status items that give you a temporary high. Instead, invest it wisely, and people who actually care about your well-being, financially and otherwise, will be attracted to you for the right reasons.

If you've been this "Hey, look at me and all my fancy stuff," type of person, it's okay. We've all been that person at one point or another. Our society is designed to push us toward consumerism and flaunting our fancy things. But we hope going forward that you put things into perspective. Down the road, that expensive car or watch could cost you thousands more in interest, lost investments, time, stress, and even relationships. So think about the long-term outcomes of your purchases so you can get to the place of the truly wealthy, quiet luxury, owning your time, and enjoying financial freedom.

Chapter 12 *Start Thinking Rich* Challenge

Now that you know the truth about why so many people have a desperate need to impress others with outward displays of wealth, do you have the courage to get honest and admit to yourself why *you* are attracted to these same status items? For example:

- Did you grow up poor and now want to treat yourself to the things you could never afford?
- Do you want to increase your sexual appeal?
- Are you hoping to garner more respect from your peers and in your community?
- Are you trying to get more likes on Instagram?
- Do outward displays of social status give you an increased feeling of safety?
- Do you feel depressed or lost and believe that owning the right material items will fill the hole you feel inside and finally bring you the happiness you want?

Most people do not have the ego strength to get honest about this. So know you're not alone. But once you get honest with yourself about your natural vulnerability to fall prey to outward displays of social status, you've got a fighting chance for success. Once you understand that the vast majority of self-made millionaires are FRUGAL and actually DOWNPLAY their wealth, the sooner you can stop looking like a fool. It may be hard to admit, but once you do, you'll be free to make choices from a rich mindset.

CHAPTER THIRTEEN

IF YOU WANT TO GET RICH, GO TO COLLEGE, GET MARRIED, AND BUY A HOUSE (OR NOT)

E lon Musk lied to you. He said you don't need to go to college, implying that college isn't worth it anymore. Meanwhile he's got two Ivy League degrees (in physics and economics) and the highest ranking jobs at SpaceX require a college degree. We wouldn't be surprised if his kids go to college someday too. This may be a tough pill to swallow for Gen Z, but if you want a better chance at becoming wealthy, you should seriously consider going to college, getting married, and buying a house (or not).

The numbers don't lie. Married couples have approximately nine times more wealth than single people. People with college degrees make at least double what people with only a high school education make annually. The vast majority of rich people own their own homes, which can dramatically increase a person's net worth. Now the details matter, which we will discuss, but these basic facts are all backed up by data, which we will share with you. Sometimes the traditional routes prove to be the best ones when it comes to accumulating wealth, IF you do them right. But there are, of course, exceptions to these tried-and-true wealth-building rules, and you can have a high school diploma, be single, rent your home, and still become rich if you know how to play the game right.

Younger generations may feel a bit disillusioned with the traditional college, marriage, and buying a house route. We get it. Predatory student loans have created a major hardship for college grads. Divorce can be a living nightmare. And with skyrocketing property prices and interest rates, buying a house may seem nearly impossible. But these things still offer major advantages if you know how to navigate the system.

GO TO COLLEGE

College isn't for everyone. But anyone on social media telling you college isn't worth it anymore is either lying or just plain stupid. But before you decide if it's right for you, we want to make sure you have all the facts from both perspectives: those of Dr. Brad, who went as high as he could on the education path, and Adrian, a self-taught internet marketer who stopped at a bachelor's degree, which in retrospect, he may have not needed.

Adrian: When Dr. Brad first pitched the title of this chapter, I was hesitant. In my field, college is too slow to keep up with the trends in the rapidly changing world of internet marketing. Let's say you write a book about affiliate and internet marketing; by the time it's finished and published, the industry will look completely different. Algorithms and tech change too fast. So, while I know Dr. Brad has some mind-blowing statistics about college and how it impacts your earnings, we both agree that there are many cases in which the best approach may not be college. My philosophy is, if you want to learn how to be good at sales, get out there and try to sell something. What you learn by trying to grow your own personal social media followers will trump anything you learn in the classroom about social media marketing. That said, I'm married to someone who has a degree in accounting, is a CPA, and that has been extremely valuable for growing our net worth and making smart money decisions.

While times may be a-changing and in the future things might be different, the stats don't lie. On average, college graduates make WAY more money TODAY than people with a high school diploma only. In a study of over 10,000 millionaires, Ramsey Solutions found that 88% of them went to college. In fact, the more education the better. People with two-year degrees (e.g. trade schools) make more than those with high school diplomas only, people with four-year degrees make more than two-year degrees, and people with graduate degrees make even more. The median earnings for four-year college grads are 88% higher, with an average of $1.2 million more earnings in their lifetime than those with a high school diploma. According to the Federal Reserve, college-educated homes have three times the income as those without college educations. College grads also weathered the Great Recession better than those with high school diplomas. The jobless rate for employees who hold bachelor's degrees is less than 2%. So you have a higher earning potential and also better chances of surviving economic downturns.

Going to college not only makes you smarter (at least theoretically), it also makes you healthier. Bachelor's degree holders are 47% more likely to have health insurance, with higher contributions from their employers than those with a high school diploma only. Even with the student loan rates as high as they are, on average, it's still worth it to get your degree. The average in-state tuition for a four-year degree is $11,000 (× 4 years = $44,000) and the average student loan debt is $29,400. And you can lessen the amounts of those loans by applying for grants and scholarships. So even when these costs are taken into account, *on average*, college is still absolutely worth it. In terms of what is best on average, college detractors have no rational argument. That said, college may be a terrible idea if you choose the wrong major.

> Dr. Brad: When I grew-up in the 1980s, the internet didn't exist. I lived in a working-class town and the people who were living the best financial lives were college grads. I worked manual labor jobs during high school and college and I quickly observed that the longer people stayed in school the more money they made and the less worn out they seemed to be at the end of the day. My summer jobs were so exhausting I thought college was an easy life, even though I worked part time too. I got to sleep in, eat as much as I wanted in the cafeteria, and got paid to play tennis.
>
> I thought my friends who complained about college were delusional, because for me it was way easier than any job I could get with just a high school diploma. I didn't have any guidance on what degree to get but I chose psychology, primarily because I was interested in figuring out how my family got so messed up so I could break the pattern in my own life. But coming from a working-class home, I knew I was on my own and I needed to make my degree worth it. As I mentioned before, I went to the library and looked up psychology jobs in the *Occupational Outlook Handbook*. This is a Department of Labor publication that shows how much money

each job makes. Anyone who is considering college MUST check this out. It is now free online. I saw that in psychology you needed to get a doctorate degree to make good money. So I decided that's what I was going to do. College is a business decision, and if you don't approach it as such, you can get wrecked.

PICK A MONEY-MAKING MAJOR

When it comes to college, there is a catch. If you want to be a high-earning college grad, you have to pick a high-earning major. Majors like arts and humanities, social work, and psychology are fun areas of study that provide tremendous value to our society. Unfortunately, the job market often disagrees, and many of these majors pay just minimum wage, and graduates often regret getting them. Before you sign up for a four-year degree and take out a bunch of student loans, it's important to research the earnings in the field you're thinking of studying. Unless your parents are rich and you don't need to worry about money, you need to approach college as a business decision. You can find information about the earning potential of college degrees in the *Occupational Outlook Handbook*, but here are the top 10 worst- and best-paying college majors within five years of graduation:

Top 10 Best-Paying College Majors (Right out of College)
- Computer Engineering: $80,000
- Chemical Engineering: $79,000
- Computer Science: $78,000
- Aerospace Engineering: $74,000
- Electrical Engineering: $72,000
- Industrial Engineering: $71,000

- Mechanical Engineering: $70,000
- General/Miscellaneous Engineering: $68,000
- Finance: $66,000

Top 10 Worst-Paying College Majors (Right out of College)
- Psychology: $40,000
- Treatment Therapy and Nutrition Sciences: $40,000
- Fine Arts: $40,000
- Miscellaneous Biological Science: $40,000
- History: $40,000
- General Social Sciences: $40,000
- Leisure/Hospitality: $39,700
- Theology/Religion: $38,000
- Performing Arts: $38,000
- Liberal Arts: $38,000

Of course, you can still study what interests you, but you may need to use that low-paying bachelor's degree as a steppingstone to a higher-paying graduate or professional degree. If that's your goal, make sure you do exceptionally well in college as there is often fierce competition to get into graduate degree programs, the best of which have limited slots. If you decide to go to college, be strategic about your degree and how you plan to leverage it to make the most money possible.

GET MARRIED

Married people are WAY richer than single people. According to the US Census Bureau, married couple homes had a median income of $110,800 in 2022, with spouseless female households having a median income of $56,000 and spouseless male households having a median income of $73,600. It turns out that being married carries major financial benefits.

You're splitting household expenses, you can get on your spouse's health insurance plan or vice-versa, and you can help each other grow up and improve saving and spending habits. The Federal Reserve Bank reported that married couples between the ages of 25 and 34 have a net worth that is nine times higher than their single counterparts. When inflation rises, that financial gap widens even further. With regard to financial well-being, being married is even more important if you have children.

Not only is marriage associated with higher income and higher net worth, Dr. Brad's research has also found that married people tend to have healthier money beliefs:

> Dr. Brad: I understand why some people have a fear around getting married. I grew up with divorced parents, so I get it. I saw what happens when a marriage doesn't work. I was also raised by a single mother for a while, and I know how difficult it is to try to raise kids and make ends meet on your own. We just weren't meant to do all of this alone. But like anything worth having, marriage takes work. It starts with a deep commitment to the entire idea, a willingness to compromise, and even some marital therapy when things get rocky. This is especially true around money, which is one of the leading causes of divorce.
>
> It's fair to say that my wife and I grew up on different sides of the tracks. She grew up in an intact family, in a home that had three bathrooms. Meanwhile, I grew up in a 1,300-square-foot, one-bathroom house, and my mom had to rent out the basement to pay the mortgage. After college, I was living well below my means because I was terrified of being poor. My focus was to pay off my student loans as fast as I could and to save as much for future financial freedom as possible.
>
> I was appalled when my future wife suggested we buy a couch. I guess she had a different vision of a comfortable living room than the ping pong table and lawn chairs that were my only pieces of furniture in the old plantation-style home I was renting on Kauai. I realized that I was so afraid of being poor, I had constructed a

lifestyle that looked poor. I was making a six-figure income but slept on a used mattress on the floor, didn't have cable, had just a couple of plates, some mismatched pieces of silverware, and drove a broken-down car. The great news is that she clearly loved me for me and the potential she saw in me and didn't marry me for my money. But she was able to hold a mirror up to me and show me my extreme relationship with money in a compassionate way. I kept telling her I didn't want to be poor, and she said, "I don't think you need to worry about being poor, you have a doctorate." Her different life experience and lack of financial trauma helped balance me out. On the other side of the coin, she was attracted to me partially because I was conscientious with money. Our different experiences around money lead to some disagreements along the way, but we have each benefited from the vision and viewpoints of the other.

Finding out the money beliefs and financial habits of a potential spouse before getting married is crucial. Someone with a low credit score today is very likely to mishandle money tomorrow. During the marriage, it must become a routine habit to check in with each other on financial goals and expenses. It's okay if you prioritize different things. A trip to the hair salon may be important to your spouse, while a cold-plunge tub may be high on your list of priorities. Some couples have a spending threshold, where if, for example, something is over a certain dollar amount, say $100, they agree to check in with their spouse before making the purchase. Adrian and his wife have a "Brambila Net Worth" meeting on the first of every month to go over all their investments and bank accounts and review income and expenses together.

WARNING: There is one major caveat to our stance on marriage and wealth. Divorce can ruin you. While marriage can increase your wealth tenfold, divorce will cut it in half (minus attorney fees). Sometimes people are in abusive relationships and need to leave for the physical safety of themselves and their children. Under those circumstances you really don't have a choice. You will likely need to sideline your financial goals for a while, but your safety is more important than financial freedom, and it is better to be broke than in danger. Trust that you can rebuild and bounce back financially in the future. If you are not in an abusive relationship but find you are regularly fighting with your spouse, spring for couples therapy. There is a good chance your relationship problems are at least 50% on you and you need to get some insight and learn and grow or you will find yourself in the same place in your next relationship anyway. In strict financial terms, it's also a lot less expensive to go to therapy than it is to get a divorce.

BUY A HOUSE (OR NOT)?

The vast majority of millionaires own their own homes, and on average, homeowners have a significantly higher net worth than renters. This is why Dr. Brad argued for having this section, even when Adrian pushed back. BUT, the fact is that owning your home can be a benefit OR a liability, depending on your situation and perspective. While we are on the same page with all other areas of this book, we have different perspectives on homeownership. As such, we are going to share both of them with you, so you can decide what is the best fit for you and your family. Fair warning, this section is going to get into the weeds as we debate our different perspectives.

ADRIAN'S TAKE

I come from a minimalist and nomadic background. I have lived periods of my life where everything I owned could fit in a backpack or in a tiny home van. To be clear, I lived this way by choice and decided to be a nomad living overseas and a minimalist after I was already a multi-millionaire, averaging an income of $100,000 per month.

I don't believe purchasing a home is the best investment, key words being "best" and "investment." Homeownership has become a cornerstone in identifying whether or not someone has "made it" by traditional standards. I had some strong judgments thrown my way when my wife and I decided to live in a van instead of purchasing a home. I was told that we were making a huge mistake by not becoming homeowners, losing out on valuable time to build equity. But I do not believe that homeownership is good and renting is bad. Actually, in strict financial terms, I believe the opposite – that homeownership can be bad and renting can be good. This argument is supported by the following three points:

1. **People Can't Control Their Egos**

   When given the choice of how much debt people can take along with the corresponding nicer homes, people usually choose bigger vs. smaller. My wife and I purchased our first property while living in Cedar Rapids, Iowa. At the time, our combined household income was around $100,000 a year. We were approved for a $350,000 mortgage. A lot of individuals use this approved number as the respective budget for purchasing a home. Their logic is that "if the bank said I can afford it, then I must be able to afford it. They are the professionals." This is a huge mistake when purchasing a home. When you take the maximum leverage possible for a mortgage it creates a lot of pressure for you (and your partner, if you have one) to maintain your income level. This decision shifts control of your life over to your mortgage payments. You won't own your home; your home will own you. Want to travel to Europe? Unfortunately you can't because of your mortgage. Want to go out to eat? Sorry, you can't because of your mortgage. Want to go see Caitlin Clark play live? Not this time; your paycheck went toward your mortgage. Want to quit your job because your new boss is a jerk? You guessed it: no, you can't. Why? Because of your mortgage!

My wife and I ended up getting a small condo for $147,000. This was below the maximum we wanted to pay. We determined our maximum budget for our home based on what we could afford off of one income, not both. This gave us peace of mind that if an event out of our control (or within our control) occurred that resulted in our collective income being cut in half, we wouldn't have to worry about our mortgage payment. We made the conscious decision to live well below our means. While a $350,000 home in Iowa in 2015 would have been bigger and more impressive, we chose financial peace of mind over the appearance of success that comes from owning a nicer home. Choosing to purchase a home that is significantly less than your approved mortgage is one of the smartest decisions you can make for your future wealth.

At this point, you may be thinking, "Well, Adrian, I only have one income stream and the maximum I can afford doesn't get me a lot where I live. Reduce this amount, and I can't even afford to buy a home." I get it; purchasing a home has become more challenging as values of homes have increased disproportionately to median household incomes. One of the easiest ways to decrease your cost of living is to get a roommate. This might not be the answer you want to hear, but it does significantly help. Or you could always just live in a van.

My wife and I sold our place in Iowa when we decided to live a nomadic lifestyle. Over the course of the next five years, our income exponentially grew while our cost of living decreased. We were making decisions that did not follow the status quo. Instead of purchasing a larger home in proportion to our increased income, we downsized and lived in a van.

Fast forward to today where we currently live in a house that we purchased for $1.2 million in 2021 at a 2.9% fixed interest rate. The mortgage payment is $4,400 a month. Despite having a more expensive home, our mortgage as a portion of our total income is less than it was in Iowa. In Iowa, our mortgage was approximately 12% of our total income. Today, our mortgage is around 4.5% of total income. Time and time again, I see friends and business acquaintances increase their income through a raise, job change, or supplemental income and immediately upgrade materialistic items in their life: home and car being the most common.

The temptation to buy bigger and nicer things only gets stronger the more money you make. Have you ever spent time online looking at $3 million or $5 million or $10 million homes? They are freaking amazing! We didn't even tour any homes outside of our strategically set budget because we knew the power of the human desire for MORE. There is no income in the world that will satisfy it! This is why I am so adamant that if you want to get a home, make sure you do not blindly use the bank's approved maximum mortgage amount as your budget. Using the approved mortgage amount is poor thinking and a sure way to become "home poor."

2. **Your Home Costs More Than You Think**

Most people call themselves homeowners but in reality they are debt owners. If the majority of your home is owned by the bank, are you really a homeowner? NO! The bank owns your home as long as you are paying a mortgage. They literally hold the deed to your home. Homeownership decisions can be very emotional. I get it. But let's focus on the numbers and set our feelings aside.

I analyzed the numbers of the average homeowner in the United States and looked at the value of the home after 30 years compared to renting (see Appendix A). To run this analysis, I had to make a few assumptions:

1. The homeowner will own the home for 30 years.
2. The property tax rate does not change over 30 years.

3. No improvements were made to the home that would increase the value in addition to the average appreciation.

4. The savings made from renting versus owning a home were invested each month.

The analysis of renting versus homeownership can be rather challenging as it requires a lot of inputs. My goal is to demonstrate that homeownership may not be the best investment.

Here are some of the key findings:

- There was not a single scenario in which the home outperformed renters who invested.
- Renters who invested resulted in a total gain of $1,565,000, whereas the homeownership resulted in a total gain of only $16,000. That is a difference of $1,549,000 in favor of renting!
- I also ran the analysis for an average homeowner in Dallas, Texas, using the same metrics. The homeowner had a net LOSS of $315,000 after 30 years.

Before you start poking holes in this analysis, I challenge you to conduct it yourself using your own realistic inputs. Do you currently own a home and your interest rate is higher or lower? Run the calculation. Is your property tax more or less? Run the calculation. And don't forget about all the phantom costs such as appliance, replacement, and repair costs. And don't forget to add in Homeowners Association (HOA) fees. Yikes! Here is a partial list of common additional phantom charges.

Appliances:

- Dishwasher
- Refrigerator
- Oven
- Washing machine
- Dryer
- Air conditioner
- Furnace

Replacement/Repair Costs:

- Painting
- Repairing a deck
- Replacing a fence
- Replacing a garage door
- Replacing siding
- Replacing windows
- Carpet
- Countertops
- Faucets and water fixtures
- Gas fireplace
- Hardwood floors
- Electric outlets

There are many scenarios in which an individual purchases a home when the value of homes was low and sold the home when the value was high. The most recent example of this was when our Austin neighbors purchased their four bedroom, four bath home in spring of 2021 for $950,000 and sold it in the fall of 2022 for $1,745,000. In just a short period of one and a half years they made $795,000. They literally purchased their home right before the Austin boom and sold it at the right time. That is amazing! But consider this:

- You just sold your home. Where are you going to live? So now you have to purchase a new home in the same market you sold your old home. Homes in the Austin area increased at the same rate as yours and therefore, other four bedroom, four bath homes of similar quality and location cost the same as yours. The extra $795,000 you "made" is just going to go back into the next home you purchase. The only way to have "made" that amount is to downsize (which most people do not do) or move to an area where the cost of living (and homes) is less. Another option is to *gasp* rent.

- Timing the purchasing and selling of a home is impossible to do. Even the best real estate gurus disagree on the housing market conditions and projections day to day. Trying to time the housing market is like trying to time a stock. You can't. And even if you could time the market, would you want the market to determine the date you sell your personal residence? I wouldn't.

What is even worse than selling your home for a profit and having nowhere to live is someone who brags that the value of their home is now significantly higher than it was when they bought it, based on some third - party real estate search engine's algorithm. Congratulations. Is your lifestyle any different because of this news? No. Do you have more cash in your pocket? No. In fact, you'll have even LESS cash because now your real estate taxes are going to increase! Unless you are retired, your home is paid off, and you are looking to downsize, the arbitrary value of your home based on real estate search engine sites means nothing in practical terms.

3. **Your Personal Residence Does Not Produce Cashflow**

In college, I was reading books like *Rich Dad Poor Dad* by Robert Kiyosaki and *I Will Teach You to Be Rich* by Ramit Sethi, who both subscribe to the idea that your home is not always a good investment. I agree. In my opinion, an investment is something that pays YOU. A personal residence is something YOU pay for each month. What do I mean when I say this? Cash is leaving your pocket each month for mortgage, utilities, insurance, the list goes on. There is no cash going into your pockets from your personal residence unless you are renting out a room. And even when you sell and the "pay day" happens, are you going to truly realize the gain by downsizing, moving, or renting? Maybe.

However, there are many forms of real estate investing that can be cash flow producing. There are lots of books on just real estate investing, and that is because there are a lot of different types of investments: single-family homes, apartment complexes, flipping homes, commercial real estate. That said, real estate investors need to be knowledgeable, put in the work, and take a calculated risk to invest in real estate.

I personally invest in apartment complexes via syndicates. This type of real estate investment makes the most sense for me based on my moderate risk level, desire to have minimal involvement in the investment, and overall financial goals. Each month, I receive cash in my pocket from these investments. My personal residence, on the other hand, does not pay me each month and therefore, I do not consider it an investment.

At this point, you may be asking, if personal residences are so bad, why do you own one, Adrian? And my answer is simple. Personal residences are not bad AT ALL. They are just not the best investment. I purchased my house because I love it. Because I own it, I am able to make changes to the home that fit my aesthetic and remodel to my desire. Owning my home gives me peace of mind, comfort, and control. That is why. And while I never want my home value to decrease, I am not considering it an investment but an expense that I would gladly continue to pay.

DR. BRAD'S TAKE

Adrian is a smart guy and makes a lot of excellent points in this section. Buying a home comes with lots of hidden costs that most people don't take into consideration. Neither Adrian nor I go around and tell random people on the internet what they should invest in or whether or not they should go to college, get married, or buy a house. These are all very personal decisions and even if most rich people do it, that doesn't mean there aren't a lot of exceptions or people who DO take this route, but don't benefit from it. That said, it blows my mind when I see financial experts on social media telling aspiring millionaires they should rent instead of buying a house. First, you shouldn't be giving that type of global financial advice to someone you don't know. Besides, it's hard to understand that stance, because by just about every metric, owning property helps build your net worth.

The fact is, most millionaires are homeowners and homeowners have much higher net worth. Ninety-five percent of millionaires own their own homes, and the value of their homes makes up a significant percentage of their net worth. The Federal Reserve Board found that the median net worth of a homeowner is $396,200, while the net worth of renters is only $10,400. I don't think this is just a coincidence. Many will also say that "a house isn't an investment." This confuses me, because an investment is simply defined as an asset that is bought with the goal of increasing in value over time. You could argue it's not the best investment, like Adrian did so well above, but it's definitely an investment, unless you change the definition of *investment* to prove yourself right.

Throughout human history, property has appreciated in value over the long term, even taking into consideration market crashes. For example, the median sales price of a home in the United States at the peak of the 2007 real estate bubble was $257,400 (Q1) and as of Q2 2024 it was $412,300, representing 62% growth since the previous crash. People who speculate in buying and selling property will periodically get crushed in real estate crashes, but over the long haul, real estate can become legacy wealth that you pass down to your children and grandchildren. The return on investment is huge, which is one of the reasons that the vast majority of rich people own their own homes.

Owning your own home is a huge net worth builder. When you buy a home, you will likely leverage about 80% of it, assuming you do a 20% down payment. For example, if you bought a $1 million home, you would put $200,000 down. However, if that home goes up 4% in value each year, which has been the historic rate of return for real estate, your net worth is not just growing 4% based on your investment of $200,000. Instead, you are getting 4% growth on the entire $1 million.

Adrian laid out a good financial analysis of why owning a home may not be the best investment. But here are 7 reasons I am a big fan of buying your own home versus renting:

1. *Forced savings and equity building.* Your mortgage is a bill you need to pay each month, and a portion of that payment goes directly to paying down your mortgage balance. As such, with each payment you own more and more equity. In other words, each month your net worth grows. While I love the idea of people saving and investing any extra money they could save each month by renting over buying, it is all too easy to *not* do that and to just spend the extra instead. This is exactly what most Americans would do.

2. *Financial security.* While certain expenses will increase over time, such as property taxes and homeowners insurance, the bulk of your payment for housing will remain stable. In contrast, since 1980, the average annual increase of rent has been 8.85%. If that trend continues, the $2,000 you are paying in rent each month this year will be $21,391.31 each month in 30 years.

3. *Inflation hedge.* Mortgage payments stay the same for 30 years but rent goes up each year due to inflation. Inflation is a renter's worst nightmare (see No. 2 above) and a homeowner's best friend. Do you really trust the government to get inflation under control? I certainly don't.

4. *Family stability.* The average renter stays in the same place for approximately just three years. Meanwhile, the average homeowner stays in their home for about 13 years. When we first moved to Colorado, my wife and I decided to rent. After our second year our landlord said she was going to sell the home to a friend of hers and we would need to get out when our lease was up. At that time there were literally no other houses for rent in our school district, and my

wife and I were in a panic. Our oldest was in third grade and we were going to be forced to change schools because we would no longer be in the school catchment area. This caused a great deal of emotional angst for us. It was the desire for stability that tipped the scale in our deciding to buy a house later that year.

5. *Tax benefits.* The game is fixed in favor of homeowners. Homeowners can benefit from tax deductions on mortgage interest, property taxes, and sometimes even on home improvement loans.

6. *A secure retirement.* A great advantage of owning a home is that if you went with a 30-year mortgage, you can have it paid off well before retirement age. Sure, you'll have to cover real estate taxes, repairs, and homeowners insurance, but this will be just a fraction of what you would need to pay each month compared to rent. For example, my parents paid off their home 25 years ago, and no longer having mortgage payments was a huge consideration in their early retirement from public school teaching.

7. *Generational wealth.* Homeownership allows you to pass down property and wealth to future generations, providing additional financial security and helping you create a financial legacy.

The bottom line is that most rich people own their own homes, and homeownership can be a wealth-building strategy that can make a massive difference in your net worth. Millionaires know this. That's why 9 out of 10 millionaires invest in real estate. They know this is a tried-and-true way to build more wealth. And real estate is on average about 40% of millionaires' net worth. Not only does buying a house increase your net worth, but it also puts you in charge of your own destiny. You won't be beholden to a landlord who may sell the house and force you to move out. You will be responsible for all home upgrades and repairs, but it's still a worthwhile investment for most people in the long run.

DO WHAT MILLIONAIRES DO

While we have different perspectives on homeownership, we agree that there are potential pros and cons. Can you be single and become a millionaire? Absolutely. Do you have to go to college to become a millionaire? Absolutely not. We know people with high school diplomas who make more than most people, even the ones with doctorate degrees. Can you spend your entire life renting and still become a millionaire? Yes! But these are the outliers. Statistically speaking, you have a much better shot at becoming a millionaire if you do what millionaires do.

Chapter 13 *Start Thinking Rich* Challenge

We just slapped you in the face with some facts, but we acknowledge there are exceptions to each rule, and you may be one of them. However, for this challenge, we encourage you to be open-minded and to be willing to play devil's advocate. Make a list of pros and cons for all three of the millionaire statistics we explored in this chapter.

- What are the pros and cons of you going to college?
- What are the pros and cons of you getting married?
- What are the pros and cons of you buying vs. renting a house?

Whatever you decide to do, we support you and we know that you can become successful. We just want you to take an honest look at how most rich people operate in these areas so you can make an informed decision.

CHAPTER FOURTEEN

RETIREMENT IS FOR DEAD PEOPLE

M alcolm Forbes nailed it when he said, "Retirement kills more people than hard work ever did." Fools retire. Smart people attain financial freedom early in life so they can spend their time on their passions (revenue generating or not). When they get sick of doing a thing they once felt passionate about, they are free to pivot to something else. Talk about a life well lived! Instead of being chained to one job for 40 years doing something they grow to hate and retiring when they're too old and depleted to enjoy it, people are joining the FIRE Movement: Financial Independence, Retire Early. But we're reframing retirement to mean owning your time at any age.

Get ready, because we are about to destroy the concept of retirement, which we are convinced is a TERRIBLE idea. There are major downsides to retirement. But there are many upsides to a conscious plan to achieve financial freedom. Adrian knows this because he went ALL IN on the financial freedom movement and lived in a van for a year while running his seven-figure business. By the end of this chapter, you'll see how it's entirely possible to save and invest up to 95% of every dollar you make and never have to sell your time again.

> Adrian: When we think about what time means, our view of it is often wrong. It's easy to fantasize about what we would do if we could retire, "Oh! I've made enough money. Now finally, I can just sit on a beach somewhere and drink Coronas or Mai Tais all day." As someone who has done that, I promise you, the good feelings won't last more than six days, seven days, max. If it's not the boredom that gets to you, it's going to be the hangovers from all those Mai Tais. When we dream of retirement, many people buy into this illusion that once we have enough money, all of our problems will be solved and we can sit around and do nothing.
>
> Now to be fair, money does solve a lot of problems, but the universal problem it can't solve is that of fulfillment. That's why you hear about lonely or unfulfilled millionaires and billionaires. You can't buy fulfillment. You can use your money to help with your fulfillment, but money won't give you purpose on its own. One of the best ways to feel fulfilled is to give. People think it's the act of slowing down and settling into your golden years that gives you fulfillment, but I disagree. I think fulfillment is the act of moving forward and pursuing the best version of your life without having money dictating your choices.

When people just stop working without finding a new purpose, they die. Sometimes that death is spiritual, but it can be physical too. That's why we're saying retirement is for dead people. There are also many people who work hard, labor-intensive jobs and they delay retirement, because they haven't figured out what to do with themselves when they stop working. It's the saddest thing. Some people's identities are so wrapped up in their work that when they think about no longer having work in their lives it's too overwhelming. So they stay in the place they know, even if they are disgruntled, it's hurting their health, and they are giving away their precious time.

RETIREMENT DEFINED

What exactly does it mean to retire? The *Oxford English Language Dictionary* defines retirement as leaving your job and *ceasing to work*. Another definition of retirement is "to go to bed." If you've been active your whole life, retiring can feel like putting your life to bed. Seclusion is often linked to retirement, since you're leaving the workforce. Work is defined as "an activity involving mental or physical effort done in order *to achieve a purpose or result*." In other words, retirement means to stop engaging in activity meant to achieve a purpose, and to just go to sleep instead.

Distill all of that down, and you could say that retirement is when:

- You're all alone,
- You're disconnected from other people, and
- You no longer engage in mental or physical effort done in order to have a reason to exist.

No thanks! That's why our plan is to retire when we are dead. Until then we will continue to work to achieve a purpose in our lives, and we highly recommend you continue to do the same.

IS RETIREMENT PSYCHOLOGICALLY HARMFUL?

Depending on the study and the year, butter and eggs are either good for you or terrible for you. One year, eggs are an essential part of breakfast to fuel you for the day. The next, eggs are clogging up your arteries with cholesterol and you should avoid them. The same is true for studies about retirement.

But here are some studies highlighting the downside of retirement, with some good tips on how to make the most of a post-9-to-5 life.

Leaving a job, especially if you've given your life to that job, can feel like a death. There may be grief involved in letting go of something you invested so much of your time, energy, and effort into. Many retirees struggle with feeling like a useful member of society and some finally have time to think about the quality of their lives. If all they've ever done is work, a life without that job can feel pretty empty. Maybe that's why one in three retirees report feelings of depression. Too many retirees experience the retirement blues. That's why it's important to create a life well lived way before you reach retirement age.

RETIRED HUSBAND SYNDROME (RHS)

Yup, you read that right. Retirement can be so bad that psychologists have made up an entire syndrome to describe it. Retired Husband Syndrome (RHS) is a stress-induced condition identified in the wives of retired Japanese men. They found the following symptoms occurred in women when their husbands retired:

1. Feeling stressed;
2. Feeling depressed; and
3. Not sleeping well.

These wives of recent retirees also experienced headaches, depression, agitation, and heart palpitations. This stress was brought on by spending more time together, increasing the chance for irritability, bringing unresolved issues to the forefront after years of being too distracted by work to address them. Not only did the husband's retirement have a negative impact on the wife's mental health, but it got worse every year of retirement. It's no wonder RHS is one of the leading causes of divorce among those of retirement age in Japan.

> Dr. Brad: I think my mom anticipated that her continuing to work when my stepdad retired would be rough for her. My stepdad had retired from the school system and she said there was no way she was going to keep working while he was retired. I think she lasted one year with him in retirement before she gave in and retired from the school system herself, which I think was beneficial for both of them. But retirement didn't mean they stopped working. My mom had a side hustle she put more time into, and my stepfather transitioned to a part-time counseling business, which my mother managed. Another thing to consider if you stop working entirely is to make sure you have a peer group that is also not working. If you're ready to golf and your friends are all at work, it may have a negative effect on your mental well-being.

One big reason for RHS is the unequal division of labor in the home. Husbands were used to being at work all day while the wives did most of the house cleaning, managing, and organizing. When the men suddenly found themselves at home all day, the wives were frustrated at them leaving messes everywhere and pretending not to see the housework piling up. For this reason, thousands of groups have formed in Japan to train retired men to be more independent and to communicate better with their wives. One group, called "Men in the Kitchen," teaches retired men how to clean and cook, and even shop for themselves. Women also felt tasked with planning hobbies for their husbands so they wouldn't lie around the house depressed all day. So if you don't want to get divorced (and we've covered how expensive divorce is – not a smart financial move), be sure to cook and clean, do fun things with your spouse, and find a post-job, fulfilling passion to pursue. If those who were once active in their jobs suddenly stop being active, it can impact their physical and mental health.

GENDER HEALTH AND RETIREMENT

Health and well-being declines for men when they lose their purpose and retire. A study in Australia found that when men retired, they experienced a 25% increase in physical dysfunction, which translates to increased health-related issues. They also had an increase in psychological distress. For women, retirement brought a 17% increase in physical dysfunction but no increase in psychological stress. Perhaps the reason for this is that they were still doing the purposeful work of caring for their home and loved ones, so they stayed active and engaged in purposeful activity for longer than their husbands. For example, retired women are more likely to be engaged in multiple social, community, religious, leisure, and caregiving activities, and are therefore less likely to feel that retirement from paid work means retiring from active life.

There are other incentives to staying active as late in life as possible. In terms of cognitive functioning, those working jobs with higher mental demands experience a slower rate of cognitive decline in their retirement years. There's also the loneliness aspect in retirement. If you experience loneliness at work and in retirement, you're more likely to be depressed after you retire. Retired men who had high-ranking jobs, or those who left the workforce early, often struggle with lower self-worth. Some people decide to volunteer after they retire, which can be good for you. But too much volunteering can also cause stress. It can only do so much for your mental and physical well-being. So many people think, "I can't wait to retire so I can finally relax." But there are many factors that decrease life satisfaction in retirement, which is why we think it's a terrible idea.

Usually, there is a honeymoon period when people first retire. For about three to six months, people feel like they're on an extended vacation. At first they tackle those tasks they may have avoided for years, such as cleaning out the garage or fixing the deck. They play lots of golf or go fishing. They may even do some travel they always wanted to do. But soon enough, their struggle for purpose sets in and they don't know what to do with themselves. The good news is, when you're not tied to a full-time job, you do have more time for leisure activities, but it turns out that too much unstructured free time is not good for your mental health.

Retirees report having a higher life satisfaction and sense of purpose when they are engaged in social leisure activities. Take pickleball, for example. Not only does a sport like pickleball keep people in good physical shape, they also get to make friends on the court, and keep their minds fresh. Many also set the goal of getting better at pickleball: taking lessons, entering tournaments, etc., adding a new sense of purpose. So if you want to retire from work someday, just know that you are going to need to find some additional "work" to keep yourself healthy and happy, even if that work is non–revenue generating.

THE FIRE MOVEMENT

We are supporters of becoming financially free as early as you can in life, so you can find fulfilling activities while you continue to grow your wealth. Some call this strategy the "FIRE Movement." *FIRE* is an acronym that stands for Financial Independence, Retire Early. "Retire" in this sense isn't about putting your life to bed. Instead, it's about securing a strong financial future when you're young enough to get out there and enjoy your life – while you're still making money. The financial mindset of the FIRE Movement is extreme. While your financial advisor might give you applause and positive remarks for saving 15% of every dollar you make, people in the FIRE movement would BOO you off stage for such a low percentage. People in the FIRE movement are investing 40% to 70% or more of their income every year so they can drastically shortcut their path to retirement.

That's what Adrian did when he and his wife got rid of all of their stuff and moved into a van. Adrian propelled himself forward financially by downsizing, cutting frivolous expenses, putting in the work, and living as minimally as possible. He took these drastic steps as an experiment to see what's possible, and it turned out to be one of the most adventurous and memorable years of his life.

Adrian: When the pandemic happened I actually didn't own a home. I had just moved back from Dublin, Ireland, and was Asia bound. Back at my parents' place for the first few months of the pandemic, my wife saw people who were living full time in tiny home vans. It seemed like a great way to keep traveling during the pandemic, so we were sold! Our all-in cost to buy a used van and convert it to a full tiny home with a bed, toilet, shower, and kitchen was $75,000. We paid cash and hit the road. We met incredible people on the road, some people traveling solo, traveling with pets, and families of five traveling in RVs and converted buses.

We discovered this whole world of people who lived beautiful lives without the need to own an expensive home. Our total cost of living in a van would sometimes be as low as $600 a month. We spent about one to two days per week finding Wi-Fi to work online on our various online businesses. Online shopping surged from the pandemic and our incomes soared. We made $1.7 million that year. Our minimalistic lifestyle, combined with our large income, allowed us to save and invest over $1 million into the stock market. Something that normally takes people a lifetime to accomplish, we did in a year from following the FIRE movement principles.

As we mentioned, Dr. Brad also made some drastic sacrifices to accelerate his path to financial freedom. Even when he was first making six figures a year, he didn't buy new clothes or furniture and alternated between those two beat-up cars. He paid off six figures of student loans in three years while fully funding his retirement accounts and saving for a house. He consistently prioritized paying himself first, and in his 40s, he reached financial freedom, where he no longer needed to work to fund his lifestyle. He gave up his job in the public school system in Hawaii and now lives in Boulder, Colorado. He continues to follow his passion of helping others improve their financial lives as a professor, financial advisor, author, and social media influencer. There are always creative ways to accelerate yourself on the path to financial freedom if you want it badly enough.

> Dr. Brad: At this point in my life, I could sell my stake in my companies and never have to work again. But I have no interest in doing so. Financial freedom gave me what I wanted most years ago, financial security and the freedom to choose where and how I want to spend my time. With regard to my "work," however, I plan on never retiring. Don't get me wrong, I love owning my time, so that I can play tennis, play pickleball, coach my boys' baseball teams, spend the summers in Hawaii with my in-laws, and vacation with my family. But I know that I will ALWAYS crave a higher purpose and will want to put in the work to make a positive impact in the lives of others. While my day-to-day activities are likely to continue to evolve and change, I plan to never retire.
>
> Instead of retiring, I think of financial freedom as being able to own more and more of my time and expanding my opportunities to fulfill my purpose in life. Not only are you likely to see further financial benefits by continuing to work, but you'll also have better physical and mental health, a better marriage, and more time to connect with people you really want to spend your time with.

Just like those studies about eggs, quitting your 9-to-5 job can be good for you or bad for you, depending on a number of factors. Your socioeconomic position, reason for retirement, life stage, physical and mental health, quality of relationships, and purposeful pursuits are all significant factors to consider well before you quit your day job. We hope that you achieve financial freedom. But take our advice, do not make "stopping work" (aka ceasing to engage in purposeful activities) your ultimate goal, because retirement is for dead people, and you have so much more to do before you die.

Chapter 14 *Start Thinking Rich* Challenge

Hopefully we have convinced you that retiring from life is not a great goal. What you want is financial security, owning your time, and the freedom to choose how you want to work. So take a moment to think about what kind of life you want to live when you are able to walk away from your 9-to-5 job. This is your time to develop an exciting plan for financial freedom and an active, enjoyable future. Picture a life in which you no longer need to work for money, and reflect on the following questions:

- How will you spend your time?
- What activities will you pursue and for what purpose? Think beyond things like travel or pursuing new hobbies. Picture your average day.
- After a few months of excitement about not having to go to your workplace, what will make you want to spring out of bed each morning with passion?
- What higher calling would you pursue if you had the time and resources to do anything you wanted?

Write out your plans in as much detail as possible.

CHAPTER FIFTEEN

ONLY POOR PEOPLE ARE AFRAID TO ASK FOR HELP

People with poor mindsets suffer from do-it-yourself-itis. In the game of life, or in this case, the game of money, it's arrogant to think you can do it all by yourself with no help. Successful people figured out long ago that it's smart to rely on experts to help them manage their money. No one becomes a millionaire without some help along the way. The secret wealthy people know is that experts and professionals help them avoid mistakes, protect their assets, and make smart, lucrative choices. There is a huge mistrust of experts among lower income people. This could be for a variety of reasons, including believing the system has failed them, having been exploited in the past, or not wanting to feel inferior in their knowledge about their finances. Our financial health is just as important as our physical health. When we need help with our health, we see a doctor. Likewise, when we need help with our finances, we should seek the help of mentors, advisors, and professionals who know what they're doing.

Most rich people have a whole team working for them, from business experts to accountants, lawyers, and advisors. They make fewer costly mistakes because they have this team in place to help them protect and grow their money. Having professionals help with a business plan, taxes, investments, and expenditures can help us achieve success in a fraction of the time it would take if we tried to do it all ourselves. When it comes to building wealth, every second counts. Dr. Brad conducted a study and found that ultra-high-net-worth individuals are much more likely to seek the advice and counsel of financial advisors, attorneys, CPAs, business coaches, and other professionals as opposed to middle- and lower-income individuals. One reason for this is that they are secure and humble enough to admit they don't know everything, and they will benefit from an expert who knows what they're doing. They are also accustomed to the idea that they don't have the time or energy to become an expert at everything. Having the resources to hire people can also be a barrier, which is obviously much less of an issue for those who have the money to spend on hired help.

But a common misconception among the middle- and lower-income groups is that expert advice is too costly. That's understandable. But the irony is, *not* having those professionals at your disposal will likely cost you even more than if you'd just consulted with an expert in the first place. Trying to do it yourself and refusing to ask for help is a guaranteed way to waste valuable time, lose large sums of money, and fill yourself with soul-crushing regret.

THE PROPER WAY TO ASK FOR HELP

You don't have to have a full-time staff of experts to be at your beck and call. You can hire experts for hourly consultation. For instance, if you're thinking of starting a business, find a CPA and ask to pay for an hour of their time. Then ask them all the questions you have about your specific business.

Some sample questions an aspiring entrepreneur might ask a CPA could include:

- What are the biggest mistakes you see people in this field make when they start their business?
- How would you recommend I start doing my bookkeeping?
- What sort of business structure would you recommend?
- What am I missing from my business plan?
- Are there any tax strategies I can implement once I am profitable?
- Which books, classes, or resources do you recommend?
- What is one thing you wish all beginning entrepreneurs knew?

Sure, buying an hour of a CPA's or attorney's time may cost you a few hundred bucks, but it could potentially save you tens of thousands down the road. There are many experts who would be willing to meet with someone for an hour, as long as you respect and pay for their time. They may even offer to consult with you for free, with the hope that you might someday hire them to do your taxes, set up a corporation, develop your estate plan, or manage your millions.

When asking for help from a potential mentor or someone you admire, it all starts with taking the initiative and putting in the work first. If they've written books, read them ALL before you approach them. Take their courses, listen to their podcast interviews, and find out as much as you can about them first. If you can show that you are ready to learn and you've already taken initiative and done the work, they are much more likely to help you.

Adrian: The first time I asked for help was in college. I had a marketing professor named Craig Marty, whom I looked up to and respected. One day, I stopped in after class and asked him when I should start investing, among other simple questions about money. My questions had nothing to do with marketing. I wanted to understand money and shared with him that I wanted to make six figures someday.

Instead of lecturing me or giving out random advice, he asked me some questions such as "Do you have a Roth IRA set up and know how much you are saving of every dollar you make?" I had never heard of a Roth IRA and the truth is I had no idea what to ask him, I just knew that there was a lot I had to learn about money and my first question helped in opening a conversation that would organically build into a lifelong relationship. I think one obstacle for people in asking for help is that they're not sure what to ask. Professor Marty asked me about my budget. I didn't have one. I was embarrassed that I didn't know some of the terms he was using, but I didn't let that stop me from finding out more. He explained that a proper budget was a way of figuring out how much money you make, by deducting your living expenses, and seeing how much you have left over. If you don't have anything left over, you're in the red and need to consider cutting expenses and/or increasing your earnings.

He also asked me about credit card debt, loans, and expenses. He took a personal interest in me because he could see my eagerness to learn and my willingness to put in the effort. He became my first mentor. Every time I go back to Dubuque, Iowa, I stop in and see him. I have so much appreciation for him and his willingness to help me. If it weren't for him and that initial after-class conversation, I know I wouldn't be where I am today and

I certainly would not be as financially sound. He pointed me in the right direction and helped me develop good financial habits that were life changing. Thank goodness I didn't let the shame and embarrassment of not knowing stop me from asking for help. As it turns out, there was nothing for me to be embarrassed about. I was a 19-year-old college kid and he was my professor. There are many people who don't understand what a budget is. Some don't even have bank accounts. So don't let your embarrassment keep you from asking for help. You're not alone. Along your journey to success, you'll discover that many wealthy people are generous and love helping others succeed.

Dr. Brad: When I was growing up, my family suffered from "do-it-yourself-itis" in a pretty extreme way. Even before I was born, my dad grew up in poverty on a farm. They didn't even have indoor plumbing and had to heat water on the stove to have a warm bath. Their philosophy was simple: "If something breaks, fix it yourself." Everything was kept in the family and the community. Neighbors helped each other fix their vehicles, my aunt who had a semester or two of college accounting classes did everyone's taxes in the family, and they'd barter and borrow before they went outside the tight community circle. They didn't look beyond that circle for help because there was a huge lack of trust when it came to outsiders. They'd rather go without than ask someone they didn't know for help or advice. They had worked hard all their lives and had been screwed over more than once, so every penny was precious to them. They weren't about to dig the coffee can out of the ground and hand over their life savings to just anybody. Not only did they have trouble trusting outsiders, which is common in close-knit Appalachian culture, but they also had money scripts playing in their minds about wealthy professionals and rich people in general being greedy and corrupt.

At my financial planning firm, we manage a lot of money for ultra-high-net-worth individuals. But the most challenging clients I have are the ones who have thousands of dollars to invest. It's much harder for them to trust us and take our expert advice than it is for clients who have us manage $10 million for them. They come back with a ton of questions and concerns and watch their accounts daily (if not hourly). It's understandable. They are new to the world of investing and working with financial experts, so it's much more difficult for them to trust ANYONE with their precious, hard-earned money. Those with $10 million are more trusting because they've had more experience working with experts. Many of them have a generational history of trusting financial advisors, who have helped them and their families grow and protect their fortunes. They've seen their parents and grand-parents hire experts to help them make the wisest investments and grow their portfolios.

But a major barrier to asking for help in middle- and lower-income individuals is not trusting that their money is in good hands with professionals. It took me years to overcome my own do-it-yourself-itis handed down to me from my family. It won't feel comfortable at first, but it's doable and if you want to join the ranks of the wealthy, it's required, unless you have the time to become a top expert in your business, get a law degree, become a CPA and financial advisor, etc. That's what the experts are there for, to help you succeed in *your* field, by letting them shine in theirs.

YOUR MENTAL BLOCKS TO GETTING HELP

When you can identify your mental blocks that prevent you from asking for help, it's easier to overcome them. It's not the same for everyone, but there are a few common ones:

- Shame or embarrassment that they are going to judge you
- An unwillingness to trust outsiders
- Not knowing WHOM to ask

- Not knowing WHAT to ask
- A fragile ego, i.e. "I know everything and don't need any help"
- A lack of initiative

If you suffer from any of these mental blocks, you're not alone. You can snap out of it, if you get honest with yourself and keep an open mind. For shame or embarrassment, the best course of action is to just act like a rich and successful person. They have NO shame in asking for help, so why should you? Keep that fact in mind as you feel a little bit of discomfort and push past it. Let your curiosity and desire to think like the rich surpass your embarrassment. If you stretch yourself, you may find a mentor or team of mentors who can change your life. The same goes for trust issues. It will be uncomfortable at first, but you can ease that discomfort by vetting professionals before you meet with them.

When looking for an expert, it's smart to properly scrutinize them so you don't fall prey to things like Ponzi schemes. Use common sense. If something sounds too good to be true, it IS too good to be true. Ask people who are a step or two closer to where you want to be for recommendations on people THEY trust. Most will be more than happy to pass along a recommendation. If your do-it-yourself-itis prevents you from taking and applying advice from experts, you're going to miss many opportunities to grow and become successful. Instead, try humbling yourself and admit that you don't know everything – and that's okay!

WHAT TO AVOID WHEN ASKING FOR HELP

When you've overcome your mental blocks to ask for help, you've won half the battle. Those with a rich mindset know there is also a proper etiquette to follow when asking for help – especially if you are looking for a mentor or advisor you aren't paying for their time. If you're looking for some free advice from a mentor, it's important to avoid the following cringeworthy behaviors:

- **Cold asks.** It's a huge turn-off when strangers hit up successful people asking for free advice without putting in the work. For example, we get hundreds of messages from strangers asking for free advice or "just 15 minutes" of our time, yet these people have never taken one of our courses or read any of our books.

- **"Can I pick your brain?"** Approaching someone at a conference after you've heard them speak and asking for more of their time so you can "pick their brain" is the fastest way to make them look for the exit. Before you approach someone, make sure you have read their books, taken their courses, and are interested in developing a relationship with them. Respect that these individuals are in high demand, have limited time, and don't know you. Put in the time to develop a clear, concise question before you approach them if you have the opportunity to speak with them.

- **Asking for free stuff.** NEVER ask a potential mentor for money. Believe it or not, we get these requests all the time and it is a huge turnoff. If you are putting together a conference or some other event, NEVER ask a notable expert to speak for free. If you approach an expert asking them for a free course or free consultation, you are asking them to give their valuable time and labor away to a perfect stranger. Why would they do that? Their time and labor are valuable, so don't ask them to give it away for free, especially when they've never met you before. By asking them to give you their time, labor, and expertise for free, you are essentially saying their work isn't worth paying for. How insulting!

You'll get much further if you prove to these experts that they're not wasting their time telling you things you'd already know if you'd taken the time to read their work, listened to their interviews, and have taken their courses. Not only is it disrespectful, but it's also annoying. Mentors want to help people who respect them enough to not waste their time. They want to know that their time and efforts will make a difference. But it's hard to believe in someone when they don't believe in themselves enough to put in the work.

WHEN HIRING A TAX EXPERT

All wealthy people hire tax experts. And it's not because they want to cheat on their taxes. Their assets are wrapped up in their net worth and we don't pay taxes on net worth. The average rich person won't purposely cheat on their taxes because they have too much to lose. In fact, people with less money have much more incentive to cheat on their taxes. Nobody wants to pay higher taxes; if anything, they just want other people to pay more in taxes. After all, the IRS has a blank on your tax return where you can donate more money to the government. Have you EVER met anyone who donated to the IRS?

The fact is, in the United States, the higher your income, the higher your tax bracket. In other words, the more taxable income you have the higher your tax rate is. As your net worth grows, chances are your financial life will become more complex. Rich people rely on experts to help them navigate their taxes, because they aren't going to waste their time trying to become a tax expert themselves, in addition to whatever else they are doing professionally. It's a common misconception that millionaires and billionaires don't pay taxes. But the truth is, they're at such a high level in the game, they're thinking of any way they can to minimize their tax responsibility. The truth is, rich people pay a lot in taxes and on your way to become rich yourself, you will find yourself paying more and more taxes, especially if you don't hire an accountant.

When Adrian increased his income by over a million dollars in 2021, he reached out to Dr. Brad, who he knew worked with a bunch of ultra-wealthy people, to see if there were any legal strategies that the ultra-wealthy use to avoid paying so much in taxes. Dr. Brad provided some suggestions, but ultimately told Adrian "the TRUTH is, rich people pay a lot in taxes."

While there is no way to avoid paying more in taxes as you become wealthier, there are ways to reduce your overall tax burden. One way to pay less taxes is to contribute to an employer-sponsored retirement plan such as a 401(k) or an individual retirement account such as a Traditional IRA. You don't pay taxes on that money until you take it out, reducing your tax burden for that year. Or you could contribute to a ROTH IRA, where you pay taxes on what you contribute this year but it grows tax free thereafter. It would be dumb for us *not* to take advantage of these tax saving and wealth building opportunities. In fact, according to Fidelity, at the end of 2023, they had 422,000 401(k) accounts at over seven figures and 392,000 IRAs with over a million dollars in them. When you have income, there's no way to avoid paying taxes. So hire an expert who can help you take advantage of tax saving strategies. That's the best way to keep as much of your money as you can.

Tax planning is even more important in high tax states. For example, in California, if you make seven figures, your state taxes are 12.3%. That means, if you make a million dollars, it costs an extra $123,000 just to live in that state. An advisor may encourage you to live in a no-income-tax state and spend that $123,000 on a house in Texas, instead. If you have a good accountant, they'll help you find the best ways to win the tax game.

If we didn't rely on the expertise of our trusted accountants and advisors, we would be forking over a lot more money to Uncle Sam. We're humble enough to admit we need tax experts who know more than we do about tax codes, we have vetted our financial team of experts, so we trust them and feel confident in their abilities, and we got over our embarrassment about asking questions. Because of our tax, legal, and financial team of experts, we save thousands of dollars each year. Wouldn't you like to save more money too?

Chapter 15 *Start Thinking Rich* Challenge

What kinds of experts do you have on your team? Have you ever consulted with a Certified Professional Accountant (CPA)? Have you ever consulted with a Certified Financial Planner (CFP®)? How about a business, real estate, or estate planning attorney? How about a business consultant or coach in your profession?

If not, what are your mental barriers to asking for help? Write them down. Now, commit to acting like a rich person and consulting with one or more of these experts within the next month. Devise a plan of action. Maybe you can talk to someone who has experience hiring professionals and they can help you vet people. Maybe it's a matter of humbling yourself and admitting that you don't know everything. Maybe it's about overcoming embarrassment.

Once you've identified your barriers and how you plan to overcome them, make a list of experts that could help you. Hire the ones you can. If you're looking for a mentor, find someone a step or two ahead of you and learn everything you can from that person. This includes reading their materials, taking their courses, and doing your homework BEFORE reaching out to them for advice. We live in an incredible time where you have the power to directly contact pretty much anyone. Find three people you look up to and reach out to them on social media with your question and see if they respond.

CHAPTER SIXTEEN

YOUR POLITICAL PARTY DOESN'T GIVE A SHIT ABOUT YOU

Let's face it, we are living in a political climate that pits us against each other. But like most things in life, how we respond to politics is all about our locus of control (we discussed this concept in Chapter 2: "Only Poor People Think the System Is Rigged"). Whenever there is a problem with the economy, those with an external locus of control will blame politicians, while those with an internal locus of control will find ways to shift and adapt. You have a choice: put your faith in politicians to save you, or save yourself.

If you're blaming the government for your problems, you've given up your personal power to create the life you want. Student loans are a perfect example of this. The hold on student loan payments provided a great deal of relief during the pandemic. The problem is, many people used that "extra" money to inflate their lifestyles. When student loan payments were reinstated, it got ugly. People who didn't save or invest that money were screwed. The truth is, we never know what's around the corner. Therefore, we need to set ourselves up to weather any storm. No government or institution will take care of you in all the ways you need. They don't even know you. Many people spend countless hours arguing about politics on social media instead of focusing on taking action to better their situations so they don't fall prey to the whims of our government. The message is, if we want to feel empowered, we have to focus on ourselves, hold ourselves accountable, and invest in ourselves.

> Dr. Brad: I grew up poor. What I've noticed is that every time there is an election, the politicians love to talk about how the system is rigged against poor people. They promise that if they get elected, they're going to make your life better. That's how they get elected. But then they get into office and they don't do shit for poor people. They have been making these promises my entire life and the percentage of people in poverty in the United States has not changed at all, no matter who has been in office. It was 12% in the 1970s and it's 11% today. If you are poor, you can't trust your politicians to save you. They don't care about you. They only care about themselves. You can't count on them to save you. You're going to need to save yourself.
>
> Adrian: I remember when my dad would share stories about when he first came to the United States from Mexico as a teenager. He didn't speak English, and back then, times were tough. Money was scarce, yet no one in the family ever took welfare. My dad didn't want to take advantage of the system. Instead, he worked hard, taking whatever manual labor jobs he could get, to make

ends meet. This may be controversial, but my dad had an extreme mindset. The aid is there to help people who need it, but he was adamantly opposed to asking for that aid because he didn't want to get stuck relying on it. You never know when a new politician will change the system and that safety net will disappear. For him, being in the United States was his advantage. To this day, he gets frustrated by able-bodied people who could work but would rather take money from the system because he knows they are just hurting themselves. I will never have to face the hardships my dad and my mom endured as they helped establish a much higher starting point for me to begin with. After having lived several years abroad, I have gained the same perspective – that being born in the United States provides a global advantage that most places don't get. I say that recognizing that the United States is not a perfect country and in many regards not even in the top 10. Regardless, the American advantage is inherited by anyone who is born or moves here. That's why the United States has more than 44 million immigrants, far more than any other country. The United States may not be perfect but it provides something unique that not many other countries do: the opportunity to get equity and build wealth. People can come to the United States, start a business, and buy property. This is the American Dream and it is still alive today.

FALLING INTO THE LEARNED HELPLESSNESS TRAP

Many of us start the day by watching or reading the news. We think it is important to be informed about what's happening in our communities, our nation, and the world. But instead of being informed, we are being manipulated by a sensationalized media that profits off of our fear, anger, distress, and despair. Our brains are hard-wired to look for danger. Media companies and politicians know this, so every day they set about to find a big bad wolf they can use to get your attention. When we're scared, the frontal lobe of our brain goes offline. This is the part of the brain responsible for rational thought and decision-making. When we ingest a steady diet of fear, anger, sadness, loneliness, and stress, we become easy to control. We do whatever we're told to keep the big bad wolf away, whether that's voting against our own best interest or subscribing to oppressive systems that limit our freedoms or harm our neighbors.

Now, with the advent of smartphones and social media, there is a constant battle for our attention. Politicians, marketers, and influencers have to try harder than ever to get your eyes on their content and messages. Many of their attention-grabbing tactics play on your cognitive biases. These cognitive biases can be devastating if you don't have the courage to take a hard look at them. They are toxic and infectious, and have kept entire families poor for generations. If you want any hope at all of changing your life, you need to snap out of the hold they have on you. Here are a few of the most common biases:

- *Confirmation bias*: When you hold a certain belief, you will subconsciously look for information that confirms that belief in your environment. Simultaneously, you will discount information that challenges the belief. For instance, if you believe you are powerless to change your financial circumstances and you watch the news, you might focus on the stories that confirm your negative beliefs about money. You'll tune your attention to the stories about the housing crisis, inflation, and the stall on wage growth. You'll wallow in the unfairness of it all. This will make you feel even more powerless and scared, so you're likely to stay at a job that doesn't pay well, because even a shitty job is better than no job at all. Instead of using your time to learn marketable skills to improve your situation, you might medicate yourself with after-work beers and complain with your coworkers about your boss, because you truly believe that you are powerless to change your circumstances. If you saw a piece of social media content that promoted personal empowerment, you'd write it off as being out of touch. Instead, you'd surround yourself with people who have resigned themselves to their "fate," and you would avoid motivated self-starters. Sadly, your confirmation bias will make you create the circumstances you are so afraid of experiencing.

- *Dunning-Kruger Effect*: This bias occurs when people overestimate their abilities or knowledge. It is painful to watch this bias in action on social media platforms. Whatever the latest tragedy, nonexpert influencers spew out their unlearned analyses as if they became overnight experts in the topic, be it the latest infectious disease, territorial conflict, environmental tragedy, or infrastructure collapse. While it is painful to see in others, it can be a success killer when it manifests within us. Ironically, this bias is more likely to occur in people who know the least about a particular subject. For example, someone who only watches one type of biased news angle may think they know everything there is to know about an issue based on the narrow views and talking points from the anchors and TV personalities. But in reality, they are playing into the hands of the people who control that media company and their narrative.

- *Self-Serving Bias*: When people do a good job at work and get a raise and promotion, this cognitive bias might make them believe it's all about their hard work, talents, and abilities. This could be a manifestation of an internal locus of control, which can be healthy if it encourages more hard work and skill development. However, the flipside of this bias is, if people get demoted or fired, many will fall prey to an external locus of control. To protect their fragile egos, they'll blame everyone and everything but themselves for the negative outcome. This is a horrific approach to coping with adversity. It is so much more helpful to shift to an internal locus of control and lovingly blame yourself, so you can identify your blind spots and overcome your weaknesses.

- *The Sunk Cost Fallacy*: Most of us hate losing. But with the sunk cost fallacy people try so hard to avoid losing that they will double down on their bad decisions to avoid the pain of admitting they were wrong and cutting their losses. Many people will drag out bad situations for longer than they should – a bad relationship, an awful job, a failing business – because they don't have the courage to make a change. Dr. Brad's research found that rich people are much more likely to just admit they are wrong and move on. For instance, let's say you make your political party your entire identity and vote with blind loyalty to the leaders in that party. And even if they let you down, you continue to vote for them because you don't want to admit you were wrong or got tricked; you might be at the mercy of this bias. It can be hard to admit you got swindled, but the sooner you admit it and cut your losses, the better off you will be.

- *Herd Mentality Bias*: Just like horses or cattle follow each other in herds, even if that's right off a cliff, people tend to do the same within their families, peer groups, and communities. We see this all the time in investing. So many people have lost money in hyped-up crypto-rug-pull schemes because they heard about a project from a shady influencer, a discord group, or from their friends. Running with the herd works well if you are a wild horse running away from a cougar, but it's not a great approach to investing.

There are ways to get around the things that trigger these biases. Propaganda only works if you're paying attention to the messages they want you to ingest and believe. But if you are so focused on your growth and progress that you miss the propaganda that is designed to trigger you into feeling helpless and hopeless, you've won a major part of the battle.

Adrian: I haven't watched the news since I was 21 years old thanks to a tip from a book called *The 4-Hour Work Week* by Tim Ferriss. This book gave me the awareness as to how bad news media is for your brain. If I had to choose between smoking cigarettes every day for the rest of my life or consuming an hour of news every day, I would happily be a chain smoker. Beyond politics, I believe that none of us have the mental and emotional capacity to handle all the stress of the world's most chaotic events every day. We aren't robot computers that can process all this negative information and continue functioning on our day, totally unaffected. The news causes stress and is designed to trigger the worst kind of emotions within us. I can't think of a more terrible way to start the day than watching the news. Any time you decide to watch the news you are telling your mental health "I want to jump into uncontrollable chaos."

The good news is, overcoming these biases is possible. The first step is identifying them and admitting to yourself that you are vulnerable. The key is to become aware of the biases you have, and put some space between the impulse to act and the action itself. If you bring awareness to the fact that you get angry when you watch the news, it might be time to ask yourself if your confirmation bias is activated. Perhaps you are looking for news that confirms your belief that things are terrible out there. Instead of watching horrible news stories first thing in the morning, think of positive ways to start your day, like listening to an uplifting podcast or affirmations. The key to combat confirmation bias is open-mindedness, so look for information that challenges your belief and seek to understand it. If you find yourself stuck in a bad situation and hear yourself say, "but I've invested so much in this," you might be at the mercy of your sunk cost fallacy. Observing your repeating thought patterns is a great way to find these biases. If you become the master of your mind, you are less likely to fall prey to those who benefit from your biases. You'll find yourself more empowered, complaining less, and working to better your own circumstances, instead of waiting for someone else to do it for you.

Dr. Brad: I grew up eating government cheese and peanut butter, but my mom was too proud to take any formal assistance from the government. So, we got our government cheese and peanut butter from my grandma. My mom grew up in Detroit, and she'll tell you that her neighborhood wasn't that bad, but I remember the house. She lived on the other side of a fence separating her house from government housing, which got broken into multiple times. She went to a high school where there were a bunch of rich kids and a bunch of poor kids mixed together. Being from the poor kids side, my mom was ashamed about not having money. She would keep a record of what days she wore each outfit, so it wouldn't look like she only had five or six outfits when that's all she had. One time, I was giving a speech and my mom was in the front row. At one point in the speech, I mentioned that I grew up "poor." I could tell by my mom's frown in reaction that she wasn't happy with that classification. So I stopped the speech, introduced the audience to my mom, and addressed her: "So mom, when I said I grew up poor, it looked like you disagreed? What would YOU say our socioeconomic class was when I was growing up?" She said, "We were middle class. . .except lower." The audience erupted in laughter, as did my mom and me. Even when we were at our poorest, my mom never saw us as poor or wanted to show it. She just did what needed to be done to support my sister and me.

FORMS OF PERSUASION POLITICIANS (AND OTHERS) USE TO MANIPULATE YOU

Those running for office have an entire staff of people dedicated to convincing you to vote for them. Experts who have made it their life's work to study your weaknesses and manipulate you to benefit their political candidate. If you don't know about the techniques they use, you're more likely to fall for them. While this list applies to politicians, it also applies to anyone who is purposely trying to manipulate you for their own gain (e.g. people trying to scam you by selling you a get-rich-quick course). Here are some forms of persuasion commonly used to manipulate:

- *Anecdotal Evidence*: Every good candidate has at least one hard-working, blue-collar "Joe the Plumber" type they bring onto the stage on the campaign trail so they can tug at your heartstrings with their story. Every get-rich-quick scam has the same – someone just like you (or often dumber and more lazy than you are) who found this amazing secret and with very little effort used it to become rich! Joe is supposed to represent you. When used by politicians, Joe will talk about sitting around the kitchen table trying to figure out how he's going to pay his bills and protect his kids. Then the candidate pitches themself as the solution to Joe's problems. But these tactics can be misleading. In fact, some of these interesting stories are completely made up, and more than one politician has been busted. Research vetted by qualified experts will trump cute little stories every time. But short, interesting stories tug at our heartstrings or fill us with hope or fear, and that's why they are so powerful. Whether it is our personal experience or a story pitched to us by a politician or some other influencer, anecdotal evidence is very dangerous because emotions take over and then the facts don't matter.
- *Ad hominem attacks*: all politicians are guilty of this one. They attack their opponent's character to make you dislike them. Oftentimes, candidates don't even say what they plan to do once they're in office. Just tearing down their opponent is enough to get them elected. Get-rich-quick scammers will use these attacks to tear down "traditional" methods for becoming rich (which are the ones that

actually work). They will try to convince you that these old methods no longer work or that only idiots would waste their time working hard, saving, and investing.

- *All-or-Nothing Thinking*: If someone is presenting you only two options that are at opposite ends of a spectrum, they're trying to trick you with all-or-nothing thinking. The truth that they don't want you to know is that most solutions fall on a spectrum. If they succeed in shutting down your imagination and your ability to see better solutions than the ones they are presenting, it's easier to convince you that they'll save you from one extreme by going to the opposite extreme.

- *The Slippery Slope Fallacy*: This is when manipulators try to convince you that if you don't vote for them or take a specific course of action NOW, it will lead to disaster. In politics, it can go something like this: "If the other candidate gets elected, it will be the end of life as we know it!" This argument requires huge leaps in logic and is also designed to scare you into taking a course of action to try to avoid an exaggerated personal or global apocalypse.

- *Strawman Fallacy*: When a manipulator exaggerates and warps their opponent's stance, essentially creating a strawman that's easier to tear down, they're using one of the oldest tricks in the book.

The best way to avoid falling prey to these fallacies is to turn off the news, read books that help you exercise your critical thinking muscles, surround yourself with open-minded people, and understand that nobody's coming to save you. You have to save yourself.

Even those who've had every possible societal obstacle stacked against them have found ways to save themselves and become rich and successful. Look at Oprah, Do Won Chang (Founder of Forever 21, an immigrant who started as a janitor), Dolly Parton, Adrian's parents, and countless other millionaires and multi-millionaires you will never hear about. They didn't let the fact that they started out poor stop them from becoming wealthy. So what's your excuse?

Politicians know that the majority of voters are middle to lower class and they know what works in getting their vote. So they perpetuate learned helplessness and pitch themselves as the only ones who can save the voters. This makes voters believe they need this powerful politician to come in and rescue them. But what they don't tell you is, they benefit from your desperation and learned helplessness, and history has shown that they are full of shit. Why would they want to change the circumstances that make you play right into their hands? So they breadcrumb you and give you just enough to get you to vote for them again – but not enough to empower you.

We could care less about which political party you choose, if you choose any at all. In full disclosure, we are both political independents. We have no delusions that politicians are going to do the right thing for the right reason. We have no delusions that politicians are even all that smart. We don't trust them or their political parties, and in each election we do what MOST Americans do – we just vote for what we see as the least worst candidate. But what bothers us is that so many people believe them, and then sit back and expect these liars to actually do something to save them, thus keeping them stuck in a poor mindset and cycle of poverty for generations. That's why you must take 100% responsibility for your life and for changing your circumstances, because the truth is: politicians and your political party don't give a shit about you.

Chapter 16 *Start Thinking Rich* Challenge

It's time to get honest. Is there a part of you that is hoping that someone or something will swoop in and rescue you from your financial situation? There is no shame if that is the case. Why wouldn't you? So many people make their money by trying to position themselves as your financial savior. Whether it's an inspiring politician, a get-rich-quick guru, a business coach, a rich husband or wife, winning the lottery, that new crypto coin, or a long-lost billionaire uncle you never heard of, it is easy to get sucked into the hope that someone or something is going to save you from your financial fate. While it can feel good to indulge in the fantasy of financial rescue, it is dangerous because it can lull you into complacency, where you are just an observer of your life instead of the creator.

Picture the next recession, losing your job, housing crisis, or stock market crash – because it IS coming. How would you fare? Start saving as if emergencies are imminent. Because they are. If you don't have a side hustle, sufficient savings, and multiple streams of income, it's time to get to work on making those things happen. Pay attention to the mental obstacles that get in your way as you're trying to improve your circumstances and confront them. Take your power back over your mind and your life.

It's time for you to take control of your mental health. If you watch the news to start your day, we challenge you to try something more productive for you like a self-help podcast or finding time to journal or meditate. If the first thing you do when you wake out of bed is grab your phone to mindlessly scroll social media, we dare you to put your phone in another room to help break the habit. Try it for a day or two and see what happens. Take charge of the thoughts and ideas that enter your mind at the start of your day. Make sure they are thoughts you consciously want to be there, and not ideas planted by people who want to take advantage of you.

CHAPTER SEVENTEEN

COMPLAINING IS FOR LOSERS

Rich and successful people avoid complainers. Complaining is like dumping trash in your house and then wondering why it stinks so bad. There are two types of people: those who complain, and those who get things done. Complainers either have no friends because nobody wants to hear constant negativity, or they have toxic friends who are always complaining too. Non-complainers have strong relationships and are respected in their community because they spend their energy improving their lives and the lives of others. Which one are you? Which one do you want to be?

If complaining worked, we would be all for it! But unfortunately, it doesn't change anything. In fact, it makes things worse. Being stuck in a constant cycle of complaint is a sure sign of an external locus of control, where you are giving your power away to every outside person and circumstance around you. Conversely, non-complainers have an internal locus of control and know when to stop whining, take responsibility, and do something to improve their situation. When we complain, we are stuck in a stinky garbage pit of *powerlessness*, which not only makes us miserable, but also easy to control.

THE THREE TYPES OF PEOPLE WHO PEDDLE POWERLESSNESS TO TRY TO CONTROL YOU

Three types of people benefit from your powerlessness, and sell it to you like hotcakes:

1. Politicians trying to get your vote;
2. Self-loathing children of rich parents who feel guilty about their economic privilege and are trying to distance themselves from "the system"; and
3. People who have *given up* on trying to make their lives better.

We've dedicated an entire chapter to why your political party doesn't care and how politicians benefit from you feeling powerless (see Chapter 16), so we are going to focus here on the self-loathing rich kids and those who are struggling and have given up.

SELF-LOATHING CHILDREN OF RICH PARENTS: "IT'S NOT MY FAULT MY PARENTS ARE RICH"

Children of rich parents often try to distance themselves from economic privilege when they grow up benefiting from the system. By the way, there's nothing wrong with growing up rich. In fact, we are all about giving our descendants a leg-up by building up some generational wealth. But quite often, these kids feel shame about their economic privilege because they see the injustices in the world and feel guilty that they were born with a leg up.

It's common for rich kids, when they go to college, to downplay how much money they have and try to hide their family wealth because they feel it separates them from their peers. They feel an overwhelming sense of guilt related to their wealth. They often feel bad about themselves when they meet self-made people. Since many of them have no idea what it takes to go from poor to rich – since they didn't do it themselves and/or their parents neglected to pass down a rich mindset and strong work ethic – they assume their family's success was just the result of an unfair system. In an ironic twist of fate, it's more comfortable for them to sell powerlessness to the poor, because it fits with their own narrative of personal powerlessness. You can't help the circumstances under which you were born, none of us can. However, selling powerlessness to the poor to feel better about yourself is not only unhelpful, but it also reinforces a poor mindset, that all but guarantees the people they feel sorry for will stay poor forever.

Now, there is truth to the belief that "life isn't fair and it's not your fault if you were born poor." But when you add, "and there's nothing you can do about it until 'they' have changed the system," that's when the belief becomes toxic. Believing that you are powerless to change your life is what keeps people stuck for generations. People comment on our social media pages all the time and we can always tell when it's a rich kid who feels guilty about their financial privilege. It's obvious because they are so adamant about selling the idea that poor people can do nothing to better their lives. Meanwhile, if you talk to the people who came from lower-income backgrounds and are finding success, you'll see that they hate those messages of powerlessness and have no respect for the people who peddle them.

There's no shame in being born rich or poor. And "the system" will never be fair, because life isn't fair. Telling people the system is rigged and there's nothing they can do about it is patently false, and it promotes helplessness. We want you to recognize and embrace your personal power – NOT perpetuate the lie that you're powerless. Refusing to make sacrifices, blaming the system, succumbing to defeat, or waiting around hoping the system changes, that's the path to chronic pain and suffering. But there's another path. The people who follow the other path know that minimum wage is just a starting point. They know that being broke is just a temporary condition that they have the power to change. Being poor is not the end of the story, it's just the beginning.

PEOPLE WHO HAVE GIVEN UP: "BEING POOR IS ALL I'LL EVER KNOW"

For those who are struggling financially and have given up trying to make their lives better, things can feel bleak. These people often make their presence known as trolls online. We get hundreds of comments a day and about 50% of those are negative. To be honest, it doesn't make us mad, it makes us sad. Most internet trolls have given up on trying to make a better life for themselves. Trolls are people who hate their lives so much that the only thing that can bring them entertainment is to try to hurt someone else. It's sad that they've embraced bitterness and hopelessness. Ironically, people who have given up find a sick kind of emotional comfort in believing that the system is rigged and that change is impossible. So when they see someone who is promoting empowerment, or even worse, someone who has transformed or is in the process of transforming their lives, they lose their minds. They will do anything they can to disparage, cut down, cancel, or otherwise try to hurt people who challenge their worldview.

When we get disparaging comments from trolls, we just imagine the person on the other side of the screen and think, "Were they always like that? Did they used to be hopeful and open minded before slipping into complaints and bitterness?" Struggling sucks, there's no denying that. You must develop a plan and make sacrifices. People don't like the idea that you have to make sacrifices to become wealthy, but that's exactly what it takes. Is it fair? Of course not! But the reality is that's just what you need to do if you want to become wealthy. What will NOT get you out of the financial suck is bitching, whining, and trying to tear other people down.

> Adrian: I've been dealing with trolls since I uploaded my first dance video on YouTube in 2008. Back then the hate comments sounded like "You shouldn't post videos with that acne" and you "suck at dancing." Today, they sound more like "you're a scammer," and "this guy is spending his parents' money." Early in my content creating career, these troll comments used to affect my entire day until I learned that one particular troll of mine had committed suicide. In 2021, I launched my first big online business training program called The Brambila Method. It went viral in the affiliate marketing space and naturally with the success came a new onslaught of trolls. One in particular went far beyond commenting on my posts. He had 40,000 followers and was so prolific with hating on me that his entire content started to change from business self-help to "hate on Adrian." After about 10 days of posting about me I had to block him. A little over a year later, I learned that he had taken his own life and immediately felt bad. Despite the fact that he said some incredibly false and messed-up things about me, I wish I had never let it bother me. It's taught me to never forget that when someone comments something negative or bad about me (or you) they are probably dealing with some serious demons. Complaining is a slippery slope!

BEING ACCOUNTABLE IS HARD; MAKING EXCUSES IS EASY

It can be so tempting to wallow in self-pity when life throws us a curveball. Our brains are wired to take the path of least resistance. It takes work to snap ourselves out of our mental ruts. That's why most people never do it. They continue on the same path they've always taken and keep getting the same results they've always been getting, over and over again. When we were cavemen, we had to conserve our energy in case we needed to run away from a threat. Our brains are still wired that way, to conserve energy or be lazy, just in case we need to run later. But there are no saber-toothed tigers coming to chase us. We have to push ourselves out of our comfort zones if we want different results, even though our primitive brains try to keep us locked in our current patterns. The bottom line is this: making excuses is far easier than making changes, and most people settle for excuses.

Dr. Brad: When I was 21 years old I wrecked my Jeep. For the first time in my life I was living with my dad, who was in South Dakota, where I was attending South Dakota State University for my master's degree. One day, I was driving from Rapid City to Spearfish. I drove my Jeep across an icy bridge, lost control, and crashed into a guard rail. Thankfully, the guard rail was there, or I would have flipped into a ravine on the other side.

My Jeep was wrecked and I was hoping for a little sympathy from my dad. Instead of offering sympathy, my dad said, "What could you do differently next time?" I was furious about his response. After all, I was going the speed limit and there was nothing I could have done about an icy bridge, right? But later, when I took some time to analyze the situation, I admitted to myself that the conditions on the road weren't great, I could have driven slower, I could have added weight to the back of my Jeep, and

I should have noticed the obvious signs on the side of the road that warned about ice forming on bridges. So even though it stung, my dad was right. Obviously, I didn't intend to wreck my Jeep. I didn't even do anything reckless or irresponsible. But there were things I could have done differently. After that experience, I tweaked my entire approach to highway driving in the winter. But to make this shift, I had to take responsibility for my crash from a psychological standpoint. In retrospect my dad was right. Ironically the State of South Dakota agreed with him and sent me a bill for the damaged guard rail. Talk about radical accountability, I paid for that mistake in a few ways.

I was raised with the mindset that I couldn't make excuses, no matter what happened. If you weren't raised that way, it makes sense to resist this approach. Sure, life is often SO unfair, and things happen that aren't our fault, all the time. But the more things you can take responsibility for in your life, the more successful you will be.

There's always going to be ice on the bridge in one sense or another. But the GREAT news is that we live in one of the few places and times in human history where people can start out dirt poor and become wealthy. There are successful people in the world who have faced seemingly insurmountable odds. They didn't make excuses or sit and mope about their obstacles, or at least not for long. They got to work and found ways to advance. When you get stuck in a cycle of complaining, it's like you're putting on blinders and can't see solutions. In fact, complainers tend to find a problem for every solution rather than solutions to their problems.

Adrian: In my line of work, I get the privilege of teaching beginners, which I absolutely love. I help people understand their finances and learn how to make money online. Out of the over 40,000 people whom I've taught, there's a small fraction of people who just start complaining, right away. And they complain about everything, from the unfairness of social media, to market saturation, to shadow banning, *blah, blah, blah.*

The difference between the complainers and the self-starters in my courses is astronomical. The ones who don't complain, who see the obstacle, understand it, and deal with it are able to overcome whatever challenges they face. Those people working and improving instead of complaining are light years ahead of the complainers in terms of success. For example, Morgan Rainey (Instagram: @cajunventures) is the first customer of mine who became a millionaire from my online training courses. She grew up in a trailer park in Louisiana, had to overcome a mountain of adversity, and often tells people across her vast social media following that complaining is for losers. My favorite kind of people are like Morgan, people who have dealt with real adversities and have every right to complain, yet choose to use their scars as fuel to propel themselves forward.

Complaining does absolutely nothing. It solves nothing. It's a drain on your time and energy. It creates a thick mud of negativity around your feet and ankles, making it harder and harder to move in the direction you want to go. Complaining is a distraction, keeping you from facing the reality in front of you. And you can't change what you won't address.

Adrian: When I played soccer in college, I was a hot-shot starter on the team. I scored a goal in my first game as a freshman. But I also started dancing at the same time. I was torn between the two passions and splitting my focus. When my junior year started, I learned I wouldn't be a starter anymore. I'd been demoted. I called my dad in a frenzy, saying I couldn't believe it. We had a new coach, so I blamed the coach and complained about the unfairness of it all, saying he didn't know what he was doing. But my dad asked me, "Well, what are *you* doing?" He said the coach was right, that if I wasn't a starter, it was because I wasn't good enough to be a starter anymore. I just sat in silence, processing what my dad said. It was a kick in the balls, but I knew my dad was right. I was spending all of my extra time dancing, so my soccer skills suffered.

By senior year I was still coming off the bench but there was a difference in my mindset and attitude. I knew my place and role on the team and it became more enjoyable for me to play while my dancing started to take off. I didn't know it at the time of my decline of on-field time, but my change in interest from soccer to dance would eventually earn me the opportunity to dance professionally for T-Pain as a 20-year-old!

Sometimes you just need a reality punch in the face to snap you into the awareness about who you are and the choices you are making. Excuses are never productive. Having awareness allows you to decide if your current interests are still worthy of pursuit.

If you let yourself get away with playing small, and you surround yourself with people who help you play small, you won't grow or improve. You'll get stuck in the mental ruts of excuses and complaints. In terms of becoming financially free, there are things that you have to do. Some of our favorite, yet most controversial social media posts start with, "You have to. . . .," or "You're not allowed to. . . ." People don't like being told what to do. But the reality is, if you don't want to do it, you are free to leave and continue experiencing the same results. But then own it, because it's nobody's fault but your own.

EXCUSES ARE FOR COWARDS; ACCOUNTABILITY FOR THE BRAVE

Excuses are like opinions, everyone has them. But they don't do anything for us other than keep us stuck right where we are. There are countless stories of people surviving horrible tragedies and going on to accomplish incredible things. The thing that sets those people apart is they don't waste time making excuses. They roll up their sleeves and get busy.

> Adrian: A friend of mine, Alex Fasulo (Instagram: @Alexandrafasulo), lost her home in a hurricane in Florida. All her possessions were wiped out. Thankfully, she made sure that her house only made up less than 10% of her net worth. She was making enough money to spring for a mansion but she didn't get in over her head. If she had used a high percentage of her finances on a home and it got destroyed in an instant by a natural disaster, she would have lost everything. Instead, she was able to withstand the devastation of losing her home because she practiced good financial habits. She didn't waste her time complaining; she turned the loss into an opportunity to travel the world. She went to Scotland and Asia and all over the United States. She now is building a new cabin home in New York, hiring the Amish to help, and documenting the whole journey.
>
> When people share how bad the 2008 housing crash was, they tend to leave out the fact that the ones who suffered the most were those living way outside their means with their residence(s). The less glamorized and more boring stories of 2008 were ones like my parents', who purchased their house for $250,000 when they were approved to buy a $600,000 home. People who lived under their means like them didn't suffer during 2008 like many did.

When the housing market crashed, people got in trouble because they were investing in real estate beyond their means. Now, some people were genuinely screwed. But there were also people buying three or four houses, investing in mortgages way beyond their net worth on the promise of lenders that the bubble would keep getting bigger. It's terrible that so many people lost their homes. But it's important to learn the lesson from the housing bubble burst so we don't make the same mistakes down the line.

We can't control everything. But we can control whether we make excuses or accept accountability for our lives. Economies crash and natural disasters happen. But if we set ourselves up to be protected and if we take responsibility for our decisions, we can bounce back faster and with less collateral damage to our lives.

YOUR LONG LIST OF EXCUSES. . .

We've heard them all, every excuse imaginable. And we've got reframes for most of them:

"I don't have time."

Is that true? Or is it just not a priority for you?

"I can't afford training or college."

Apply for grants and scholarships, work nights and save for school, go to Community College.

"Life's not fair."

That's 100% true. Focus on what you're going to do about it.

"My parents didn't teach me about money."

Now that you're an adult, it's your responsibility to teach yourself about money.

"I'm not a trust fund baby."

Neither are most self-made millionaires.

"It takes money to make money."

Wrong. Many people go from poor to rich.

"They have x, y, and z so it's easier for them than it is for me."

Many people have started with more or less than you have. Use what you've got, your skills, gifts, resources, and talents, to go after what you want.

"My life is hard."

Perhaps your life HAS been harder than most people you know. Get a therapist, have a good cry, then focus on how you're going to start getting what you want.

There's usually one sentence that can cut through any excuse: You can improve your circumstances, and if you don't, it's probably just not enough of a priority for you to do what it takes.

If you want someone to tell you you're powerless and your life is hopeless, you've come to the wrong place. We would never insult you like that. In fact, that's about the cruelest thing you could say to someone. Of course, there are circumstances of severe mental and physical disabilities, awful tragedies, and terrible setbacks that happen in people's lives. If you are "lucky" enough to live a long life, just about everyone you know will die. We're not heartless to those struggles. In fact, we have experienced tragedies ourselves. But even people who have lost everything, people who come from horrible poverty and have experienced awful situations can build a better life if they have the courage to focus on taking action instead of making excuses.

THE WORLD IS GROWING RICHER

Even with economic downturns and market crashes, the world is actually getting richer than it's ever been. While some hold tightly to the belief that going from poor to rich is a lost cause, the facts tell a very different story. When it comes to quality of life, we have been on a historically unprecedented upswing for the last few centuries. For example, since the 1800s, the number of people in extreme poverty has decreased astronomically. According to the World Bank, it was estimated that 80% of people in the world were in extreme poverty. Now, that number has fallen to under 20%. When you think of it in global terms and the resulting massive reduction in human suffering, that's an unbelievable shift.

Chart from World Bank

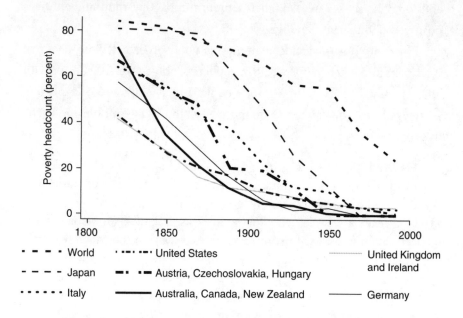

Even though poverty rates have never been lower, there IS a dark side of money and many examples of people taking advantage of others. For example, rich investors have bought buildings and evicted the tenants, moving them out for gentrification purposes. If you've seen this happen, you might be inclined to think that all rich people are evil. Adrian's friend Josh Trent (Instagram: @JoshTrentOfficial) saw this happen and came to that conclusion. He grew to hate the idea of money, thought the entire game was corrupt, and that businesses are evil. He said, "You know what, screw it. I'm just going to put myself in $80,000 worth of credit card debt and then declare bankruptcy because it's a game I can't win." Later, he realized there can be a good side to money, where wealthy people donate their resources to combat disease, establish libraries, provide education to the disenfranchised, and promote human rights and social justice. Then he changed his mindset that money's not good or evil, it's just a tool. After shifting his mindset, Josh's *Wellness and Wisdom* podcast started to grow, and today he makes over $30,000 a month impacting thousands of lives positively about health and wealth mindsets.

It's up to you to decide if money is good or bad. If you have evil intentions and you become wealthy, you'll probably make evil choices with your money, like exploiting poor people. But if you're a good person, money is a tool you can use to do more good things in your life and in the lives of others.

> Dr. Brad: When I was growing-up I didn't know any rich people. I didn't know any doctors, lawyers, or successful entrepreneurs. But I knew that my family consisted of smart, hardworking, God-fearing people who for some reason had been poor for generations. Some of my ancestors came over on the Mayflower. We had been in America for centuries, so why didn't we own any property? Why weren't we educated at the best schools? Why did my grandparents, on both sides, live in trailer parks? None of it made any sense to me, except for one theory: the system was rigged by rich people who were purposely keeping us down. It wasn't until I became a psychologist that I realized we had not climbed the socioeconomic ladder due to our own lack of financial literacy and beliefs about money. When we feel bad about our position in life, it is much easier to blame others than to take an honest, and often painful, look at ourselves.
>
> Now I see the truth of it. I have seen poor people who are generous and poor people who are evil. I have seen rich people who are generous and rich people who are evil. Money doesn't make someone bad or good. It's just a personality exaggerator. If you are a good person, more money can give you the power to do even more good in the world. If you are a bad person, you can use money to hurt others. Money is just a too, no more, no less.

When we hear people complaining, it's like nails on a chalkboard. We're allergic to it. It repels us immediately, because we know how contagious it can be. Some people get together and complain as a way to bond with one another, circulating a never-ending cycle of powerlessness and hopelessness. We're challenging you not only to refrain from complaining, but also to remove yourself from environments where others are complaining. Distance yourself from complainers, as if they have a disease and you don't want to catch it. Your life and your energy are too precious to waste. Life isn't fair, people can be mean, and there will always be reasons to complain. Don't dwell on those things. Instead, keep the vision of the life you want bright and clear in your mind. If you do this, success will follow you. It's hard to find optimism and solutions when you're drowning in a sea of complaints. So get out of that mucky water, dry yourself off, and get to work. No complaints. No excuses.

Chapter 17 *Start Thinking Rich* Challenge

We have spent this entire chapter trying to convince you to stop complaining. So this challenge may come as a bit of a shock.

Step 1: Make a list of all of your complaints. Write down ALL the things that aren't fair in your life and in the world. Take some time to do this. Get a piece of paper and write them all down. If you are using an electronic device, print out your list when you are done. We will help you get started with a list of complaints that apply to most people, but make sure to get specific and add more to the list that apply specifically to you. Get creative, because your list could be, quite literally, endless:

1. Life isn't fair.
2. Success takes hard work.
3. Life is easier for people who have more resources, connections, friends, etc., than me.
4. Some people have gotten more opportunities than me.

5. Some people were born richer, smarter, stronger, taller, and better looking than me.

6. Some people were born without the same mental or physical limitations and/or challenges as me.

7. Some people had a better education than me.

8. Some people have/had a healthier and more supportive family than me.

9. Some people didn't have to endure the same stress, mistreatment, and/or trauma as me.

10. Some people were born into better circumstances than me.

11. I have been mistreated, lied to, betrayed, insulted, overlooked, taken for granted, etc., by others.

12. Some rich people are evil.

13. The government, schools, traffic, technology, the economy, the weather, public transportation, etc., sucks.

14. Relationships are hard and I have been mistreated (more than once I might add) by my significant other.

15. Some people have a bigger house, nicer car, nicer clothes, etc., than me.

16. I don't get the level of respect, understanding, compassion, etc., that I deserve.

Did we miss anything? If so, write them down. Write them ALL down. Once you have a comprehensive list (and this might take hours or days for you if you take this assignment seriously), move on to Step 2.

Step 2: Take this list of complaints and hold it in your hands. Play some music that really helps you get in touch with your emotions. You could play some sad music, or perhaps some angry music. As the music plays, read through your list. Allow yourself to get in touch with your sadness and anger around this list of complaints. After all, life truly IS NOT FAIR, and the fact is, that reality often SUCKS. If you are sad, have a good cry.

Make it a deep, sobbing cry, like you are wringing out a wet sponge. If you are angry, let it out in a safe way. Punch a pillow, or lay down on your mattress and throw a tantrum, where you flail around (in a safe way), banging your arms and legs on the mattress. Sometimes these emotions will come in waves, so keep this going until you have utterly exhausted yourself and you have curled up into the fetal position.

Step 3: Now that you have expressed your deepest emotions around how much it sucks that life isn't fair and all the ways you have specifically experienced this, it is time to let it go. Take your list and rip it up, burn it, or in some other way destroy it.

Step 4: Read the next chapter of this book.

CHAPTER EIGHTEEN

GET A ROOMMATE, GET ON THE BUS, GET SOBER, GET BALD, AND GET A SIDE HUSTLE OR SHUT UP ABOUT BEING BROKE

The average American can EASILY become a millionaire, and we are about to prove it to you. Fair warning: if you really want to start thinking rich and building your wealth, some sacrifices will be necessary. Most people don't have the discipline and resolve to pull it off, but you'll be glad you did it in the long run. Sure, roommates can be annoying. And you do look cool in your new whip. Of course people like to blow off steam at the bar after a hectic work week. And not everyone can pull off the bald look in such a strikingly attractive way like Dr. Brad can (he wrote that). And you may be too tired to even think about starting a side hustle. But some discomfort is a price you will need to pay if you want to create an extraordinary life. People tell us all the time they "can't afford" to invest. But we are going to prove that they can if they really want to. In fact, if you get a roommate, ride the bus, get sober, and shave your head, in 25 years you will have a nest egg of close to $3 million and that's BEFORE we even talk about how you can increase your income with a side hustle. So sit back and open your mind because you are about to get educated.

GET A ROOMMATE

If you "can't afford" to invest, get a roommate. If you've already got a roommate helping you pay rent and you still can't afford to invest, then get another one, and another one, and another one. If you are lucky enough to have parents who are still alive and love you, move back in with them. See, we can do this all day.

If you're past your college years, it may seem strange to think of getting roommates again. Most Americans seem to prefer to live alone or with their families. But rent/mortgage is the biggest percentage of most people's living expenses. For low- to moderate-income families, rent makes up 40% of their living expenses. If you get roommates, you could lower that to just 13% of your expenses. And you'll also save on utilities and water.

If you want to invest in a property, consider going in on it with trusted friends. Three of you could invest in a condo and rent it out to cover expenses. If you travel for work, consider renting out your home as a short-term rental. There are many ways to reduce your living expenses. Adrian lived in a van with his wife for a year and saved 95% of his income. Crash on a couch if you have to, stay in your nephew's tree house, do whatever it takes (as long as it's legal). In reality, most rich people don't live luxurious lifestyles anyway. They live on a fraction of their income. They make their money work for them instead of grinding for money. If you want to go from poor to rich, you have to be willing to live a minimum-wage lifestyle, at least for a while. If Adrian can live in a van for a year, then you can cut a few corners too.

Americans suffer from a strange mindset. We think we are supposed to "have our own place." This is just a made-up concept. The idea of living alone is foreign to our ancestors and for most of the people in the world. Rent or mortgage payments are often the biggest monthly expense we have, and a roommate can free up hundreds or even thousands of dollars a month for you. The math is very simple. The average rent in the United States is around $2,000. If you pay $2,000 a month in rent, a roommate can free up $1,000 a month for you. If you invested that $1,000 a month and got an average annual investment return of 10% (compounded monthly), in 25 years you would have $1,337,890. But if you got 3 roommates, you would get even richer. We created a chart below for you to see how much richer you would be if you got more roommates. Easy, peasy, lemon squeezy.

Number of Roommates	Money freed-up each month you invest assuming total rent = $2,000/month	How much it would be worth in 25 years at 10% average annual return (compounded monthly)
1	$1,000	$1,337,890
2	$1,333	$1,783,408
3	$1,500	$2,006,836

So getting a roommate alone would give you an extra $1,337,890 in just 25 years. Congratulations, you are already a millionaire!

Get a roommate: $1,337,890

Total: $1,337,890

GET ON THE BUS

If you "can't afford" to invest, sell your car and ride the bus. Maybe it's your emotional attachment to your car that is keeping you poor. Your ancestors lived just fine for hundreds of thousands of years without a car, so what makes you think you have to have one? Also, aren't cars destroying the earth or something like that? So wouldn't you be doing the earth a favor if you got rid of yours? The fact is, if you really "can't afford" to invest but you want to get rich, get rid of your car.

If you think you need it because you have a long commute, just rent a place within walking distance or bike-riding distance to your job, or just take the bus. Between gas, car payments, maintenance, and insurance, the average American pays around $894 a month for their car. If you invested that money instead, and got an average annual investment return of 10%, in just 25 years you would have another $1,196,074. So by getting a roommate and riding the bus, you'd be a multi-millionaire in just 25 years. But wait, we aren't done yet!

Get a roommate: $1,337,890

Get on the bus: $1,196,074

Total: $2,533,964

GET SOBER

If you "can't afford" to invest, stop drinking alcohol. People waste a ton of money, time, energy, and resources on things that make their lives worse, not better. Roughly 45% of drinkers say they regretted overspending on alcohol and partying, 17% admit that drinking has led to debt, and 45% of Gen Z say alcohol has negatively affected their finances. Not only are you spending money when you go out partying, but you're also spending time and energy that could be used to level up and learn a side hustle. There's a saying that nothing good happens after 10 p.m. If you're out drunk late at night, you put yourself at risk for other consequences, financially and physically. When we drink, our guard is down, leaving us susceptible to being robbed, assaulted, or tricked into spending more money than we want. Those dumb enough to get behind the wheel of a car wind up spending tens of thousands of dollars on a DUI, do jail time, and run the risk of losing their jobs and driver's license. Binge drinking and partying is like taking a sledgehammer to your ankle right before running a marathon. People who do this on a regular, or even occasional, basis are seriously disabling themselves in the game of becoming wealthy, and in all other areas of life.

> Adrian: I stopped drinking and partying after I lied to my parents about how college was going when I came home after the first semester. I told them I'd been working really hard on my classes and GPA when in reality I was binge drinking and partying like everyone else. When I got back to college my second semester at University of Dubuque I knew I needed to find a new hobby to replace the time I spent partying. I started watching videos online of people learning how to dance the robot and breakdance. To put in perspective how much time college kids are partying, I spent enough time the next two years learning how to dance the robot from the internet that I actually got good enough to dance professionally for T-Pain!
>
> The true cost of drinking isn't just the cost of the alcohol, it's the opportunity cost of killing your brain cells, wasting the night and the next morning or day, and destroying your energy and drive to do something fulfilling with your life. Giving up alcohol changed my life, from learning how to dance, dancing for T-Pain, dancing on *America's Got Talent* with my old dance crew The Body

Poets, becoming an influencer, saving, and investing so much money that I became a millionaire by the time I turned 30. One of my most recommended books I give to people is *This Naked Mind* by Annie Grace, which is the best book I've ever read that will help you see how life without alcohol is game changing.

Did you know that millennials spend an average of $110 on alcohol per month? If you invested that $110 a month and got an average annual investment return of 10%, in 25 years you'd have $147,168. And that's just the money you wasted on booze. So that brings our total to:

Get a roommate: $1,337,890

Get on the bus: $1,196,074

Get sober: $147,168

Total: $2,681,132

GET BALD

If you "can't afford" to invest, get bald. Okay, fine, you don't want to shave your head, so let's compromise: learn to cut your own hair or get a friend to do it. You can learn how to cut hair for free on YouTube. While you're at it, do your own nails too. Americans spend so much money on both and you've got to ask yourself, would you rather be poor with nice hair, or rich and bald? For example, some surveys have shown that the average American woman spends approximately $1,800 a year on salon visits. If you invested that money instead, and got an average annual return of 10% (compounded monthly), in just 25 years you'd have $200,684. Now shaving your head may be a last resort, but you're the one who said you couldn't afford to invest, and we are just here to help you get honest about your priorities.

Get a roommate: $1,337,890

Get on the bus: $1,196,074

Get sober: $147,168

Get bald: $200,684

Total: $2,881,816

GET A SIDE HUSTLE

So, we have just shown you how the average American can EASILY build up a nest egg of $2.9 million in 25 years by making a few sacrifices. Now, if you don't want to make any of those sacrifices, we can't really blame you. So instead of cutting back costs, if you "can't afford" to invest, consider getting a side hustle. If you don't want to get a roommate, ride the bus, get sober, or shave your head but you still want to get rich, then you should increase your income. It's time to level up and diversify your income streams. Now, we are of the opinion that creating multiple streams of income is a good idea for everyone. Economic downturns, the pandemic, and market crashes have shown us just how unreliable that 9-to-5 job can be. As soon as CEOs get wind of a recession, they start hacking away at jobs to save themselves. Layoffs, business failures, and corporate restructuring are an inevitability. So you need to make yourself financially bulletproof. For example, if you got a side hustle that generated an extra $1,500 a month and invested the money at 10% average annual return, in 25 years you would have over $2 million.

Ask any financial advisor and they'll tell you not to put all your eggs in one basket. So why would you do that when it comes to your income streams? The best financial advice is to diversify your portfolio. But you should also be diversifying your earning opportunities. If you have multiple streams of income, you become practically invincible to the whims of the economy. If your boss fires you but you already have an established side hustle that's pulling in five figures every month, you're not going to feel the pain of losing everything the way someone would if that was their only way of making money.

People balk at this and say things like, "What kind of world do we live in where I have to get a side hustle to survive?" To that we say, the world is indeed unfair, we didn't create it, but if you want to have a better life, you need to learn how to beat the system. Working at a side hustle doesn't have to be an arduous suck fest. In fact, we think it should be fun, like a game where instead of points, you're racking up financial freedom. If you spend just 30 minutes to an hour every day playing the side hustle game, you can start the momentum to build a sizable income.

We all have different goals. Maybe you don't want to be a full-time entrepreneur like Adrian. Maybe you're not interested in being a college professor and financial planner like Dr. Brad. But whatever your interests, it's a fair bet that most of us would say, "Hey, I'd like an extra 500 bucks per month." Think of it as an extracurricular activity. Instead of partying, you're spending an hour a day learning how to make money online.

Now is the best time to get involved in making money online. The opportunities are endless. Adrian can attest to personally trying every single legitimate and ethical way of making money online from selling T-shirts and selling on Amazon, to creating content. We are constantly surprised at the ways we've seen people make money on the internet. There's a niche for absolutely everything. In the next chapter we will dive into side hustles that you can start today. But just to prove that anything is possible here are some of the more *ridiculous* things we've seen people make money online doing:

- Setting up a camera so people can watch them sleep. Yes, this is a real thing and yes, people are literally making money in their sleep doing it.
- ASMR (Autonomous Sensory Meridian Response) videos. People get a nice microphone and film themselves whispering, chewing, crinkling wrappers, or creating other sounds. It's really weird when you first see it, but some people love the tingling sensation they often feel when exposed to these audio stimuli, which they find relaxing. People love watching it!

- Playing video games. There are tons of people making money by filming themselves playing the latest video games. They don't even have to be good video games or be good at playing them. Many people love watching these for entertainment.
- Travel blogs. Some have found ways to make money doing what they love, like traveling.
- Palm reading and psychic readings. You don't even need a corner shop with a neon sign to make money as a psychic. The internet is all you need.
- Acting like an NPC (non-player character). In video games there are characters whom you can't control who robotically repeat the same actions or phrases over and over. People in real life are pretending to be them online and making a fortune in the process.

There are many ways to make money with the accessibility of the internet. And there are no gatekeepers. Adrian has had customers who couldn't find work because they had a criminal record. But they were able to start their own business online instead of waiting to be hired and checking that box at the bottom of the application that asks if they'd been convicted of a crime. Stay-at-home moms with gaps in their resumes can make money as bloggers and influencers. You don't even have to show your face online to make an income. The internet doesn't care, as long as you're serving a niche. No college degree or clean record required. You just have to learn how to do the skills required to make money online. We'll dive deeper into this in Chapter 19: "People Who Binge Netflix Without a Side Hustle Will Be Poor Forever."

Adrian: After taking a couple of my courses, Rachel Nader went from being a part-time stay-at-home mom and part-time special-needs teacher to an online business owner making $8,000 a month. Her brand (Instagram: @spendymom) is a healthy combination of her bright personality sprinkled with offers of helping business owners manage their social media. Kylie Landis

(Instagram: @kylielandis) from Cedar Rapids, Iowa, had a successful career working a corporate job. With the news of her second child on the way, she had a desire to quit her job to spend more time at home with her children. As she started to prepare for what her financial life would look like going from two household incomes to one she took one of my online content creation classes. Two months later she made $6,600! She now makes a full-time income as a stay-at-home mom without the burden of logging 40 hours a week. People like Rachel and Kylie represent what is possible for mothers across the world who have internet access, desire to learn, and a little bit of extra time (visit StartThinkingRich .com/earn to get access to the same updated training they received).

Dr. Brad: I have never had just one source of income. Your company doesn't care about you. Even government jobs aren't immune to layoffs. I've always felt that having just one job put me at economic risk, but the main reason for having multiple sources of income was that I wanted to make more money so I could invest more money so that I could achieve financial freedom in my 40s. I was able to do it, and now I have over 10 distinct sources of income. If I get annoyed or bored with any of them, I can just shut it down. In fact, I could quit them all and be just fine. But since I think that retirement is for dead people, I'm always looking for my next side hustle, as long as it fits with my life's purpose. If you have a face and are comfortable showing it on camera, there's a way for you to make money. If you'd rather not show your face on camera, there's a way for you to make money. If you have professional expertise or just know how to do one random thing in a particular field, there's a way for you to make money. Getting a side hustle has never been easier.

There's no excuse for you NOT having a side hustle that brings you additional income. If you don't know how to do anything, research what people are looking to learn and then learn that thing and teach it to others online. You don't need to be the world's leading expert to help people learn. After all, the biggest market for learners in any area are beginners, and many advanced experts have forgotten the challenges of first starting out. If you can teach people how to go from Point A to Point B, you can create a useful learning product. Adrian taught robot dancing on YouTube for his first online side hustle. Dr. Brad got speaking and consulting gigs and created educational products (e.g. books and online courses) to supplement the income he was making from his public school job. You can become a virtual assistant or help a business with their social media posts. Do data entry. Film your cat every day (people love pet videos). Find the thing and commit to it consistently. What do you have to lose? More importantly, what do you have to gain?

Getting a side hustle isn't completely risk-free. For example, even though many online side hustles now can be launched with little to no upfront financial commitments, you are going to need to invest your time and energy. You are going to need to be okay with failure. You are going to need to be okay with it taking months or years before they start paying off. Being successful at side hustles, especially online, requires learning, executing, trial and error, paying attention to trends and algorithms, and researching the market. But what were you doing anyway? Wasting your precious time scrolling Instagram? Puking in the bushes after a night partying with friends? Whining and complaining? If you want to get rich, you need to start thinking rich, and putting your energy where success can find you!

Adrian: My very first side hustle was creating a hip-hop clothing brand called Dance Saves Lives. After I clocked out at 3 p.m. from my call center job in Dubuque, I'd spend five hours, from 4 p.m. to 9 p.m. every night, learning how to build a website where I could sell apparel. I saved $3,000 and spent it all on the inventory of the custom-branded apparel. I was so excited to launch and was devastated when it finally happened and no one made any purchases. Days turned into weeks and then years where boxes and boxes of Dance Saves Lives apparel sat in a closet unsold. It took moving to Ireland to finally get rid of them where I dropped them off at a local Goodwill. The classic saying from the movie *Field of Dreams* of "If you build it, the will come" is not true for side hustles! Despite the failure of my first side hustle I kept trying and failing. It took two years until I finally made any money online. The $0.43 I made that day felt like a million dollars. After numerous other failures that $0.43 a day turned to $43, then $433 and sometimes there are days where I make $43,000, in one day. The truth is I failed way more times than I succeeded. I'm optimistic about people like you reading this book starting a side hustle and the future of side hustles. Technology like no-code websites and AI is only making it easier for you to start!

YOU CAN AFFORD TO INVEST!

This is your invitation to get creative and level up. This is a huge life hack that, if you're willing to do what it takes, will make you massively successful. So if you've been saying to yourself "but I can't afford" to invest, it's time to get serious. As we have so clearly demonstrated, you can create an extra $2.9 million in net worth by simply getting a roommate, riding the bus, getting sober, and shaving your head. Or, if you don't want to do that, cut your expenses or just get a side hustle. For example, if you created some additional income and invested an extra $1,500 a month, you would have an extra $2 million in 25 years. OR you can do both! If you started this at 22, by age 47 you could have a nest egg of $4.9 million. Here's the breakdown:

Get a roommate: $1,337,890

Get on the bus: $1,196,074

Get sober: $147,168

Get bald: $200,684

Get a side hustle: $2,006,836

Total: $4,888,652

If you aren't willing to do any of this because it seems like too much work, please stop complaining about being broke. If you want an extraordinary life, you need to go to extraordinary measures to make it happen. We suggest you start investing at least 30% of every dollar you make. If you can't afford it and you don't want to take extreme measures to cut your expenses, then it is time to start your side hustle. In the next chapter we're going to break down some of our favorite ways for people to start making money online, right now!

Chapter 18 *Start Thinking Rich* Challenge

Can you start saving and investing 30% or more of your income right now? Ideally, before you get your first job you would have had that mindset and you'd be well on your path to becoming a multi-millionaire. But unfortunately, many were not raised to have a rich mindset, and set up their expenses (e.g. buying a car, renting a place, etc.) *before* setting aside money for their financial freedom. So if that's you, don't worry, you're not alone, but if you want to get rich, you need to get busy. As we have demonstrated, the fastest way to free up cash would be for you to get a roommate (or three). If you would rather not make that adjustment or the other ones we have mentioned, you might want to make cuts in other areas. Here are four steps to get you started:

1. Make a list of your expenses. Better yet, track them for a month or two to see where your money is going. This exercise alone can be transformational, because you might not even know how your money is disappearing.

2. After you have a clear picture of your expenses, get creative on how to slash your expenses as much as possible. Read books and follow social media profiles committed to minimalism. Make it a game – how much can you cut your living expenses?

3. Design your minimalist lifestyle while you get your side hustle going. Perhaps you need to get a cheaper car or move to a cheaper place. Perhaps you need to stop eating out so much.

4. Make a list of side hustles you want to explore. List your skills, assets, and knowledge. Research skills and ideas the internet is seeking and find your niche. It can literally be anything. In the next chapter, we'll show you how to get that side hustle off the ground.

CHAPTER NINETEEN

PEOPLE WHO BINGE NETFLIX WITHOUT A SIDE HUSTLE WILL BE BROKE FOREVER

There are a million obstacles ready to separate you from your money, your time, attention, energy, and resources. We live in an attention economy. When you waste an hour on your phone, business owners and investors get richer, and you get poorer because you've done nothing to advance your own prosperity. Streaming platforms love it when you binge-watch TV shows instead of learning a new skill or creating a side hustle. They're getting rich off of your laziness (more on this one later). If you're constantly doom scrolling and watching the news, you're killing your creativity and making media moguls richer instead of using your precious time and creative energy to come up with innovative ways to save money and grow your wealth.

So how can you immediately increase your income by 40%? Stop watching Netflix and invest time in a side hustle. We're not exaggerating. Traditional side hustles like consulting, mowing the neighbor's lawn, etc., are great, but in this chapter we are going to focus on online side hustles. It's the modern-day gold rush on the internet and we are seeing people making fortunes online. So cancel your Netflix subscription and get in the game (sorry Netflix).

If you don't know where to start, consider the top-paying side hustles. At the time of writing this book we found the five top-paying side hustles to be coding, web design, graphic design, mobile app development, and website development. When Dr. Brad shared this information with his followers on social media, he was stunned at the blowback. People were appalled that these side hustles required some expertise. Apparently people want side hustles that don't require any skill or knowledge. Apparently they have bought into the lie that getting rich is easy and that launching successful side hustle requires no expertise at all. But those don't exist. We got rich because we're eternal students, constantly reading and learning how to expand our thinking, enhance our skills, and grow our wealth. It takes time, effort, and lots of hard work to educate ourselves on new skills and methods. Nobody delivered a pile of money to us on a platter, and nobody is going to do that for you either.

But you don't have to be a tech wiz or graphic design genius to start a side hustle. In fact, you can build a side hustle with the time and money you waste binge-watching your favorite TV shows. In this chapter, we will provide practical, tactical information on how to start one or more of these side hustles. Americans spend an average of three hours watching TV every day. We waste even more time on social media. If you invested just one hour of that time every day on educating yourself and learning new skills to start a side hustle, the impact on your life would be enormous. Adrian's clients have shared numerous success stories that started with them turning off the screens and turning on the hustle. The irony of us telling people to turn off social media when we have hundreds of thousands of followers taking our advice on our channels is not lost on us. The truth is, we'd be happy if we had zero followers because they were all too busy improving their lives. So let's break this down.

STRANGER THINGS OR SIDE HUSTLE KING?: MINI-PROJECT-BASED SERVICES

The award-winning Netflix series *Stranger Things* takes 21 hours and 49 minutes to watch. That's the same amount of time it would take for you to learn how to create an online gig. This gig would be a mini-project-based service, which you could list for sale on a marketplace like Fiverr. The options for gigs are endless on Fiverr. You could create a proofreading gig, do logo design, do translations, architectural designs, or even tattoo designs. All you have to do is pick a thing you know how to do and create a profile. The great thing about a site like Fiverr is that it already has a built-in marketplace full of buyers ready to buy your service. All you have to do is tap into that buyer system. And while it may look like it's not lucrative because there's pressure to keep service fees low, you can absolutely grow that out to a million-dollar business, like our friend Alex Fasulo (IG: @AlexandraFasulo) did. She has already made over a million dollars doing copywriting gigs. Go onto Fiverr or any other marketplace for digital services and see what's selling, find out who the top sellers are, and look around for ideas on your niche in this marketplace. Then set up your profile and start selling.

LUCIFER OR LUCRATIVE?: USER-GENERATED CONTENT

Binge-watching *Lucifer* on Netflix would take you 2 days, 1 hour, and 57 minutes. Or you could start thinking rich and learn about the world of UGC, aka User Generated Content. This is an incredibly easy side hustle in which you create product reviews for the things you already have around the house. For example, if you bought a new toaster recently on Amazon, you can get paid to review it. And they don't just pay you once. They could pay you dozens of times over several years for your reviews.

> Adrian: I learned about how much you can make from Amazon product reviews after I uploaded my first one. I happened to post it in the month of Black Friday and Cyber Monday. That November, I made over $15,000 from the stuff I'd already purchased and had around the house. It's been two years and I've not uploaded a single video since then. But in the last 30 days, I still made $2,500 from my reviews.

Adrian has experimented with Amazon product reviews testing the concept before he started telling others about it, but our friend Morgan Rainey (IG: @cajunventures) went all in on this side hustle. In her first 12 months she made over $158,000. If you have a phone and can point it at a product and you can talk about that product and say a few things about why you like it, that's all it takes. Not only that, but Amazon has an influencer program. Walmart is also developing one that's in the beta stages. This is a potential goldmine. The future of online shopping is going to be full of regular people making product reviews to help the buyers decide which thing to buy. So instead of watching *Lucifer*, you could potentially make five figures if you learn how to use these programs.

PUNISHER OR PROFITS?: E-BOOKS, TEMPLATES, AND GUIDES

Marvel's *The Punisher* would take 22 hours and 51 minutes to watch. Or you could learn how to create an e-book or guide to sell. This product is one of the lowest-risk, most profitable businesses you could start, because it costs nothing but your time. It's a digital product you can create using a website, like Canva. You can create the entire thing for free. Just brainstorm ideas on an e-book that people will find helpful, such as setting up a LinkedIn page, a guide for buying a good used car, or writing a resumé. Just think of the problems people have in specific situations, industries, or niches. If you know helpful tips and tricks, create a tactical e-book that you can sell for anywhere between $7 and $27 that will make a small but significant impact on their lives. We're not talking about an autobiography here. This e-book should be focused on the person who's buying it. Maybe it will make a task easier or teach them a valuable skill in a short amount of time. For instance, a realtor may create an e-book teaching other realtors how to get more listings. If you're not sure where to start, try compiling a list of things you know how to do and start there. The goal of these e-books is to solve people's problems or teaching from your area of expertise. Use a search engine to see what people struggle with the most in your particular niche to get ideas. Adrian has personally sold thousands of these mini-books online and believes it's a way to add great value to customers.

QUEER EYE OR RICH GUY?: ONLINE COURSES

It would take over 55 hours to binge-watch *Queer Eye*. Or, in that same amount of time, you could learn how to create your own online course. For this, you'll have to do a screen-recording or get comfortable talking on camera. Pick something to teach in a course, such as building a website or setting up your Facebook profile. Remember that the biggest potential audience is beginners, so you don't need to be the world's leading expert to do this. It doesn't have to be this big masterclass either. It can just be a mini-course to solve one minor problem. There are many people around the world who are still just getting access to the internet for the first time. Those of us who are used to navigating apps and websites take that knowledge for granted. For some, these things are completely new and they need to learn how to use them. People on the internet are constantly seeking new knowledge. Google gets 8.5 billion searches per day. If you know how to do something – almost anything – you can make money teaching it on the internet.

> Adrian: In 2013, I created dance video tutorials to make money on courses. It was my first class ever and all I did was teach people how to do the robot and the arm wave. That was 11 years ago and I still made $500 last month from those tutorials. You can keep making money on these classes for as long as people buy them. The only downside is, when the customer buys my dance videos, they see a much younger Adrian. That's the only risk about creating a course. It's going to be on the internet forever. So, even after I die, people might be learning how to do the robot from my videos.

Even if you think it's a small thing that you can teach, take the shot and create the course. Maybe you know how to make the best homemade tortillas. Film it and sell it as a course! Teach people how to knit, ski, paint, sing, whatever. There's no limit to what you can teach and how much you could make. So turn off *Queer Eye* and start creating your course.

GREY'S ANATOMY OR GROW FINANCIALLY?: CONTENT CREATORS

Grey's Anatomy has about 343 hours' worth of content. It's been running forever and it's a good show. But instead of bingewatching *Grey's*, you could become a content creator. This one is highly recommended because by 2027, it's expected to become a $480 billion industry. Most people who use the internet don't create content. So the demand for content is at an all-time high (you saw how many searches there are every day on Google). There are many different ways to make money as a content creator. YouTube pays a pretty penny once you meet their qualifications for monetizing. But there is much more beyond YouTube. You can create a newsletter or start a Substack and sell subscriptions. You could start a blog, create exclusive content for your audiences, or create private membership groups.

> Dr. Brad: When the pandemic hit, someone close to me lost their job. So I called my buddy Adrian and picked his brain around ways I could help them make money online. Following Adrian's advice, within a couple of months we launched a private membership group. The group takes about five hours a month to manage and brings in over $55,000 a year.

Once brands recognize that you are reaching the same audience that they want to reach, they'll pay you to mention their products. For example, our personal finance creator friends Matt Gresia (IG: @RealMattGresia), Seth Godwin (IG: @SethGodwin) and Gina Zakaria (IG: @SavingWhiz) have multiple streams of income as full-time content creators, and all average multiple six figures a year in brand deals alone! Once you've earned the trust of your audience and grown your following, businesses will come out of the woodwork to offer you money for promoting their products.

> Adrian: I have an amazing partnership with a brand called "High Level." It's a software that I use to run all my businesses. Since I have a strong following and I create good content, they offered me a two-year contract that pays $10,000 per month. And the return on the investment is worth it for them because I've brought them new business tenfold. I'm not biased toward one content creation platform or another. I think people should do them all, especially anywhere you can create vertical videos. And by the way, you don't have to show your face. A lot of content creators out there never show their faces. So don't let that lame excuse hold you back.

With all the advances in AI and technology, it's ridiculously easy to create content. There are many platforms you can use and the demand is out there for your content. Businesses will pay big bucks for content creators who have put in the time and effort to build a following. So stop watching the latest fake emergency on *Grey's Anatomy* and get your content up and running!

BREAKING BAD OR BANKING BUCKS?: AFFILIATE MARKETING

In the 60 hours it would take you to watch every episode of *Breaking Bad*, you can learn affiliate marketing. This is the side hustle that's made Adrian the most money. This side hustle is tied with becoming a content creator, because you need content and a following to become a successful affiliate. In this side hustle, you get paid a commission for selling someone's product online. It's the easiest form of sales possible. There's no cold-calling, you don't have to go door-to-door, and you can reach massive amounts of people with just the click of a button. If you're promoting a good product with a good offer to an audience who trusts you, this side hustle could make you a millionaire. Let's say you have 10,000 people following you and you're selling a backpack. Even if only 10% of your followers buy this backpack, that's 1,000 sales. If you make a $5 commission on each purchase, you just made $5,000 from a social media or blog post. Do a few product posts per week and you could be bringing in up to $15,000 every week. This is way easier than building your own backpack business, testing the product, buying the materials, and stocking the inventory. All you have to do is sell a product that's already there. You don't have to bother with product design, manufacturing, inventory, shipping, or customer service. You just get them to click and buy, and you're done!

It's important to note that affiliate marketing is not a stand-alone hustle. You have to be a content creator first. That's why we listed content creation before affiliate marketing. But once you build your following, the potential is there to make a lot of money.

> Adrian: I've made most of my money through affiliate marketing, just by promoting products that I already use. I've been an affiliate for over 500 companies, and I'm the number-one affiliate for most of them. I do this work primarily through blogging and short-form videos. Occasionally, I'll do ads. It's been incredibly rewarding. I was taught in college that if you know how to sell, you'll always have a job, but I believe if you know how to sell online, you'll never need one.

So while *Breaking Bad* is a great show, it's not going to make you rich. But affiliate marketing can, if you put the time and effort into it. Walter White found his side hustle. Don't you think it's time you found yours?

There's no excuse for you to sit back, watch TV, and stay poor. There is money just waiting to be earned in the magical world of the internet. If you're not getting in on this, you're missing out. And other people will be getting rich while you watch Netflix. Every minute you have is precious. If you could exchange your TV time for dollars, wouldn't you do it? Because you can. So do it.

Chapter 19 *Start Thinking Rich* Challenge

Cancel your streaming services and put restrictions on your social media so you won't be tempted to waste your time in a wealth-killing never-ending scroll tornado. Then set aside at least one hour of every day to learn one of the side hustles mentioned in this chapter. Brainstorm ideas for e-books, courses, and content and start creating. If you feel you don't have anything you can teach, use that time to learn a new skill. Learn from the masters about building a successful side hustle and multiple streams of income, do Amazon reviews, and create gigs on marketplaces like Fiverr. Build your knowledge and skill set. Then monetize it every way you can. Pay attention to where you started versus where you are in a year after spending 365 hours (an hour per day for one year) creating your side hustle empire.

CHAPTER TWENTY

YOU'RE NOT ALLOWED TO USE YOUR CREDIT CARD IF YOU DON'T PAY IT OFF EACH MONTH

Want to know one of the fastest ways to piss people off on social media? Just tell them: "You're not allowed to use your credit card if you don't pay it off each month." Little did we know there is a toxic lie about credit cards that has gone viral on the internet: "If you want a good credit score, you need to carry a balance on your credit card each month." Adrian got a lot of heat for telling people not to carry balances on their credit cards on Facebook. Here's some of what people said:

- "No. That's not how it works. In fact that won't help your credit at all."
- "You don't have any clue how the credit card system works. Do you?"
- "If you could pay it off in one payment, why bother with a credit card?"
- "This is actually a BAD IDEA. You need to keep at least a $10 balance on your card at all times. A $0 balance doesn't help your credit at all."
- "If you keep a $1,000 balance and pay some interest and just pay half of it off, your credit score will jump."

Credit card debt is a huge problem for Americans. People in the United States carried an average of $6,500 in credit card debt in 2023. The average credit card interest rate is 23.56%, meaning the average American throws away roughly $1,400 in interest fees every year. Over a 25-year period, if that $1,400 a year had been invested at an average annual return of 10% (compounded monthly), it would be worth $156,000. That's $156,000 of YOUR money flushed down the toilet. Congratulations, you just made banks a whole lot richer and yourself a hell of a lot poorer.

Everything in society is set up to extract your resources from you. There are entire teams of scientists who sit around working to come up with devious strategies to separate you from your money. Take Las Vegas slot machines, for instance. Scientists in labs discovered that sporadic incentives will keep rats pressing the reward button, even if it's ultimately detrimental to them. For us, they play the most pleasing musical notes to the human ear in the slot machines, pump in scents to create positive emotions, and hire scantily dressed women to bring you "free" drinks. Do you know those confusing patterns on the floor at casinos? They are there by design to get you to look up and see all of the possibilities for you to give them your money. It's no accident that you have to go through a maze of slot machines to find a bathroom. There's also a reason there are no clocks on the walls. They want to keep you on that floor for as long as possible, unaware of the time passing as you dump your hard-earned money into their pockets. The entire environment is set up to extract more money from you. The same is true for grocery stores, where items are strategically located and displayed to maximize your vulnerability to impulsive purchases.

Credit card companies also know how to keep you spending on their high-interest cards. They offer all kinds of incentives and perks to make you think you're getting good deals, such as airline points and membership rewards. But it's all designed to get you spending in the hopes that you will carry a credit card balance from month to month so that they can rack up interest fees before you can pay off your balance. Credit cards can be a useful tool if you know how to use them and stay vigilant about paying them off, but for most Americans, it is clearly not worth taking the chance. As soon as you let your guard down, you could be at risk of a vicious cycle of compounding debt that's difficult to pay off and you'll be spending thousands on fees and interest.

If credit card debt wasn't bad enough, PayDay loans charge upwards of 400% interest. People who fall prey to these predatory loans are usually poor and struggling to pay their bills. These companies know that their borrowers might be just one setback away from not being able to pay their rent or feed their families. That's why they can get away with charging so much in interest. They've got their borrowers over a barrel. When we get in a financial bind, we become susceptible to scams. That's why we must be extremely diligent with our finances and always assume that if something seems too good to be true, it almost certainly is.

HOW TO PLAY
THE CREDIT GAME

Credit card companies literally bank on the hope that their users won't be financially literate enough to reap the benefits of having their card without paying interest. In today's society, you can't do much without having a credit card. You need them for checking into hotels, making online purchases, renting a car, etc. But just because they've made it so you have to use their products, doesn't mean you have to get scammed by high interest and fees. Here's a few ways you can outsmart the banks and win the credit game:

1. Recognize that the credit card game is dangerous.

   Credit cards are so popular because the banks are counting on you to be a financial idiot, just like the average American. You need to have the right mindset to win. That starts with understanding that every time you swipe the card you are borrowing money from the bank at an extraordinary interest rate. The money is not yours, it's theirs and every time you use your credit card you are borrowing money from them.

2. Don't use over 30% of your available credit.

   If you don't have the money and you've already used over 30% of your available credit, don't make the purchase. Going above 30% could hurt your credit score, but more importantly, that $50 shirt could wind up costing you $100 if your credit card balance starts to spin out of control.

3. Pay off your credit card balances IN FULL each month. Period.

   Carrying a balance on your credit card is like stuffing your hard-earned money into the pockets of a bunch of rich bankers. It's the worst kind of loan you could get (aside from PayDay loans). If you need a loan (and you probably don't), get a lower-interest loan from your bank. Don't use your credit cards as a loan that you pay off over time. This is the fastest way to stay poor.

4. NEVER use your credit card for cash advances.

Not only does the bank charge you a higher interest rate on cash advances (up to 25%), but they also charge cash advance fees, anywhere from 3% to 5% of the advance. They start charging you interest right away, because there's no grace period, like there is for purchases. You'll lose money from the moment you get the advance, and if you need one, you've got much bigger problems. Instead of getting the cash advance, cut up your credit card and close your account. In your situation your credit card is your very worst enemy.

5. Don't be stupid.

Don't put purchases on your credit card unless you know you're able to pay the balance off within the statement month. Some credit cards require you to use their card to get deals on airline purchases, for instance. But you should only buy those tickets if you have the money in your account to pay off the balance. Don't rely on credit cards for emergencies. Doing so is like grabbing onto an anchor while you're drowning. Your credit card won't help keep you afloat. It will drag you down to the bottom of the ocean. Just imagine all the stuff you would need to do if your cards were all maxed out and start doing that NOW. Then, when you get a handle on things, you can start putting money aside in an emergency savings account and use that instead.

YOUR CREDIT SCORE

Credit card debt hurts your credit score, and having a low credit score can cost you money. The lower your credit score, the harder it will be for you to get low-interest loans and buy property. Your credit score is negatively impacted when you carry a balance of more than 30% of your credit allowance on your account. But do not get confused! Your credit score is NOT helped if you carry a balance of 30%, or any balance at all for that matter. This is a bizarre belief that costs people thousands. This falsehood is so prominent, we often wonder if it wasn't a rumor started by the credit card companies themselves to increase their profits.

Not only does a low credit score keep you from getting good loans with lower interest payments, but they could also affect your insurance premiums. It can even determine what types of jobs you get. In most states, employers are allowed to pull your credit report when they're making hiring and promotion decisions (another great reason to have a side hustle). Landlords might not want to rent to you if you have a low credit score. Once you do find a place to rent, utility and internet companies may require a deposit before they'll give you access to their services. Even the military takes notice. For example, more than one Special Forces candidate has been rejected because of bad credit. The thinking goes, if you can't even manage your own personal finances, why on earth would we trust you with making good decisions on the battlefield? Since you are such a financial wreck, you could also be vulnerable to betraying your country for money. You may argue that credit scores are bullshit and we shouldn't have them. But the reality is, they're a part of our system and they can have a real impact on your life. So keep in mind that your financial health requires you to be strict with yourself when it comes to your credit score.

MANAGING DEBT WHILE INVESTING IN YOUR FUTURE

Managing debt is an important financial skill. And credit card debt is one of the worst kinds of debt. While credit card debt is a serious concern, you can pay it down while also saving and investing. This can be a smart move, because if you're only focused on paying off debt without saving and you encounter an emergency, you'll have no savings and will have to rack up debt again to take care of it.

Do not try to pay off all of your debt before you start investing. Why? Because for many Americans, becoming debt free won't happen until they are old and gray, and the most important ingredient in investing is time. For example, even if you tackle credit card debt, student loan debt and mortgages can take decades to pay off. Your financial freedom demands that you not wait – you need to start investing ASAP. For example, even if you are paying most of your discretionary income to high-interest debt payments, at least start saving and investing 1% of your income. After you have paid off your credit card debt, you can use that money to increase your investing.

One way to ensure you're saving and investing in your future while also paying off your debt, is to allocate a percentage of your income to each item. For instance, you may have the goal of reserving 30% of your income for paying off debt, saving, and investing. You could pay 20% of that toward your debts and put 10% into investments. If the bulk of your debt is high interest, you might need to allocate 29% to debt and just 1% to investing to get started. Once your debt is paid off, you'll have the freedom to put the full 30% toward investments. As long as you're making consistent progress on your debt, and you're not racking up any more, you'll be able to pay it off while still building up your investments. This will give you more time to generate higher returns. If you stay committed and consistent, you'll be able to manage your debt and prevent yourself from carrying credit card debt in the future.

MAKE A SPENDING PLAN AND STICK TO IT

In the age of the internet, there's no excuse for not knowing how to make a spending plan. The word "budget" sounds too much like the word "diet," which is all about cutting out delicious things in your life. Instead of that, we like to approach it as a spending plan – where you focus on spending your money where you want it most – directed toward your financial freedom. Start with your top 3 (or more) financial goals and allocate a percentage of your income to each. For example, your top 3 financial goals might be:

1. Financial Freedom at age 40: 30%
2. Down payment on a 3,000-square-foot home in Boulder, Colorado: 20%
3. Family European Vacation: 5%

Once you've decided where you want the money to go, you can then just make cuts in areas you don't care so much about. There are plenty of free budgeting spreadsheets online to get you started. Once you have your spreadsheet, it's time to go through all of your expenses. Scour your credit cards to find subscriptions you didn't know you still had. Add up how many coffees you bought at the local coffee shop. Find all the places you can cut back, cancel memberships and subscriptions, and stop unnecessary spending. If you can't pay off your credit cards every month, everything must go. No streaming services, no Amazon purchases, no eating out or getting iced coffees, no new clothes. This is for your own good. You need to have eagle-eye focus on one thing and one thing only, paying off your credit cards as fast as possible. Borrow books from the library instead of buying them, wear hand-me-downs, work on that side hustle, do whatever it takes. Credit card debt is like financial slavery. You're not free until you've paid it all off. Is that iced coffee really worth your financial freedom?

Figure out how much you can save and what percentage of your income you can allot to debt, emergency savings, savings for other goals, and investing for your financial freedom. Everything else is second priority. If you need to move back into your parents' house, get a few roommates, get a second job, or get a side hustle to increase your income, do it. Figure out how long it will take you to reach your goal of paying off your debt according to how much you can pay each month and stick to it. Put your spending plan up in a place you will see it every day. If vision boards are your thing, put pictures of your financial goals and what being financially free looks and feels like to you to keep you motivated. Treat credit card balances like a financial illness that you must concentrate all of your time, energy, and effort into curing.

HOW TO STOP CREDIT CARD SPENDING

If you lack self-control when it comes to credit card spending, we recommend you dive into Dr. Brad's other books about financial psychology, such as *Mind Over Money* or *Money Mammoth*, to figure out why you're prone to sabotaging yourself financially. But in the meantime, there are ways you can help yourself when you feel compelled to spend more than you have.

- Delay gratification – this is when you delay spending by prioritizing your values over what feels good in the moment. You can delay gratification with credit card purchases by putting your credit card in a block of ice in the freezer so you have to wait for it to thaw before you can make the purchase.
- Pay for everything with cash – If there is a larger purchase you want to make, like for an appliance, save the money and buy it with cash instead of using your credit card. Teach yourself to wait until you have the money before you make purchases. Studies show we spend less when we use cash, because it makes our spending more conscious.

- Write your financial goals on sticky notes and put them in your wallet and in the drawer where you keep your credit cards. Make sure you look at your goals and affirm your values every day, so you're not just refraining from spending in the moment, but also choosing something better in the long run.
- Lower your expenses and stick to a budget – When it comes to credit card debt, a major reason people carry debt is because they live beyond their means. Is that new pair of shoes or fancy dinner worth sacrificing your financial goals?

We challenge the nay-sayers who spread misinformation that you HAVE to carry a credit card balance in order to have good credit. The opposite is true. Credit scores tank when you carry balances on your credit cards. If you want to start thinking rich, you'll have to free yourself from the debt cycle so you start building wealth.

Chapter 20 *Start Thinking Rich* Challenge

Make a get-out-of-debt payment plan so you can free yourself from financial slavery. Get strict and creative! Make it a game to pay off your debt as quickly as possible so you save and invest more. Use the snowball method, where you tackle the highest interest debt first and work your way down to the lowest. When you have finished paying off the highest interest debt, move on to the next highest, combining those payments to the debt and so on until you have wiped them out. If you keep getting into trouble with your credit cards, cut them up and delete them from your online retail accounts. By the end of this challenge, you should have a firm rule that unless you have the ability to pay off your credit card balances each month, you're not allowed to use credit cards.

CHAPTER TWENTY-ONE

YOU'LL BE POOR FOREVER IF YOU DON'T START THINKING RICH

While money doesn't solve all of life's problems, it sure does solve a lot of them. The famous psychologist Abraham Maslow theorized that our motivation in life is driven by physiological and psychological human needs. He summarized this theory in what has come to be known as Maslow's Hierarchy of needs. Maslow identified five human needs that go from basic to complex. You need to resolve the most basic ones before you even care about the others.

But one thing is consistent with all five needs – in today's world you need money to meet them. But the fact is, having financial abundance can set you up to go far beyond just meeting them. Wealth gives you the opportunity to enhance and maximize your experiences in life. We truly believe that everyone reading this book can become rich. In this chapter we have an honest discussion about how money can be used to enhance your experiences in life. We want this for you, and if you are willing to put in the work, we think you deserve it.

LEVEL 1: BASIC SURVIVAL

It's hard to think about investing when you are worried about where you will get your next meal. These are the basics of human survival: clean water, nourishing food, adequate clothing, warmth, and sleep. It is easy to forget in America, but most people throughout human history and around the world today do not have enough money to meet these very basic needs. But wealth can take you beyond just basic survival. You can enjoy fine dining, high-quality clothes, and even better sleep on a more luxurious mattress.

LEVEL 2: SAFETY AND SECURITY

We all need protection from the elements, physical security, law, order, and freedom from a daily fear of survival. You have to have money to put a roof over your head, to live in a safe neighborhood, and/or to escape from a dangerous country to one that provides basic safety and security. Beyond physical safety, wealth can help us feel safe in other ways.

- *Financial security*. With wealth you are no longer worried about being able to meet your basic needs or to cover unexpected expenses. Wealth can offer a peace of mind that is priceless.
- *Health security*. Wealth will not only allow you to afford health insurance, top-notch healthcare services, access to specialized treatments, and wellness programs, ensuring you and your family receive the best possible care.

LEVEL 3: LOVE AND CONNECTION

When we are no longer worried about our basic survival, we can shift to focusing on our emotional needs. These needs include having close and supportive relationships with family, friends, and an intimate partner.

- *Mate selection*. As sad as it may seem from an idyllic romantic point of view, money (or the promise of future money) is often needed to attract a quality mate, especially for men.
- *Investing in relationships*. Money helps us stay connected with family and friends. Wealth can help us travel to spend time with family without worrying about the costs, but perhaps even more importantly, can free up our time so we can spend it nurturing our relationship with family and friends.
- *Legacy building*. Wealth offers the opportunity to leave a lasting legacy for future generations. Whether through inheritance, philanthropy, or establishing foundations, you can make a meaningful impact that extends beyond your lifetime.

LEVEL 4: SELF-ESTEEM

Social status and feelings of accomplishment are important to our happiness. This includes having a meaningful career and role in society. Money plays a big part in this, as it can give us the opportunity to pursue the education and training we want to give us a sense of purpose and make a name for ourselves. Wealth can help you raise your self-esteem needs in several ways.

- *Exclusive opportunities.* Wealth can give you access to exclusive opportunities. These can include access to prestigious schools, exclusive memberships, or unique networking opportunities. This can lead to personal and professional growth as well as expanding your social network.
- *Investment opportunities.* Wealth makes it possible to invest in diverse opportunities, potentially leading to even greater wealth. This includes traditional investments such as stocks, but also real estate, start-ups, buying into businesses, and other private equity ventures.
- *Luxurious experiences.* Wealth can give you access to higher-end goods, services, and experiences that enhance your comfort and convenience.

LEVEL 5: REACHING YOUR HIGHEST POTENTIAL

The highest human need in Maslow's hierarchy is focused on self-fulfillment. It involves immersing ourselves in creative endeavors and achieving our full potential. Wealth can help us achieve our full potential in several ways.

- *Freedom of choice.* With freedom of choice, we can pursue hobbies, travel, or other experiences without being worried about lost income or not being able to afford it.
- *Freedom of time.* Wealth allows you to prioritize activities that bring you joy and fulfillment, whether it's spending time with loved ones, pursuing passions, or traveling.
- *Ability to support causes.* Wealth allows you to transcend worries about yourself and your immediate family. It gives you the opportunity to contribute to charitable causes, support research, or fund projects that align with your values so that you can feel a sense of purpose and make a positive impact on society.

Without money it is impossible for us to adequately meet our needs. But having an abundance of resources can help us expand our experiences and truly invest in our sense of passion and purpose and connection with others. As we discussed in Chapter 1, being poor sucks. But the fact is, being rich is awesome. And if you are willing to start thinking rich and doing what rich people do, you can become rich too.

Adrian: Two years after graduating college with a business degree my salary was just $33,000. I drove a used Camry, lived in a small duplex, got groceries at Walmart, and rarely ate out. I taught hip-hop dance as a side hustle and performed every weekend at the local Diamond Jo Casino 80s club night from 8 p.m. to 1 a.m. Fridays and Saturday nights (which paid me $25 an hour, much more than my day job). The extra money I'd make from my two side hustles allowed me to start saving and putting away money into my Roth IRA.

Despite being one financial hardship away from being broke I was making enough money to put food on the table and a roof over my head. I was making a small positive impact in the world with the resources I had. I was trying to live the best version of my life at that time and if you were to ask people what I was like, they would have said Adrian is "happy, positive, and energetic." I was a dreamer but also ambitious and disciplined enough to spend countless hours learning how to become a full-time internet entrepreneur.

I used to dream of a day where I didn't have to clock in and out of work, where I didn't have to worry about money, and where I could retire my parents. Today, every two weeks I make what it used to take me a whole year to make. I have several millions of dollars invested that pay dividends high enough to cover my entire cost of living. I buy my vehicles in cash. I hired both my parents and my wife and what I do to make money doesn't feel like "work," because of how much I enjoy it. I recently took a three-month trip to Asia flying first class, fully embracing lifestyle design, making decisions based on "wants" instead of just needs, and the freedom of time to travel long and slow. The positive impact I make in the world today goes beyond what I had ever thought was possible.

If you met me today, you would probably describe me as "happy, positive, and energetic." I am the same person as before, just with more experience. I am still trying to live my best life. I am grateful that I started thinking rich at the age of 20. I dream of a day where I can say I've helped millions of others *Start Thinking Rich* too.

Dr. Brad: I know what it is like to go to bed hungry. I know what it is like to feel ashamed because you can't afford to wear nice clothes. I know what it is like to see tears in your mother's eyes when she tells you she is sorry you can't take a karate lesson because she can't afford it. I know what it is like to be stuck on the side of the highway for hours, because your piece-of-shit car broke down and you couldn't afford a mobile phone to call for help. I know what it is like to see the smirk on the face of a gas station attendant when you hand him $2.50, because that was all the money you had to put gas into your tank. I know what it is like to leave school with $100,000 in student loan debt. I know what it is like to sleep on a mattress on the floor and to work 70 hours a week. I know what it is like to feel so desperate that you fall for get-rich-quick scams and lose what little money you have. The fact is, being poor sucks and I want you to become rich instead.

But I don't care how much money you make: if you don't own your TIME, then you ain't rich. If you can't choose how to spend your most valuable resource – your time – then your big mansion is just your prison. I have been able to go from a net worth of negative $100,000 to multi-millionaire in two short decades, but I'm just getting started. What I am most proud of, though, is that I can use my time to write this book for you. I can go on vacation with my family and not worry about mortgage payments. I can take a day, or a week, or a month off and not be stressed about making ends meet. I can go to my boys' school events and coach their Little League baseball teams without losing money. I want you to own your time so that you can spend it doing what matters most to you. Like Adrian, I am a minimalist at heart, and I have focused on designing my life so that I can have the best possible experiences. If you have seen me on social media, you have probably seen my tagline: *experiences > stuff*. If you don't own your time because you're a slave to your Tesla payments, big fat mortgage, and credit card debt, your addiction to stuff is keeping you from having great experiences. Don't get derailed on your road to wealth with an obsession on the latest gadgets and most expensive cars you can buy.

If you want to have the awesome experience of being rich, don't act like the average American. Instead, focus on making investing for your financial freedom your top financial priority, so you can own your TIME. Stay focused on what matters. Being rich is awesome, you deserve it, and it is well within your grasp. We believe in you. You've got this. And please stay in touch to let us know how you are doing along your journey and whatever challenges you are facing along the way by going to StartThinkingRich.com.

ABOUT THE AUTHORS

Bradley T. Klontz, PsyD, CFP® is an expert in financial psychology, financial planning, and applied behavioral finance. He's an Associate Professor of Practice at Creighton University Heider College of Business, Co-Founder of the Financial Psychology Institute, and Managing Principal of YMW Advisors. Dr. Brad has over 1.4 million followers on social media, where he creates content aimed at increasing financial wellness. You can connect with Dr. Brad on social media @DrBradKlontz and learn more about him at www.BradKlontz.com.

Dr. Brad is a Fellow of the American Psychological Association, and a Former President of the Hawaii Psychological Association. He was awarded the Innovative Practice Presidential Citation from the American Psychological Association for his application of psychological interventions to help people with money and wealth issues and his innovative practice in financial psychology for practitioners across the country.

Dr. Brad has been a columnist for the *Journal of Financial Planning*, *On Wall Street*, and PsychologyToday.com. His work has been featured on ABC News's *20/20, Good Morning America*, and in *USA Today, Wall Street Journal, New York Times, Washington Post, Los Angeles Times, Time, Kiplinger's, Money magazine,* NPR, and many other media outlets and professional magazines and journals.

He was appointed to the CNBC Financial Advisor Council in 2023 and received the 2018 and 2021 Montgomery-Warschauer Awards from the Financial Planning Association, honoring the most outstanding contribution to the betterment of the financial planning profession. Dr. Brad has partnered with organizations including Capital One, JP Morgan Chase, Mutual of Omaha, and H&R Block in efforts to help raise public awareness around issues related to financial health and financial psychology.

Dr. Brad is co-author/co-editor of nine books on the psychology of money: *Start Thinking Rich* (Wiley, 2025) with Adrian Brambila, *Psychology of Financial Planning* (Wiley, 2023) with Drs. Ted Klontz and Charles Chaffin, *The Practitioner's Toolkit* (Wiley, 2023) with Drs. Ted Klontz and Charles Chaffin, *Money Mammoth* (Wiley, 2020) with Drs. Ted Klontz and Edward Horwitz, *Facilitating Financial Health* (NUCO, 2008; 2016) with Dr. Ted Klontz and Rick Kahler, *Financial Therapy* (Springer, 2015) with Drs. Kristy Archuleta and Sonya Lutter, *Mind Over Money* (Broadway Business, 2009) with Dr. Ted Klontz, *Wired for Wealth* (HCI, 2008) with Dr. Ted Klontz and Rick Kahler, and *The Financial Wisdom of Ebenezer Scrooge* (HCI, 2005; 2008) with Dr. Ted Klontz and Rick Kahler.

Adrian Brambila, an internet entrepreneur and former professional dancer for T-Pain, has become a leading figure in online marketing. With over 1.7 million followers on social media, Adrian's transition from the entertainment industry to digital entrepreneurship is remarkable. As a professional robot dancer for T-Pain, he captivated audiences, but his entrepreneurial spirit set him apart.

Adrian is recognized as one of the top affiliate marketers in the world, having generated tens of millions in revenue. His journey to success took an unconventional turn during the pandemic when he lived in a van and traveled across the United States. Documenting his experiences, he showcased how he was making upwards of $100,000 per month online and how wealth and minimalism can coexist. This unique approach resonated with many, turning him into a viral sensation and a source of inspiration for aspiring entrepreneurs.

Adrian's story and various online business ventures have been featured on prominent platforms such as *America's Got Talent*, Shopify, Alibaba .com, *Vox*, *Entrepreneur*, and *Business Insider*. His ability to generate substantial income through innovative online strategies has made him a sought-after speaker and consultant in the digital marketing world.

Adrian grew up in Fallbrook, California, and graduated from the University of Dubuque in 2011. He is the founder of Bramify, The Brambila Method, and Affiliate Automation. To learn more about Adrian and to receive free money tips sent to your inbox weekly, sign up for his email newsletter on Adrianbrambila.com.

ACKNOWLEDGMENTS

ADRIAN'S ACKNOWLEDGMENTS

The first person I want to thank is my wife, Ashley. As my dad likes to joke: "Adrian knew he was going to be an entrepreneur and make a lot of money, which is why he needed to marry someone who was going to be a CPA!" That is not a real thought I ever had, but it's a family joke that always gets my wife to roll her eyes with a smile.

My wife is my true partner in all things, including the making of this book. She is my CFO in life and business. She jokes that I make the bread, but she "turns it into a mother f***ing bakery" and I couldn't agree more.

I have to thank my mom, Leticia, and dad, Tony. You both instilled such great financial habits in me at a young age, and watching you as a kid work hard to improve our quality of life as a family shaped me to be the person I am today. It's because of both of you I have a strong work ethic and am disciplined with my money. Thank you both for being the best role models on what it takes to come from nothing and earn your success.

A major thanks to everyone who bought this book because you knew me from my past or from watching my content. I hope the gifts of knowledge in this book deliver as much value to you as my gratitude for you.

DR. BRAD'S ACKNOWLEDGMENTS

Many thanks to my wife, Joni. Thank you for your dedication to our relationship and for helping to create a stable, loving, nurturing, and supportive home for our children. I feel so lucky to have you as a partner and to be on this journey with you.

I would also like to express my deepest love to my sons, Logan and Ethan. You both inspire me to be a better person. Special thanks to Ethan for helping us choose the title of this book!

I want to thank my loving sister and parents and stepparents: Brenda, Wanda and Jim, and Ted and Marjorie. I am so blessed to have your enduring love and support.

Lastly, I want to acknowledge you, the reader. You bought this book because you want to create a better life for yourself and your family. I am truly inspired by your courage to face harsh truths, your commitment to self-improvement, and, by extension, your dedication to making the world a better place. Through these pages I am dedicated to telling you the truth and bringing you love, joy, and abundance.

APPENDIX

ADRIAN'S ANALYSIS OF THE COST OF A HOME VERSUS RENTING

HOMEOWNERSHIP METRICS:

In summary, below are the metrics used and the basis behind each amount:

Metric	Fixed or Variable	Basis
Purchase Price	Fixed	Average Today
Down Payment	Fixed	Average (6% & 17%)
Interest Rate	Fixed	Average Past 30 Years
Property Taxes	Variable	Today's Rate + Adjusted for Inflation
Home Insurance	Variable	Average Today + Adjusted for Inflation
Annual Rent	Variable	Average Today + Adjusted for Inflation

Home Value Purchase Price – The home value was determined by the average home value cost in the specific area based on available information.

Down Payment – The average first-time homebuyer pays about 6% of the home price for their down payment while repeat buyers on average put down 17%, so I performed the analysis on both 6% and 17%. Private mortgage interest (PMI) is required when a down payment on a home is under 20%. I have incorporated PMI into the analysis when 6% and 17% was used as the down payment. Private mortgage insurance rates typically range from 0.19% to 2.25% of your mortgage and can vary based on credit score. Most home mortgage calculators use an average of 0.5% as a default for PMI costs. I did the same in my analysis.

Interest Rate – A challenging metric to determine is the interest rate. Interest rates fluctuate daily and are based off an individual's credit score. The average credit score for first-time homebuyers is in the mid-700s. At the timing of writing this book, the interest rates for home mortgages with a good credit score is around 7%. The average interest rate over the course of thirty years is 5.71%. Since interest rates are constantly changing, I felt it best to use the average over the past 30 years of 5.71%.

Property Taxes – *Ouch*, no one likes to talk about taxes and property taxes is no different. Property tax rates are different based on location but are typically calculated using the home value base multiplied by a specific rate annually. The changes in tax rates year over year depends on the local jurisdiction laws. After an election year, you may see your property rate increase or decrease. Or your county may choose to appraise your home so the home value base increased (therefore, increasing your total property tax). For example, in Travis Country (Austin, Texas), your home value can increase by a maximum of 10% every year if the housing market supports this increase! Additionally, it can increase beyond the maximum 10% if improvements were made to the property. That hurts! I used the average property tax rate available for each location and adjusted for inflation. The 30-year Breakeven Inflation Rate was 2.26% in February 2024, according to the United States Federal Reserve. In the analysis, I used an annual increase in home insurance premiums of 2.25%.

Home Insurance – Another metric that can be difficult to determine is the cost of home insurance. Each year, your home insurance premium can increase based on a number of factors: claims history, location of home, home's age and condition, and increase in cost of materials. It can be expected that even without any claim history your home insurance premiums will increase over the course of 30 years. For purposes of this analysis, the home insurance premium will increase over time close to the rate of inflation. As mentioned previously, the 30-year Breakeven Inflation Rate was 2.26% in February 2024, according to the United States Federal Reserve. In the analysis, I used an annual increase in home insurance premiums of 2.25%.

Closing Costs – The transaction of purchasing and selling a home results in closing costs. Closing costs can be negotiated, especially in the buying position. However, the seller usually pays an average of 10% of sale price in closing costs.

Appreciation of Home – I used the average appreciation rate of homes in the United States over 30 years. The average appreciation rate is 3.8%.

RENTING METRICS:

Annual Rent – Let's state the obvious. We can assume that rent will not remain the same over the course of 30 years. Determining the appropriate rent increase each year can be tricky. If you have rented before, you can imagine the difficulty in pinpointing the annual rent increase to be used in this analysis as you probably have experienced fluctuations in your own experience. Are you renewing your lease? If yes, you may not see a rent increase at all. Or you may see a rent increase aligned with inflation. Are you changing apartment complexes? You will most likely see a larger jump in rent costs.

In this analysis, we are assuming that the homeowner is staying in the same home for 30 years. As such, we are going to assume the same thing about the renter – that they would be renting the same place for 30 years. While average rent increase has outpaced inflation over the past 30 years, this metric uses all rent increases, including vacant doors, not just lease renewals. The 30-year Breakeven Inflation Rate was 2.26% in February 2024, according to the United States Federal Reserve. I used an annual rent increase of 2.5% for my analysis, slightly above the inflation rate of 2.26%.

To evaluate whether owning a home is the best investment, I determined the average monthly cost of owning a home compared to the average monthly cost to rent. In each scenario run, the person renting would save money each month if renting. Next, I took the money from the down deposit and the average monthly savings and invested them in an index fund that mirrors the S&P 500. Using the average rate of return for the S&P 500 over the past 30 years and the average appreciation value of the homes in the specific area, I calculated the net value of each investment after 30 years. Did the homeowner's house investment or the renter's index fund investment have a higher value after 30 years?

As you can see from the analysis, there was not a single scenario in which the home outperformed the index fund. Not even close. I even took it a step further and looked at increasing the rent rates annually by 8.86%. I kept the conservative increase in home insurance and property taxes to mirror inflation over the past 30 years. The only metric that changed was rent. Due to the compounding effect of the rent increase, you would eventually start to pay more each year in rent compared to homeowner- ship. However, the initial down deposit amount and subsequent monthly rent savings in those initial years produced a greater net return in the index fund compared to the home investment.

USA Average 6% Down Payment

Location	USA Average
Home Value	$417,000
Down Payment (6%)	$25,020
Mortgage	$391,980
Mortgage	30 Year Fixed
Interest	5.71%
PMI	108 Months

Other Metrics Increased Each Year:

Insurance Year 1	$2,151.00
Property Tax Rate	1.02%
Property Tax Year 1	$4,253.40
Rent Year 1	$20,556.00

After 30 Years:	Home Ownership
Original Home Value	$417,000
Annual Appreciation Rate	3.80%
Appreciated Value	$1,276,605
Cash Spent:	
Down Payment	$25,020
Mortgage Payments	$837,553
Insurance Payments	$90,762
Property Taxes	$179,473
	$1,132,808
Closing Costs on Sale (10%)	$127,661
Total Gain on Home Ownership	**$16,137**

After 30 Years:	Rent Savings Invested in S&P500
Initial Contribution	$25,020
Total Costs Rent vs Owning	
Rent Total Cost	-$902,464
Mortgage Payments	$837,553
Insurance Payments	$90,762
Property Payments	$179,473
Total Savings	$205,324
Monthly Savings	$570
Investment (10%)	$1,795,547
Cash Spent	$230,344
Total Gain on Renting	**$1,565,203**

USA Average 17% Down Payment

Location	USA Average
Home Value	$417,000
Down Payment (17%)	$70,890
Mortgage	$346,110
Mortgage	30 Year Fixed
Interest	5.71%
PMI	31 Months

Other Metrics Increased Each Year:

Insurance Year 1	$2,151.00
Property Tax Rate	1.02%
Property Tax Year 1	$4,253.40
Rent Year 1	$20,556.00

After 30 Years:	Home Ownership
Original Home Value	$417,000
Annual Appreciation Rate	3.80%
Appreciated Value	$1,276,605
Cash Spent:	
Down Payment	$70,890
Mortgage Payments	$728,438
Insurance Payments	$90,762
Property Taxes	$179,473
	$1,069,563
Closing Costs on Sale (10%)	$127,661
Total Gain on Home Ownership	**$79,382**

After 30 Years:	Rent Savings Invested in S&P500
Initial Contribution	$70,890
Total Costs Rent vs Owning	
Rent Total Cost	-$902,464
Mortgage Payments	$728,438
Insurance Payments	$90,762
Property Payments	$179,473
Total Savings	$96,209
Monthly Savings	$267
Investment (10%)	$2,014,853
Cash Spent	$167,099
Total Gain on Renting	**$1,847,754**

Dallas, Texas, Average 6% Down Payment

Location	Dallas, TX
Home Value	$308,000.00
Down Payment (6%)	$18,480.00
Mortgage	$289,520.00
Mortgage	30 Year Fixed
Interest	5.71%
PMI	108 Months

Other Metrics Increased Each Year:

Insurance Year 1	$3,200.00
Property Tax Rate	2.22%
Property Tax Year 1	$6,837.60
Rent Year 1	$18,900.00

After 30 Years:	Home Ownership
Original Home Value	$308,000
Annual Appreciation Rate	3.35%
Appreciated Value	$827,685
Cash Spent:	
Down Payment	$18,480
Mortgage Payments	$618,624
Insurance Payments	$135,025
Property Taxes	$288,514
	$1,060,643
Closing Costs on Sale (10%)	$82,769
Total Gain on Home Ownership	**-$315,726**

After 30 Years:	Rent Savings Invested in S&P500
Initial Contribution	$18,480
Total Costs Rent vs Owning	
Rent Total Cost	-$829,761
Mortgage Payments	$618,624
Insurance Payments	$135,025
Property Payments	$288,514
Total Savings	$212,402
Monthly Savings	$590
Investment (10%)	$1,711,397
Cash Spent	$230,882
Total Gain on Renting	**$1,480,515**

Dallas, Texas, Average 17% Down Payment

Location	Dallas TX
Home Value	$308,000.00
Down Payment (17%)	$52,360.00
Mortgage	$255,640.00
Mortgage	30 Year Fixed
Interest	5.71%
PMI	31 Months

Other Metrics Increased Each Year:

Insurance Year 1	$3,200.00
Property Tax Rate	2.22%
Property Tax Year 1	$6,837.60
Rent Year 1	$18,900.00

After 30 Years:	Home Ownership
Original Home Value	$308,000
Annual Appreciation Rate	3.35%
Appreciated Value	$827,685
Cash Spent:	
Down Payment	$52,360
Mortgage Payments	$538,031
Insurance Payments	$135,025
Property Taxes	$288,514
	$1,013,931
Closing Costs on Sale (10%)	$82,769
Total Gain on Home Ownership	**-$269,014**

After 30 Years:	Rent Savings Invested in S&P500
Initial Contribution	$52,360
Total Costs Rent vs Owning	
Rent Total Cost	-$829,761
Mortgage Payments	$538,031
Insurance Payments	$135,025
Property Payments	$288,514
Total Savings	$131,810
Monthly Savings	$366
Investment (10%)	$1,872,919
Cash Spent	$184,170
Total Gain on Renting	**$1,688,750**

REFERENCES

CHAPTER 1

Falvey, J. R., Hajduk, A. M., and Keys, C. R. (2022, February 21). *Association of Financial Strain with Mortality Among Older US Adults Recovering From an Acute Myocardial Infarction.* Jama Network. https://jamanetwork.com/journals/jamainternalmedicine/fullarticle/2788997.

Kahneman, D., Deaton, A. High income improves evaluation of life but not emotional well-being. *Proceedings of the National Academy of Sciences* 107, 16489–93 (2010).

Killingsworth, M. A. (2021). Experienced well-being rises with income, even above $75,000 per year. *Proceedings of the National Academy of Sciences, 118*(4). https://doi.org/10.1073/pnas.2016976118.

Luby, J., Constantino, J., and Barch, D. (2022, March 1). Poverty and developing brain. *Cerebrum: The Dana Forum on Brain Science.* https://www.ncbi.nlm.nih.gov/pmc/articles/PMC9224364/.

Oacas Library Guides: Poverty and Child Welfare: Effects of poverty on families. Effects of poverty on families – Poverty and child welfare – OACAS Library Guides at Ontario Association of Children's Aid Societies. (n.d.). https://oacas.libguides.com/c.php?g=702168&p=4992460.

Shrider, Emily A., Creamer, John. (2023b, September 12). *Poverty in the United States: 2022.* Census.gov. https://www.census.gov/library/publications/2023/demo/p60-280.html#:~:text=The%20official%20poverty%20rate%20in,and%20Table%20A%2D1.

CHAPTER 2

"Capitalism Definition and Meaning." Merriam-Webster. Accessed April 17, 2024. https://www.merriam-webster.com/dictionary/capitalism.

Klontz, Bradley T., and Sonya L. Britt. "How Clients' Money Scripts Predict Their Financial Behaviors." Financial Planning Association, November 1, 2012. https://www.financialplanningassociation.org/article/journal/NOV12-how-clients-money-scripts-predict-their-financial-behaviors.

Klontz, Bradley T., Paul Sullivan, Martin C. Seay, and Anthony Canale. "The Wealthy: A Financial Psychological Profile." *Consulting Psychology Journal: Practice and Research* 67, no. 2 (June 2015): 127–43. https://doi.org/10.1037/cpb0000027.

Taylor, C. D., Klontz, B., and Lawson, D. (2017). Money disorders and locus of Control: Implications for assessment and treatment. *Journal of Financial Therapy*, 8(1). https://doi.org/10.4148/1944-9771.1121.

CHAPTER 3

Berger, Rob. "What Is the 4% Rule for Retirement Withdrawals?" *Forbes*, February 19, 2023. https://www.forbes.com/advisor/retirement/four-percent-rule-retirement/.

McBride, G. (2023, May 2). Target-date funds: What they are, how they work. *Bankrate.* https://www.bankrate.com/retirement/target-date-funds-pros-and-cons/.

Staff, F. (2023, September 12). 70% of millionaires work with advisors, Northwestern Mutual says. *Financial Advisor.* https://www.fa-mag.com/news/financial-planning-is-top-of-mind-for-millionaires--study-says-74597.html.

CHAPTER 4

"18 Bible Verses About Wealth and Prosperity." Kenneth Copeland Ministries. Accessed January 26, 2024. https://www.kcm.org/real-help/finances/apply/18-bible-verses-about-wealth-and-prosperity.

Klontz, B. T., Sullivan, P., Seay, M. C., and Canale, A. (2015a). The wealthy: A financial psychological profile. *Consulting Psychology Journal: Practice and Research*, 67(2), 127–43. https://doi.org/10.1037/cpb0000027.

Klontz, B., Britt, S. L., Archuleta, K. L., and Klontz, T. (2012). Disordered money behaviors: Development of the Klontz Money Behavior Inventory. *Journal of Financial Therapy*, *3*(1). https://doi.org/10.4148/jft.v3i1.1485.

New American Bible, revised edition © 2010, 1991, 1986, 1970 Confraternity of Christian Doctrine, Inc., Washington, DC, 1 Timothy 6:10.

New American Bible, revised edition © 2010, 1991, 1986, 1970 Confraternity of Christian Doctrine, Inc., Washington, DC, Matthew 19:24.

New American Bible, © 1960, 1971, 1977, 1995, 2020, The Lockman Foundation, La Habra, CA, Matthew 19:21.

Ramsey Solutions. (2023, April 12). *The National Study of Millionaires*. https://www.ramseysolutions.com/retirement/the-national-study-of-millionaires-research.

CHAPTER 5

Gillespie, L. (2023, January 13). Average American debt statistics. Bankrate. https://www.bankrate.com/personal-finance/debt/average-american-debt/#average-american-household.

Reinicke, C. (2022, January 20). 56% of Americans can't cover a $1,000 emergency expense with savings. CNBC. https://www.cnbc.com/2022/01/19/56percent-of-americans-cant-cover-a-1000-emergency-expense-with-savings.html.

Schroders, Working Americans aged 45+ say it will take $1,100,000 saved to retire comfortably, but only one in five will get to a million. Homepage. (2023, April 4). https://www.schroders.com/en-us/us/individual/media-center/working-americans-aged-45-say-it-will-take-1-100-000-saved-to-retire-comfortably-but-only-one-in-five-will-get-to-a-million-/.

Statista Research Department. (2024, April 9). Monthly job losses U.S. 2024. Statista. https://www.statista.com/statistics/217824/seasonally-adjusted-monthly-number-of-job-losers-in-the-in-the-us/.

CHAPTER 8

Horowitz, Juliana Menasce. "How Americans View Their Jobs." Pew Research Center's Social & Demographic Trends Project, March 30, 2023. https://www.pewresearch.org/social-trends/2023/03/30/how-americans-view-their-jobs/.

CHAPTER 9

Burton, Neel. "The Psychology of Laziness." *Psychology Today*, October 25, 2014. https://www.psychologytoday.com/us/blog/hide-and-seek/201410/the-psychology-of-laziness.

Nickerson, Charlotte. "Learned Helplessness Theory in Psychology (Seligman): Examples & Coping." *Simply Psychology*, November 9, 2023. https://www.simplypsychology.org/learned-helplessness.html.

Psychology Today Staff. "Learned Helplessness." *Psychology Today*. Accessed February 26, 2024. https://www.psychologytoday.com/us/basics/learned-helplessness.

Taylor, C. D., Klontz, B., and Lawson, D. (2017). Money Disorders and Locus of Control: Implications for Assessment and Treatment. *Journal of Financial Therapy*, 8(1). https://doi.org/10.4148/1944-9771.1121.

CHAPTER 10

Denworth, Lydia. "Brain Waves Synchronize When People Interact." *Scientific American*, July 1, 2023. https://www.scientificamerican.com/article/brain-waves-synchronize-when-people-interact/.

CHAPTER 11

"Clothes and Jewelry." National Museum of Denmark. Accessed February 27, 2024. https://en.natmus.dk/historical-knowledge/denmark/prehistoric-period-until-1050-ad/the-viking-age/the-people/clothes-and-jewellery/.

Smeets, Paul, Whillans, A.V., Bekkers, Rene, and Norton, Michael I. "Time Use and Happiness of Millionaires: Evidence from the Netherlands." *Social Psychological and Personality Science* 11, no. 3 (April 2020): 295–307.

CHAPTER 12

"What Happens to Unpaid Debt after 7 Years." Chase. Accessed February 28, 2024. https://www.chase.com/personal/credit-cards/education/basics/what-happens-to-debt-after-7-years.

Dickler, Jessica. "At a Time When Most Americans Are Living Paycheck to Paycheck, the 'Quiet Luxury' Trend Takes Over." CNBC, June 10, 2023. https://www.cnbc.com/2023/06/10/quiet-luxury-may-be-americans-most-expensive-trend-to-date.html.

Landau, Elizabeth. "Study: Experiences Make Us Happier than Possessions." CNN. Accessed February 28, 2024. https://edition.cnn.com/2009/HEALTH/02/10/happiness.possessions/.

Loudenback, Tanza. "7 Psychological Traits of the Super Rich." *Business Insider*. Accessed February 27, 2024. https://www.businessinsider.com/psychological-traits-of-the-super-rich-2016-9#7-they-are-more-vigilant-about-their-money-7.

CHAPTER 13

"20 Famous Real Estate Investing Quotes." RealtyMogul, December 1, 2023. https://www.realtymogul.com/knowledge-center/article/20-famous-real-estate-investing-quotes.

"How Does a College Degree Improve Graduates' Employment and Earnings Potential?" APLU, February 23, 2024. https://www.aplu.org/our-work/4-policy-and-advocacy/publicuvalues/employment-earnings/.

Average length of homeownership: Americans spend less . . . (n.d.). https://www.thezebra.com/resources/home/average-length-of-homeownership.

Changes in U.S. family finances from 2019 to 2022. Federal Reserve. (n.d.). https://www.federalreserve.gov/publications/files/scf23.pdf.

Crew, Kcm. "Homeowner Net Worth Has Skyrocketed." *Keeping Current Matters*, November 7, 2023. https://www.keepingcurrentmatters.com/2023/11/07/homeowner-net-worth-has-skyrocketed/.

Kaplan, J. (n.d.). Meet the typical millionaire: They're over 55, have a house worth nearly 7 figures, and are probably moving to Scottsdale. *Business Insider*. https://www.businessinsider.com/who-are-americas-millionaires-white-gen-xers-boomers-educated-stocks-2024-1.

Kelly, Jack. "The Making of a Millionaire, and Why $100k Is No Longer the Benchmark Salary for Wealth in America." *Forbes*, February 20, 2024. https://www.forbes.com/sites/jackkelly/2023/05/23/the-making-of-a-millionaire-and-why-100k-is-no-longer-the-benchmark-salary-for-wealth-in-america/?sh=54e836b8af28.

Klontz, B., Britt, S. L., Mentzer, J., and Klontz, T. (2011). Money Beliefs and Financial Behaviors: Development of the Klontz Money Script Inventory. *Journal of Financial Therapy, 2*(1). https://doi.org/10.4148/jft.v2i1.451.

Guzman, G. and Kollar, M. (2023, August 15). *Income in the United States: 2022.* Census.gov. https://www.census.gov/data/tables/2023/demo/income-poverty/p60-279.html.

Lenihan, Ron. "U.S. Net Worth: How Much Wealthier Are Married Couples?" *The Street,* July 28, 2023. https://www.thestreet.com/personal-finance/us-net-worth-wealth-data-married-vs-single.

Median sales price of houses sold for the United States. FRED. (2024, January 25). https://fred.stlouisfed.org/series/MSPUS.

Planet, T. (2021, September 14). How long does a tenant stay? Tenant Planet, Inc. https://tenantplanet.com/blog/how-long-does-a-tenant-stay/#:~:text=So%2C%20how%20long%20does%20a,which%20to%20judge%20your%20performance.

Ramsey Solutions. (n.d.). The National Study of Millionaires. https://www.ramseysolutions.com/retirement/the-national-study-of-millionaires-research.

Trends in college pricing and student aid 2023. (n.d.). https://research.collegeboard.org/media/pdf/Trends%20Report%202023%20Updated.pdf.

Winters, M. (2024, March 24). The best- and worst-paying college majors, 5 years after graduation. CNBC. https://www.cnbc.com/2024/03/24/best-and-worst-paying-college-majors-5-years-after-graduation.html.

CHAPTER 14

"Retired Husband Syndrome." ABC News/GMA, January 10, 2006. https://abcnews.go.com/GMA/AmericanFamily/story?id=1491039.

Bertoni, M. and Brunello, G. (2017). Pappa Ante Portas: The effect of the husband's retirement on the wife's mental health in Japan. *Social Science and Medicine.*

Bjälkebring, Pär, Georg Henning, Daniel Västfjäll, Stephan Dickert, Yvonne Brehmer, Sandra Buratti, Isabelle Hansson, and Boo Johansson. "Helping out or Helping Yourself? Volunteering and Life Satisfaction across the Retirement Transition." *Psychology and Aging* 36, no. 1 (February 2021): 119–30. https://doi.org/10.1037/pag0000576.

Byles, Julie E. et al. "Gender, Mental Health, Physical Health and Retirement: A Prospective Study of 21,608 Australians Aged 55–69 Years." *Maturitas* 87 (May 2016): 40–48. https://doi.org/10.1016/j.maturitas.2016.02.011.

Fisher, Gwenith G. et al. "Mental Work Demands, Retirement, and Longitudinal Trajectories of Cognitive Functioning." *Journal of Occupational Health Psychology* 19, no. 2 (2014): 231–42. https://doi.org/10.1037/a0035724.

Oxford English Dictionary, "Retire."

Oxford English Dictionary, "Work."

Segel-Karpas, Dikla, Ayalon, Liat, and Lachman, Margie E. "Loneliness and Depressive Symptoms: The Moderating Role of the Transition into Retirement." *Aging and Mental Health* 22, no. 1 (September 13, 2016): 135–40. https://doi.org /10.1080/13607863.2016.1226770.

Watson, S. (2023, July 28). The emotional shock of retirement. WebMD. https:// www.webmd.com/healthy-aging/features/emotional-shock-retirement.

CHAPTER 15

Guagenti, Calogero. (n.d.). California Tax Calculator 2022-2023: Estimate Your Taxes. *Forbes Advisor*. Retrieved April 15, 2023. https://www.forbes. com/advisor/income-tax-calculator/california/?deductions=0&filing=single& income=1000000&ira=0&k401=0.

Hannon, K. (2024, February 27). Soaring number of Americans are now 401(k) millionaires. *Yahoo! Finance*. https://finance.yahoo.com/news/soaring-number-of-americans-are-now-401k-millionaires-100001736.html.

Klontz, B. T., Sullivan, P., Seay, M. C., and Canale, A. (2015b). The wealthy: A financial psychological profile. *Consulting Psychology Journal: Practice and Research*, 67(2), 127–43. https://doi.org/10.1037/cpb0000027.

CHAPTER 16

Arnsten, Amy, Carolyn M Mazure, and Rajita Sinha. "This Is Your Brain in Meltdown." *Scientific American*, April 2012. https://www.ncbi.nlm.nih.gov/ pmc/articles/PMC4774859/.

Desmond, M. (2023). *Poverty, by America*. Allen Lane.

Dwyer, Christopher. "12 Common Biases That Affect How We Make Everyday Decisions." *Psychology Today. September 7*, 2018. https://www.psychologytoday. com/us/blog/thoughts-on-thinking/201809/12-common-biases-that-affect-how-we-make-everyday-decisions.

Klontz, B. T., Sullivan, P., Seay, M. C., and Canale, A. (2015a). The wealthy: A financial psychological profile. *Consulting Psychology Journal: Practice and Research, 67*(2), 127–143. https://doi.org/10.1037/cpb0000027.

CHAPTER 17

A measured approach to ending poverty and boosting shared prosperity: Concepts, data, and the twin goals. World Bank. (2014). https://www.worldbank.org/en/research/publication/a-measured-approach-to-ending-poverty-and-boosting-shared-prosperity.
Beauchamp, Z. (2014, December 14). The world's victory over extreme poverty, in one chart. *Vox.* https://www.vox.com/2014/12/14/7384515/extreme-poverty-decline.

CHAPTER 18

Davis, Maggie, and Della Costa, Chloe. "Over a Quarter of Drinkers Admit Alcohol Has Negatively Affected Their Finances, With 37% Planning to Cut Back This Year." Edited by Dan Shepard. *LendingTree*, February 12, 2024. https://www.lendingtree.com/credit-cards/study/alcohol-spending/.
Keuren, M. V. (2024, February 26). The average cost of owning a car. *Yahoo! Finance.* https://finance.yahoo.com/news/cost-owning-car-190604240.html.
Lyte, B. (n.d.). You Won't Believe How Much the Average Person Spends on Salon Visits Each Year. https://www.wisebread.com/you-wont-believe-how-much-the-average-person-spends-on-salon-visits-each-year.
Mayer, Yanling. "US Rent Affordability Drops to Lowest Level in Decades." *CoreLogic®*, October 26, 2023. https://www.corelogic.com/intelligence/us-rent-affordability-drops-lowest-level-decades/.

CHAPTER 19

"How Many People Use Google? Statistics & Facts (2024)." RSS. Accessed April 8, 2024. https://seo.ai/blog/how-many-people-use-google.

CHAPTER 20

Maxwell, Tim. "How to Minimize the Cost of a Cash Advance." *Bankrate*, March 8, 2022. https://www.bankrate.com/finance/credit-cards/how-to-minimize-the-cost-of-a-cash-advance/.

Sommer, Constance. "Average Credit Card Debt in the U.S." *Bankrate*, February 14, 2024. https://www.bankrate.com/finance/credit-cards/states-with-most-credit-card-debt/.

CHAPTER 21

Mcleod, S., (2024, January 24). Maslow's hierarchy of needs. *Simply Psychology*. https://www.simplypsychology.org/maslow.html.

INDEX

Page numbers followed by *f* refer to figures.

Charles Schwab corporation, 52, 53
Children of rich parents, 198–200
Choice. *See also* Freedom of choice
  advice on, 173
  as cause of poverty, 54
  excuses about, 205
  importance of, xvi
  jobs' effect on, 96–98
  and poor mindset, 110
  and rich mindset, 42
  in spending, 72, 210
Clark, Caitlin, 152
Clinical psychology, 80
Closing costs, 265
Cognitive functioning, 168
Cold asks, 180
Collective neuroscience, 113
College, 143–147
College majors, 147–148
Competition, 31
Complaining, 197–211
  avoiding, 119
  cycle of, 203–204
  and excuses, 205–208
  futility of, 73, 204
  and locus of control, 197
  and mindfulness, 191
  and powerlessness, 73, 189
  psychological effects of, 113
Conditional relationships, 141–142
Confirmation bias, 188–189, 191
Consumer play, 39
Content creators, 235–237
CPAs, 22, 29, 145, 174, 175, 178
Credit card debt:
  and budgeting, 248
  effect on credit scores, 243
  enslavement to, 140, 246, 255
  hacks for, 49
  and investing, 244–245
  of lower-wage workers, 95
  and money worship, 43

national average of, 240
and payday loans, 241
paying off, 31–32
racking up, xvii, 19, 24
wiping out, 29
Credit game, 242–243
Credit play, 38
Credit scores, 20, 150, 239–240, 242–244, 248, 264
Crypto rug pull schemes, 100, 190

D
Dance Saves Lives clothing brand, 225
Day trading, 20, 54, 100–103
Delayed gratification, 128, 133, 138, 247
Deloitte, 90
Department of Labor, 16, 98, 164
Do-it-yourself-itis, 177–179
Dollar cost averaging, 133
Doorman, Christina and Walter, 139
Down payments, 28, 29, 159, 246, 264, 267*f*
Dunning-Kruger Effect, 189
Dweck, Carol, 104

E
Earner skills, 68
E-books, 233, 238
Ego, 12, 115, 131, 142, 152–154, 179, 189
Employees, 15–16
Entrepreneurs:
  and choice, 97–98
  expert advice for, 59
  freedom of, 93
  internet, xv, 253
  mentorship of, 55
  parental views on, 63
  poor mindset view of, 43
  questions for, 175
  self-funded, 84
  Silicon, xvi
  studying, 124